GUINNESS

Book of the

Marathon

Roger Gynn

GUINNESS

Book of the

Marathon

Roger Gynn

GUINNESS

Book of the

Marathon

Roger Gynn

Editor: Beatrice Frei
Design and Layout: David Roberts
Maps: Eddie Botchway

**Copyright © Roger Gynn and Guinness
Superlatives Ltd, 1984**

Published in Great Britain by
Guinness Superlatives Ltd, 2 Cecil Court,
London Road,
Enfield, Middlesex

Set in Times 10/11pt.
Filmset by Fakenham Photosetting Ltd,
Norfolk
Printed and bound in Spain by Mateu Cromo
Artes Graficas, S.A. Pinto (Madrid)

British Library Cataloguing in Publication
Data

Gynn, Roger
The Guinness book of marathon.
1. Marathon running
I. Title
796.4'26   GV1065

ISBN 0–85112–410–0
ISBN 0–85112–422–4 PBK

ABBREVIATIONS

ft—feet; in—inches; yd—yards; m—metres;
km—kilometres

AAA—Amateur Athletic Association
AAU—Amateur Athletic Union (USA)
ATFS—Association of Track & Field Statisticians
CG—Commonwealth Games (from 1966)
dnf—did not finish
dsq—disqualified
EC—European Championships
E Cup—European Cup
EG—Empire Games (to 1962)
FOT—Final Olympic trial race
IAAF—International Amateur Athletic Federation
IOC—International Olympic Committee
NC—National Championship
NUTS—National Union of Track Statisticians
OG—Olympic Games
OT—Olympic trial race
Pol/Poly—Polytechnic Harriers' marathon
RRC—Road Runners' Club
TAC—The Athletics Congress (USA)
WC—World Championship
WCCA—Women's Cross Country Association (GB)

Nations

Arg	Argentina	Ind	India
Aus	Australia	Ire	Ireland
Aut	Austria	Irq	Iraq
Bel	Belgium	Ita	Italy
Bol	Bolivia	Jam	Jamaica
Bul	Bulgaria	Jap	Japan
Bur	Burma	Ken	Kenya
Can	Canada	Kor	Korea
Chl	Chile	Lat	Latvia
Col	Colombia	Les	Lesotho
CRC	Costa Rica	Lib	Libya
Cub	Cuba	Lux	Luxemburg
Cze	Czechoslovakia	Mex	Mexico
Den	Denmark	Mor	Morocco
Ecu	Ecuador	NC	New Caledonia
Egy	Egypt	Nor	Norway
Eng	England	NZ	New Zealand
Est	Estonia	Pak	Pakistan
Eth	Ethiopia	Pan	Panama
Fij	Fiji	Phi	Philippines
Fin	Finland	PNG	Papua-New Guinea
Fra	France	Pol	Poland
GB	Great Britain & N Ireland	Por	Portugal
		PR	Puerto Rico
Ger	Germany	PRK	North Korea
GDR	German Democratic Republic	Qat	Qatar
		Rho	Rhodesia
GFR	German Federal Republic	Rom	Romania
		SAU	Saudi Arabia
Gre	Greece	SA	South Africa
Gua	Guatemala	Sco	Scotland
HK	Hong Kong	Sov	Soviet Union
Hol	Netherlands	Spa	Spain
Hon	Honduras	Sud	Sudan
Hun	Hungary	Swa	Swaziland
Swe	Sweden	Uga	Uganda
Swz	Switzerland	Uru	Uruguay
Syr	Syria	USA	United States
Tan	Tanzania	Ven	Venezuela
Tun	Tunisia	Yug	Yugoslavia
Tur	Turkey	Zam	Zambia

USA States

AL	Alabama	NJ	New Jersey
CA	California	NM	New Mexico
CO	Colorado	NY	New York
CT	Connecticut	OH	Ohio
DC	District of Columbia	OR	Oregon
FL	Florida	RI	Rhode Island
LA	Louisiana	VA	Virginia
MA	Massachussetts	WI	Wisconsin
MO	Missouri		

Notes

TABLES of winners etc relate to men unless stated.

ACCENTS are confined to acute (´), circumflex (ˆ), grave (`) and Umlaut (¨) in French, German and Scandinavian names.

INDEX relates to entries in text only. Wherever possible, full dates of birth are given. Dates of death are omitted due to difficulty in obtaining accurate information.

STRUCTURE of European chapter: Great Britain is followed by the Nordic nations, then the Western nations which do not qualify for either the Balkan or Mediterranean Games. Eastern bloc nations are next, except for Yugoslavia, Romania and Bulgaria which are contained in the Balkan section for which they qualify, as well as Greece and Turkey. The latter also contest the Mediterranean Games in which Spain and Italy also compete.

Conversion Table

miles	kilometres
26 miles 385 yd	42.195 km
25 miles	40.2 km
24.85 miles	40 km
21.75 miles	35 km
20 miles	32.2 km
18.6 miles	30 km
15 miles	24.1 km
12.4 miles	20 km

CONTENTS

INTRODUCTION

Except for some early historical references, the marathon in this book relates entirely to that race held over a distance of 26 miles 385 yd (42.195 km) which was first run in the 1908 Olympic Games between Windsor and the White City stadium and which became standard in the Olympics from 1924. Marathon times cannot be interpreted in the same way as for track events but such results can supply the reader with some insight into the top performers of the day whether on a national or international scale, ancient or modern. Thus the varying topography of all the courses (flat, net uphill or down, rolling etc) as well as climatic conditions (temperatures, shade or sun, and humidity) make each race as much a battle against these factors as against fellow competitors.

In this book the phrase 'marathon record' is frequently used to indicate best performances. This is done purely as a convenience measure for at least two reasons. First, many national sports bodies identify a fastest marathon time as simply that—a 'best' performance—and do not give such time official 'record' status. Second, the IAAF itself does not recognise marathon 'record' performances for the obvious reasons noted above. Similarly, statistics buffs may note small discrepancies among finish times given in this book when compared to periodicals and newspapers. In most of today's races modern timing systems allow recording of finish times to tenths or hundredths of a second. It is IAAF policy for such finish times to be rounded upward to the next second if the tenths or hundredths are, respectively, greater than 0.1 or 0.01. Press deadlines, improper rounding of times and other complications frequently interfere with accuracy of reporting which is often cleared up only upon publication of official results, weeks or months later. In this book, prior to 1980 when the IAAF rounding rule took effect, exact times as recorded are presented wherever known, and in the interests of maintaining an exact historical record this practice is continued here after 1980 as well, especially when knowledge of such detail adds useful information. As much material as possible that has not appeared previously in print has been included with an emphasis on regional Games, international runners and races, and national championship results. With some historical data included, it is hoped that an acceptable balance has been achieved.

Roger Gynn

ORIGINS

No book on the marathon would be complete without some reference to the ancient legends which caught the imagination of Michel Bréal (Fra) in 1894, and prompted him to suggest that a distance race be held in the 1896 Olympic Games and be called the Marathon. The common belief passed down through the years, that in 490 BC an Athenian soldier named Pheidippides or Philippides ran from Marathon to Athens with news of victory over the invading Persians before dropping dead, was the basis on which Breal's idea was formulated. However, the only historian of the day to have recorded anything remotely resembling that belief was Herodotus (485–425 BC) and he wrote his piece some fifty years after the battle. The historian, who had the advantage of being able to converse with veterans of the battle, related that Pheidippides, a *hemerodromoi* or trained runner, was sent from Athens to Sparta, which he reached the next day, to get help. It is therefore assumed that the distance of some 136 miles (219 km) was covered by the runner in rather less than 48 hours. There is no direct mention of any return to Athens. Plutarch (*c* AD 46–120) wrote of a soldier, possibly wounded, who brought the first news of victory at Marathon to the Elders with the words 'Hail! We are victorious' and then

expired. Lucian, a 2nd-century satirical writer, attributes the run to Philippides who ran from Marathon in a single day with the result of the battle. There is no doubt that there were trained messengers used to running very long distances, yet in the ensuing ancient Greek Games there was no race that in any way could be construed as being a distance event which at least would have given some evidence to substantiate the legend.

A remarkable sequel to the original story has recently been unearthed by historian Dave Terry who has revealed that a very similar occurrence took place in the Holy Land in approximately 1080 BC. At that time a Hebrew messenger from the tribe of Benjamin ran from the battlefield at Even-Heazer, near Aphek, to Shiloh a distance of 35 km. He too carried news of a battle, which was between the Philistines and the Israelites, for the information of the High Priest and which he delivered the same day. The history of the modern marathon foot race, as devised by Bréal, thus commences with the original races held over the 40 km route between Marathon and Athens in 1896.

Historical Highlights

25 Nov 1892 Baron Pierre de Coubertin made a statement at the Sorbonne in Paris regarding the revival of the ancient Olympic Games.

1894 Michel Bréal wrote to de Coubertin suggesting

Original Athens Olympic stadium.

that the Olympic programme include a distance race.

16 Jun 1894 International Olympic Committee convened in Paris.

Feb 1896 Two runners left Athens at 8 am to run to Marathon. G Grigoriou finished in 3:45:00, ten minutes after J Vanoulis who had taken a lift in a cart for 5 km during the run.

10 Mar 1896 The first official marathon to be held over the Marathon to Athens route, and the first national championship race.

24 Mar 1896 The second authenticated marathon to be held as part of the Pan-Hellenic sports celebrations, acting as an Olympic trial.

Mar 1896 The first woman, Stamatis Rovithi, to run the distance.

10 Apr 1896 The first modern Olympic Games marathon took place with one runner from each of Australia, France, Hungary and the United States, as well as those representing Greece.

19 Jul 1896 The first marathon to be held outside Greece from Paris to Conflans, France. The winner received 2000 French Francs, plus another 2000 Francs for bettering the 1896 Olympic winning time.

Len Hurst (GB) wins the first marathon to be held outside Greece in 1896, from Paris to Conflans.

20 Sep 1896 The first marathon to be staged in the Western Hemisphere from Stamford, CT to the Columbia Oval, New York, over 25 miles.

19 Apr 1897 The first Boston marathon from Ashland to Exeter Street. Distance 24 miles 1232 yd (39 km).

30 Aug 1904 First Olympic marathon to be held outside Europe at St Louis.

28 Nov 1907 First Yonkers, NY marathon.

11 Apr 1908 First marathon to be held in the African continent at Cape Town over 25 miles.

9 May 1908 First marathon in Great Britain at Coventry over 25 miles.

24 Jul 1908 Olympic Games marathon from Windsor to the White City over a distance of 26 miles 385 yd for the first time.

10 Oct 1908 First professional marathon in Great Britain over the Olympic course.

25 Nov 1908 First professional marathon in the United States at Madison Square Garden, New York.

12 Apr 1909 First marathon in the Australasian continent held at Sydney.

26 May 1909 First Polytechnic Harriers' marathon for the *Sporting Life* trophy over 26 miles 385 yd from Windsor to Stamford Bridge.

18 Dec 1909 First indoor marathon in Great Britain held at the Royal Albert Hall over 524 laps of a thick coconut matting track.

24 May 1910 First professional marathon to be held in South America at Buenos Aires.

19 Nov 1911 First Open marathon in Asia. Staged at Tokyo over 25 miles as the Japanese Olympic trial.

17 Jul 1912 Formation of the International Amateur Athletic Federation.

27 May 1921 The fourth IAAF Congress meeting at Geneva, by which time the World Records Committee had proposed that the standard distance for the Olympic marathon be 26 miles 385 yd.

28 Oct 1924 First Kosice marathon. International from 1925.

19 Apr 1925 First AAU marathon championship at Boston.

30 May 1925 First AAA championship marathon from Windsor to Stamford Bridge.

12 Oct 1925 Al Michelsen (USA) first runner to better 2:30 for full distance with 2:29:01.8 at Port Chester.

21 Aug 1930 First British Empire Games' marathon at Hamilton.

9 Sep 1934 First European Championship marathon at Turin.

10 Feb 1938 First marathon in the Central American and Caribbean Games at Panama City.

10 Feb 1946 First Mainichi marathon at Osaka.

12 Jul 1947 First Enschede marathon.

7 Dec 1947 First Asahi marathon.

11 Sep 1949 First Nordic championship marathon at Stockholm.

6 Mar 1951 First Pan American Games marathon at Buenos Aires.

11 Mar 1951 First Asian Games marathon at New Delhi.

20 Jan 1952 First Beppu marathon.

13 Jun 1953 First sub 2:20 time by Jim Peters of 2:18:40.2 between Windsor and Chiswick.

12 Sep 1953 First sub 2:20 time on an out and back course. Jim Peters ran 2:19:22 at Enschede.

2 Oct 1955 First Athens Classical marathon.

1 Dec 1956 First Olympic Games marathon to be held in Australasia (Melbourne).

21 Oct 1964 First Olympic Games marathon to be held in Asia (Tokyo) when Abebe Bikila (Eth) became the first to win two gold medals in the event, both in world record time.

7 May 1967 First Karl Marx Stadt marathon.

3 Dec 1967 First sub 2:10 time by Derek Clayton at Fukuoka in 2:09:36.4.

20 Oct 1968 First Olympic marathon to be held at high altitude, at Mexico City.

21 Apr 1969 First field of over one thousand runners (at Boston).

1971 For the first time over one hundred marathons held in the United States in one year.

17 Apr 1972 Women officially accepted to run at Boston.

14 Jan 1973 First marathon to be held at the African Games at Lagos.

28 Oct 1973 First all-women's marathon at Waldniel, GFR.

22 Sep 1974 First women's international marathon at Waldniel.

12 Oct 1975 First sub 2:40 marathon by a woman; 2:38:19 by Jacqueline Hansen at Eugene.

24 Oct 1976 First New York marathon through the five boroughs.

19 Mar 1978 First Avon women's marathon.

Jim Peters (GB), setting his first world record in 1952. (H W Neale)

21 Oct 1979 First marathon with over 10 000 runners at New York. Grete Waitz became the first woman to better 2:30 with 2:27:32.6.

29 Mar 1981 First London marathon.

13 Sep 1981 First European Cup marathon at Agen, France.

7 Mar 1982 First IAAF Golden marathon from Marathon to Athens.

12 Sep 1982 First women's marathon to be held in the European Championships.

1982 For the first time over 100 marathons held in Great Britain in one year.

Aug 1983 First World Championship marathons for men (14 Aug) and women (7 Aug) at Helsinki.

The
International
Games

Spiridon Louis (Gre), first Modern Olympic marathon champion, 1896. (Hulton Picture Library)

The Olympic Games

1896 Athens 10 April

The staging of the 1896 Games was the culmination of de Coubertin's dreams and the marathon, the brainchild of Bréal, was held on a perfect spring day. The 18 competitors had been transported to the village of Marathon the previous day and of the four foreign entrants only Gyula Kellner (Hun) had run the distance prior to the Olympic race. The Frenchman Albin Lermusiaux led for the first half of the event but began to fade as the road climbed. Edwin Flack (Aus), gold medal winner in both 800 m and 1500 m, took over at the front but by 30 km had been joined by the Greek Spiridon Louis who had been running conservatively in the dusty conditions. Louis had only managed fifth place in the trial held over the same 40 km course 17 days earlier. With the finish in sight Louis broke away. On arrival at the marble Panathenaic stadium he was greeted by a deliriously happy crowd and was personally welcomed by members of the Greek Royal family. Louis won Greece's only gold medal of the Games with a lead of 7 min 13 sec, still the greatest winning margin in the Olympic marathon. Greece would have secured a complete sweep of the medals had not Spiridon Belokas been disqualified for allegedly taking a lift during the race. Eight other runners failed to finish.

1	**Spiridon Louis (Gre)**	**2:58:50**
2	**Charilaos Vasilakos (Gre)**	**3:06:03**
3	**Gyula Kellner (Hun)**	**3:06:35**

First and second names of winner are sometimes recorded as Spyros and Loues in different combinations.

1900 Paris 19 July

The Olympic events were staged as part of the Universal Paris *Exposition* and spread over some five months. The marathon was run over an intricately routed, poorly marked 40.26 km (25 miles) course which looped from the stadium into the Bois de Boulogne and through many side streets before finishing back at the stadium. The day was very hot and was reported to be 39°C (102°F) whilst traffic was extremely heavy and sheep as well as pedestrians wandered in the path of the runners. The winner was

Emile Champion (Fra), 1900 Olympic silver medallist, takes a drink ahead of colleague and eventual winner Michel Théato.

Michel Théato who was believed to be a baker's roundsman and had a first-hand knowledge of the roads. He did not know that he was the Olympic champion until 12 years later. Ernst Fast (Swe) was well in the lead but with 5 km remaining he and his accompanying cyclist took a wrong turn. In finishing third he is at 19 years 179 days the youngest ever Olympic marathon medal winner. Fourth placed Arthur Newton (USA) claimed later that he had led from the half-way stage and no one had passed him, thus adding to the controversy which surrounded the race. Seven of the 13 starters finished and it is interesting to note the fourth and fifth finishers Eugène Besse (Fra) and Newton who clocked 4:00:45 and 4:04:12 respectively.

1	Michel Théato (Fra)	2:59:45
2	Emile Champion (Fra)	3:04:17
3	Ernst Fast (Swe)	3:37:14

1904 St Louis 30 August

After the chaos of the 1900 celebrations it was unfortunate that the next Olympics would once more be attached to a similar exhibition, this time the St Louis World Fair. Again the marathon runners received little consideration as horsemen cleared the way over a dust-ridden course which had no less than seven hills for the 32 runners to negotiate. It was purported to be 25 miles in length but modern reconstruction shows that it was nearer 26. Among the early leaders on another very hot day was Fred Lorz but he retired at 10 miles with cramp and Sam Mellor became the new pace setter until he too gave in at 16 miles (25 km). Next it was Thomas Hicks' turn at the front but he was only kept going by

the continual supply of strychnine, brandy and eggs administered by his followers. Always up with the front runners Hicks, who had placed second at Boston in April, almost retired more than once but no more so than just after 18 miles when a fresh Lorz overtook him. It took a great deal of persuasion on the part of Hicks' supporters to keep him going to the finish where he eventually learnt that he had won as Lorz had quite rightly been disqualified for taking a car ride. The medal winners are all shown as being from the United States but whilst the Birmingham (GB) born winner Hicks had become an American citizen, it appears that second placed Corey was still a French national. Two South African tribesmen employed at the Fair were ninth and 12th of the 14 finishers, the first black African competitors in an Olympic marathon.

1	Thomas Hicks (USA)	3:28:53
2	Albert Corey (USA)	3:34:52
3	Arthur Newton (USA)	3:47:33

1906 Athens 1 May

The extra Olympic marathon between Marathon and Athens attracted 53 runners from 14 nations and was at that time by far the most international marathon to have been held. For some unknown reason the distance was over 41.86 km (26 miles) and once more the day was warm as the field left Marathon at 3 pm. The favoured Italian Dorando Pietri was a clear leader until stomach trouble forced him to retire at 24 km (15 miles) and soon afterwards the eventual winner William Sherring went to the front. John Svanberg (Swe) finished strongly to take the silver medal as George Blake (Aus), who had been contesting that position with William Frank (USA), fell back to finish sixth. Three years later Svanberg turned professional and competed in

St Louis 1904. Runners at start of marathon from left include: Tom Hicks (USA, 20) winner, Fred Lorz (USA, 31) disqualified, Sid Hatch (USA, 39) eighth, Felix Carvajal (Cub, 3) fourth, Albert Corey (USA, 7) second, Christos Zehouritis (Gre, 6) tenth, and Arthur Newton (USA, 12) third.

the United States. Only 14 runners are recorded as having finished.

1	William Sherring (Can)	2:51:23.6
2	John Svanberg (Swe)	2:58:20.8
3	William Frank (USA)	3:00:46.8

1908 London 24 July

The race started on the east lawn of Windsor Castle and in order that the finish could be in front of the Royal box at the White City stadium, an extra 385 yd was added to the course length of 26 miles. Fifty-six athletes lined up on a warm, humid afternoon. After members of the favoured British squad had suffered from setting too fast an early pace (1:15:13 at 13 miles) the South African Charles Hefferon led two miles later. At 25 miles Dorando Pietri (Ita) who had always had the leaders within view, took over the lead with the Americans John Hayes, Alton Welton and Joseph Forshaw in close contention. The heat was sapping every ounce of strength from the runners and as Pietri entered the stadium he stumbled and fell. After collapsing on the cinders for the fifth time he was helped across the finishing line and thus had to be disqualified. Hayes crossed the finish 32 seconds later to take the first prize whilst Queen Alexandra presented a suitably inscribed gold cup to the gallant Italian. Less

than half (27) of the field finished, the first European being John Svanberg (Swe) in eighth place. Top runners from the United States (first, third, fourth and ninth) and Canada (fifth, sixth, seventh and eleventh) all finished before the first British runner, William Clarke, 12th in 3:16:08.6.

1	John Hayes (USA)	2:55:18.4
2	Charles Hefferon (SA)	2:56:06
3	Joseph Forshaw (USA)	2:57:10.4
Disqualified—Dorando Pietri (Ita)		**2:54:46.4**

Johnny Hayes (USA), winner of the 1908 Olympic marathon. (Hulton Picture Library)

1912 Stockholm 14 July

A record number of 19 nations entered 68 contestants for the Stockholm marathon, once more held in very warm weather. The course, 40.2 km, for the first time went out to a turn (at Sollentuna) and back over the same road to the stadium. Christian Gitsham (SA), second in the Polytechnic Harriers' marathon in May, led at the half-way in 1:12:40 by 15 seconds from Tatu Kolehmainen, second of the famous Finnish brothers. Another South African Kenneth McArthur was third. Kolehmainen made a desperate bid to catch Gitsham on the return but paid the penalty and was forced to retire. This left the two Africans in the lead and it was not until two miles from the finish, as Gitsham took a drink, that McArthur broke away. The older McArthur, who took no refreshment during the race, won by nearly a minute and thus maintained his unbeaten record over the distance. Gaston Strobino, his feet rubbed and bleeding, finished powerfully to take the bronze medal, having been only 12th at Sollentuna. Once more the Americans packed well with third, fourth and seventh through tenth places, as the first European to finish was again a Swedish runner, Sigge Jacobsson in sixth. Jacobsson, who had trained arduously for the race, made the mistake of wearing new racing shoes and suffered accordingly. In the final kilometres the young Portuguese champion Francisco Lazaro collapsed and died in hospital the following day, the only such disaster in Olympic marathon history.

1	Kenneth McArthur (SA)	2:36:54.8
2	Christian Gitsham (SA)	2:37:52
3	Gaston Strobino (USA)	2:38:42.4

1920 Antwerp 22 August

For the first time in an Olympic marathon, conditions were favourable, the day being wet and cool and the roadway soft. But yet again there was no standard distance, this time the course was the longest ever at 42.750 km (26½ miles). One of the pre-race favourites was the silver medallist of eight years earlier, Gitsham. He had trained hard over the course in the weeks before the race and he led in the early stages, but soon after the mid-point (1:13:10) he was joined by Hannes Kolehmainen (Fin). Kolehmainen, star of the track at Stockholm, began to force the pace and even Gitsham could not respond, eventually retiring shortly after 35 km. In the meantime, the Estonian champion Jüri Lossmann had been steadily making up ground on the leaders and at the finish had closed to within 13 seconds of Kolehmainen's winning world record. For the first time since the inaugural Games marathon European runners took the first six positions. Of the 33 finishers 17 were timed in under 2:50.

1	Hannes Kolehmainen (Fin)	2:32:35.8
2	Jüri Lossmann (Est)	2:32:48.6
3	Valerio Arri (Ita)	2:36:32.8

1924 Paris 13 July

At the time of the 4.10 pm start the weather was sunny and there was a cool breeze as opposed to the heat-wave conditions which had prevailed the day before. For the first time since 1908 the course measured 42.195 km and from then on that would be the standard marathon distance. Whilst defending champion Kolehmainen never featured and failed to finish, it was another Finnish athlete Albin Stenroos, a woodcutter, who showed at the front before half-way. He was 35 years old and won a bronze medal in the 10000 m in 1912, yet his

Paris 1924. Albin Stenroos (Fin) en route to his one and only marathon victory.

marathon races were few and far between. Stenroos gradually pulled away from his rivals until at the finish in Colombes stadium he had a near six-minute advantage over Romeo Bertini (Ita). Clarence De Mar (USA), who had been in the silver medal position for much of the race, finished third as Sam Ferris became Britain's best ever finisher in fifth place in only his second marathon. Thirty of the 58 starters completed the race which was held for the most part over a very good road surface.

1	Albin Stenroos (Fin)	2:41:22.6
2	Romeo Bertini (Ita)	2:47:19.6
3	Clarence DeMar (USA)	2:48:14

1928 Amsterdam 5 August

Marthinus Steytler, a one-armed South African farmer who had set a national record of 2:41:35 earlier in the year, led the 68 strong field out of the stadium under leaden skies on a chilly afternoon. After a succession of early leaders Joie Ray (USA), winner of the New York trial after finishing third in his marathon debut at Boston, featured briefly at the front before the turn. After the half-way two Japanese runners, Kanematsu Yamada and Seiichiro Tsuda, began to force the pace and by 35 km Yamada, the national champion, led from Ray with Martti Marttelin (Fin) third ahead of Tsuda. Four kilometres later Yamada was being pressed by the Algerian El Ouafi, running for France, with the Chilean Manuel Plaza just behind. It was not long before El Ouafi overtook Yamada and the latter was soon passed by Plaza and Marttelin, thus being shunted out of the medals as the top positions remained unchanged at the finish. Delighted Chilean supporters wrapped Plaza in the national flag as he won his country's one and only Olympic medal. With Ray fifth of the 57 who completed the flat course, runners born in different continents took the first five places.

1	Boughera El Ouafi (Fra)	2:32:57
2	Manuel Plaza (Chl)	2:33:23
3	Martti Marttelin (Fin)	2:35:02

1932 Los Angeles 7 August

The Los Angeles marathon attracted only 29 starters, the lowest since the Paris débâcle of 1900 and once more race-day was hot. This should have been Paavo Nurmi's marathon but the Finnish star, already the holder of 12 assorted Olympic medals, had his entry refused on the eve of the Games on allegations of professionalism. The white capped Argentinian hope Juan Zabala was first out of the stadium and, in touch with the leaders all the way, was first back to take the gold medal although completely exhausted. The battle for the minor places was an enthralling one. Lauri Virtanen (Fin), who had won two bronze medals on the track, led from 21 km to 30 km before he began to waver. Duncan

Wright (GB), fourth at that juncture, fought his way to the front at 35 km but Zabala soon wrested the lead from him. Armas Toivonen (Fin) held third just ahead of Seiichiro Tsuda (Jap) but then Sam Ferris (GB) began a late charge to take the silver medal as Wright faded to finish fourth in 2:32:41. For the first time in an Olympic marathon the first four finishers were all on the track at the same time. In ninth place the third of the Japanese, Korean-born Taika Gon, collapsed when within five yards of the tape, but managed to recover and cross the line without help.

1	Juan Zabala (Arg)	2:31:36
2	Sam Ferris (GB)	2:31:55
3	Armas Toivonen (Fin)	2:32:12

1936 Berlin 9 August

The race was run on another warm day but more than three-quarters of the marathon course was sheltered to some extent. Defending champion Zabala was among the leaders as the 56 runners left the stadium at 3 pm, and by 15 km he led by over a minute and a half. By half-way, reached in a fast 1:11:29, Zabala had begun to slow and his lead was under a minute but he rallied to increase his advantage. In close pursuit were Kitei Son (Jap) and Ernie

1936 Olympic marathon. Kitei Son (Jap, 382), wearing distinctive running shoes, and Ernie Harper (GB), the gold and silver medal winners.

Juan Zabala (Arg), an exhausted winner of the 1932 Olympic race.

Harper (GB) and at 28 km (17 miles) Son went clear in second. Just past this point Zabala stumbled and fell, to be passed by Son but the Argentinian recovered briefly only to retire at 32 km (20 miles). Son, holder of the world's fastest recorded time, continued to stretch his lead over Harper to two minutes at the finish, as he became the first to better 2:30 in an Olympic marathon. Shoryu Nan, like Son Korean-born, was only seventh at 20 miles yet took the bronze medal with a strong finishing burst. Erkki Tamila, third in the Finnish trial held over 36.5 km (22½ miles), finished fourth and with Väinö Muinonen (fifth) and Mauno Tarkiainen (ninth), the latter running his first full distance marathon, gave Finland the unofficial team prize.

1	**Kitei Son (Jap)**	2:29:19.2
2	**Ernie Harper (GB)**	2:31:23.2
3	**Shoryu Nan (Jap)**	2:31:42

1948 London 3 August

After a 12-year break the Games resumed, with London having the unenviable task of hosting them. The marathon course was a tough one, wending its way out into the country before returning to the finish at Wembley stadium, and the fact that it was a dull and humid day did not help the 41 runners. The Belgian champion Etienne Gailly held on to an early lead through 30 km with an advantage of half a minute. Korean Yoon Chil Choi then made a supreme effort to go from third to first in the space of five kilometres but it cost him dearly and he soon retired. Delfo Cabrera (Arg), who had also overtaken Gailly, found himself at the front. However,

Delfo Cabrera (Arg) overtakes a tired Etienne Gailly (Bel) on the track to win the 1948 Olympic title. (Keystone)

the gallant Belgian fought back to regain the lead and enter the stadium first but he was unable to counter the finishing speed of first Cabrera and then Tom Richards (GB). The exhausted Gailly had to be content with the bronze medal. The Argentinian trio, who rarely competed over the full marathon distance as half-marathons were the vogue in their country, performed extremely well as in addition to Cabrera, Eusebio Guinez finished fifth, and Alberto Sensini, ninth.

1	Delfo Cabrera (Arg)	2:34:51.6
2	Tom Richards (GB)	2:35:07.6
3	Etienne Gailly (Bel)	2:35:33.6

1952 Helsinki 27 July

Sixty-six athletes from a record 32 nations lined up for the marathon in the stadium where earlier the 1920 Olympic marathon champion Hannes Kolehmainen had lit the flame on top of the stadium tower. Jim Peters (GB), holder of the world record of 2:20:42.2 set the previous month, took up the early running and was joined by Gustaf Jansson (Swe) at 15 km. In third place was the Czecho-slovakian track genius Emil Zatopek, making his marathon debut, who had already won the 5000 m and 10000 m events the same week. He caught up with Jansson by 20 km and together they passed Peters, who ten kilometres later was forced to abandon the race due to a severe attack of cramp. Zatopek was soon on his own and heading for a most popular and exciting victory, his winning time being the fastest yet recorded over a regular out and back course. Reinaldo Gorno (Arg) overtook a tired Jansson for the silver medal as the Swedish star only just held off Yoon Chil Choi (Kor) who had left his final burst too late. The first seven all finished inside Son's 1936 time, whilst Cabrera, having been in fourth position towards the latter part of the race, became the highest placed defending champion in finishing sixth.

1	Emil Zatopek (Cze)	2:23:03.2
2	Reinaldo Gorno (Arg)	2:25:35
3	Gustaf Jansson (Swe)	2:26:07

1956 Melbourne 1 December

The story of the Olympic marathon has tended to be one synonymous with hot weather, and 1956 was certainly no exception as the temperature soared into the 80°F (27°C). Another first was recorded in the stadium as one of the 46 starters caused a false start. No real break occurred until the leaders approached the half-way point and then the French Algerian Alain Mimoun made a decisive break on one of the hills. He held on to his position and was never seriously challenged in his gold medal bid. Mimoun, who had won three Olympic track silver medals behind Zatopek, was the third consecutive champion to have made his full marathon debut in

Emil Zatopek (Cze) and Gustaf Jansson (Swe) overtake Jim Peters (GB) at Helsinki, 1952. (AP)

Alain Mimoun (Fra) with Emil Zatopek after Mimoun had won the gold medal at Melbourne in 1956. (AP)

Barefoot Abebe Bikila (Eth) wins the 1960 Olympic marathon in world record time. (Keystone)

the Olympic event. The silver and bronze medallists held their places from 35 km, whilst defending champion Zatopek equalled Cabrera's feat of four years previously in finishing sixth. Thirty-three runners endured the trying conditions and completed the hard course as European athletes took the first three places for the first time since 1920.

1	Alain Mimoun (Fra)	2:25:00
2	Franjo Mihalic (Yug)	2:26:32
3	Veikko Karvonen (Fin)	2:27:47

1960 Rome 10 September

This marathon was notable for a number of firsts, namely, the first Olympic marathon to start and finish outside the athletic stadium, the first to start as late as 5.30 pm, and the first to result in a world record outside the inaugural 42.195 km record set in 1908. In addition the largest field yet gathered in an Olympic marathon, 69 in all, was present. The experienced Belgian champion Aurele Vandendriessche was prominent in the first half of the race but by 20 km two Africans, one completely

unknown and the other a converted track runner, took to the front relegating the Belgian to third. Abebe Bikila (Eth), barefooted, went ahead at 41 km to finish in the fastest time then recorded, ahead of Rhadi (Mor) and Barry Magee (NZ). None of the nations taking the first three places had taken an Olympic marathon medal before. The previous record holder Sergey Popov (Sov), one of the pre-race favourites, was disappointing in only fifth place behind his colleague Konstantin Vorobeyev.

1	Abebe Bikila (Eth)	2:15:16.2
2	Rhadi ben Abdesselem (Mor)	2:15:41.6
3	Barry Magee (NZ)	2:17:18.2

1964 Tokyo 21 October

For the first time the Olympic Games were staged in Asia and on race day conditions for the marathon field were overcast and extremely humid. Australian Ron Clarke sped away from the start to be joined by Jim Hogan (GB) at 10 km and defending champion Abebe Bikila five kilometres later. The Ethiopian had undergone an appendix operation the previous month and was not expected to run, let alone pose a threat. However, at the turn (1:04:28) Bikila had opened a slight lead and from then on was unchallenged, increasing his advantage with every step he took. Kokichi Tsuburaya (Jap) moved into second as Clarke fell back eventually to finish ninth in 2:20:26.8, and Hogan retired at 35 km. Inside the stadium Bikila clocked another record time in the first ever successful defence of an Olympic marathon title. He was delighting the crowd with an exhibition of callisthenics as Tsuburaya entered the stadium, closely followed by

Basil Heatley (GB) snatches the silver medal from Kokichi Tsuburaya (Jap). Tokyo 1964. (Keystone)

Mamo Wolde (Eth), pictured after securing Ethiopia's third gold medal in successive Olympic marathons. (Keystone)

record, and 'low' altitude country athletes surprisingly took three of the first five places, as Bill Adcocks (GB) progressed from eighth to fifth in the last two kilometres. World record holder Derek Clayton (Aus) could only manage seventh place in 2:27:23.8.

1	Mamo Wolde (Eth)	2:20:26.4
2	Kenji Kimihara (Jap)	2:23:21
3	Mike Ryan (NZ)	2:23:45

1972 Munich 10 September

The marathon course came in for some criticism due to the abundance of corners and quality of the road surface which in places was uneven. There was a record 73 runners at the start, one more than at Mexico City, and by 10 km all the top athletes were in the leading pack. Soon afterwards Frank Shorter (USA) put in a spurt and by 15 km was out alone. Karel Lismont (Bel), the current European champion, held second position at 20 km but then began to suffer and slipped to fifth as defending champion Mamo Wolde took up the challenge. The Belgian rallied and overtook Wolde in the closing stages but could make no impression on Shorter who won with a clear two minutes in hand. Just before Shorter entered the stadium a German student, Norbert Sudhaus, ran on to the track towards the finishing tape before being led away by officials. Meanwhile Shorter had made his appearance and seemed bemused by the hesitant applause and laughter which was dying away. The United States, with Kenny Moore fourth and Jack Bacheler ninth, had their most successful Olympic marathon since 1912.

1	Frank Shorter (USA)	2:12:19.8
2	Karel Lismont (Bel)	2:14:31.8
3	Mamo Wolde (Eth)	2:15:08.4

1976 Montreal 31 July

Conditions were muggy and damp for the marathon, and with the boycott by 22 African nations, many favoured Frank Shorter to repeat his win of four years earlier. Bill Rodgers (USA), nursing a foot injury, was still courageous enough to lead the front runners in the early part of the race. At 15 km the leaders numbered 12 dropping to eight in the space of five kilometres as Shorter began to force the pace. The champion led at 20 km but Waldemar Cierpinski (GDR), who had been in touch the whole time, moved to the front at 30 km and after a brief tussle shook off Shorter. For the first time 2:10 was bettered in the Olympics and Cierpinski's 2:09:55 made him fourth equal fastest of all time alongside Bill Rodgers. The other medallists each took a position one lower than in 1972. Lasse Viren (Fin), 5000 m and 10000 m winner, made an impressive marathon debut in fifth (2:13:30) one place ahead of the disappointing home favourite Jerome Drayton.

the British and former world record holder Basil Heatley. Off the last bend Heatley, who had been fifth at 25 km, sprinted by to take the silver medal. Tsuburaya never recovered from this defeat which he considered a personal humiliation; unable to run the distance again due to Achilles tendon problems he became severely depressed and committed suicide in 1968. With Brian Kilby fourth and Ron Hill 19th Britain edged out Japan for the unofficial team prize.

1	Abebe Bikila (Eth)	2:12:11.2
2	Basil Heatley (GB)	2:16:19.2
3	Kokichi Tsuburaya (Jap)	2:16:22.8

1968 Mexico City 20 October

The marathon was held over a point to point course starting in the southern suburbs of Mexico City and finishing in the Olympic stadium. For the first time the Games were staged at altitude and because of this factor there was no firm pre-race favourite, especially as Abebe Bikila had problems with an ankle injury. At 15 km Tim Johnston (GB) and Nedo Farcic (Yug) had a small lead, and two kilometres later Bikila retired from the affray. Naftali Temu, Kenyan winner of the 10000 m, took up the front running at 25 km with Mamo Wolde (Eth) close behind, but it was Wolde who was clear five kilometres later and from then on was never threatened. Ethiopian runners thus made it three successive gold medals in the Olympic marathon, a

1 Waldemar Cierpinski (GDR)	2:09:55
2 Frank Shorter (USA)	2:10:45.7
3 Karel Lismont (Bel)	2:11:12.6

1980 Moscow 1 August

The Soviet Union became the first Eastern European nation to stage the Games but it was unfortunate that due to political wrangling Japan and the United States were among the absentees. Their presence was sorely missed in the marathon. Vladimir Kotov, the Soviet champion and new record holder, was responsible for much of the work in the first half of the race. Rodolfo Gomez (Mex) made the first real break at 23 km and stayed in front until just after 35 km when he was overtaken by Cierpinski and the European record holder Gerard Nij-boer (Hol). The GDR runner proved the stronger on the final run-in and in winning by 17 seconds equalled Bikila's feat of the 1960s. The Soviet trio of Dzhumanazarov, Kotov and European champion Leonid Moseyev, one of the favourites, finished in third, fourth and fifth, ahead of the first non-European finisher Gomez, as the first seven finishers all bettered 2:13.

1 Waldemar Cierpinski (GDR)	2:11:03
2 Gerard Nijboer (Hol)	2:11:20
3 Satymkul Dzhumanazarov (Sov)	2:11:35

European Championships 1946. From left: Stylianos Kyriakidis (Gre), Väinö Muinonen (Fin), Henning Larsen (Den), Squire Yarrow (GB) and eventual winner Mikko Hietanen (Fin).

European Championships

1934 Turin 9 September

Since 1919 Turin had staged an annual marathon which from 1921 had been over a course of 42.750 km (26½ miles) and was not an easy one. Conditions were unfavourable for the 15 starters, as it was a hot day. At half-way Thore Enochsson (Swe) led from the 1932 Olympic bronze medallist Armas Toivonen (Fin). The Finn went into the lead at 30 km from Enochsson and Aurelio Genghini (Ita), winner of the Turin race the year before, and the order remained unchanged at the finish. There were no British entries.

1	**Armas Toivonen (Fin)**	**2:52:29**
2	**Thore Enochsson (Swe)**	**2:54:35.6**
3	**Aurelio Genghini (Ita)**	**2:55:03.4**

1938 Paris 4 September

The Belgian champion Felix Meskens, winner of *L'Auto* international marathon at the same venue in 1934, made the early running but by half-way had dropped away. Squire Yarrow (GB), who had finished second in the Poly in his debut, went into the lead at 31 km (19 miles) shadowed by Väinö Muinonen (Fin). Four kilometres later Muinonen went to the front and took the gold medal in front of Yarrow and Henry Palmé (Swe), the latter having been fifth at 35 km.

1	**Väinö Muinonen (Fin)**	**2:37:28.8**
2	**Squire Yarrow (GB)**	**2:39:03**
3	**Henry Palmé (Swe)**	**2:42:13.6**

1946 Oslo 22 August

The first post-war championship race at Oslo was over the normal Scandinavian short marathon distance of 40.2 km. For the first time there was an entry from the Soviet Union but one of the favourites was Stylianos Kyriakidis (Gre), winner at Boston and fastest European, who had suffered during the occupation of his country in the war. After John Systad (Nor) and Pierre Cousin (Fra) had taken turns at the front, Mikko Hietanen (Fin) came from 12th at 10 km to first at 30 km. Muinonen, the 1938 winner, took the silver behind Hietanen, at the age of 47, but Kyriakidis never featured and retired at 30 km.

1	**Mikko Hietanen (Fin)**	**2:24:55**
2	**Väinö Muinonen (Fin)**	**2:26:08**
3	**Yakov Punko (Sov)**	**2:26:21**

1950 Brussels 23 August

Local hopes were pinned on Etienne Gailly, hero at London two years earlier, and for the first 10 km he

Jack Holden (GB), winning the 1950 European title. (AP)

Veikko Karvonen (Fin), taking the 1954 European gold medal in Berne. (Popperfoto)

son showed at the front of a six strong group. Veikko Karvonen, no better than ninth at the mid-point, joined the Soviet duo and the three were clear by 40 km. On approaching the stadium, the Finnish star moved into second as Filin sprinted away to what seemed a certain win. Once in the stadium, Filin turned the wrong way and before he could right himself had lost over 100 metres, to be overtaken by both Karvonen and Grishayev.

1	Veikko Karvonen (Fin)	2:24:51.6
2	Boris Grishayev (Sov)	2:24:55.6
3	Ivan Filin (Sov)	2:25:26.6

1958 Stockholm 24 August

The Stockholm course was quite hilly and race afternoon wet as the field of 25 set off on the marathon. Soviet champion Sergey Popov soon went to the front, closely followed by Olympic champion Alain Mimoun. By 30 km Popov had a clear lead over Fred Norris (GB) as both Mimoun and the Melbourne silver medallist Franjo Mihalic (Yug) retired. Popov's winning time sliced more than two minutes off Peters' world record set in 1954 and his winning margin of 5 min 33.6 sec remains the greatest recorded in the European championship event.

1	Sergey Popov (Sov)	2:15:17
2	Ivan Filin (Sov)	2:20:50.6
3	Fred Norris (GB)	2:21:15

1962 Belgrade 16 September

In extreme heat it was little wonder that no single runner was keen on cutting out the opening pace and it was left to Stanislaw Ozog (Pol) to lead the field through the half-way point. Then the Soviet runner Nikolay Rumyantsev had a spell at the front and he led at 30 km before dropping out. Brian Kilby (GB), who had been running economically, went into the lead soon after and won comfortably, thus equalling Holden's feat of 1950 in taking both the Commonwealth and European titles the same year.

1	Brian Kilby (GB)	2:23:18.8
2	Aurele Vandendriessche (Bel)	2:24:02
3	Viktor Baikov (Sov)	2:24:19.8

1966 Budapest 4 September

Hungary, whose officials were the instigators of the European championship idea, at last staged the event. With 20 km of the marathon covered, there was still a bunch of 12 runners together and these were whittled down to seven as Gyula Toth (Hun) led them through 30 km. Jim Hogan (GB) held the first clear advantage at 40 km and kept going to register his first major victory. Vandendriessche

Right:
Brian Kilby (GB), winning the 1962 European Championship marathon. (AP)

did not disappoint his followers. The weather was cool for the evening race as rain had fallen just prior to the runners leaving the stadium. As Gailly dropped back the British champion Jack Holden shook off Charles Cérou (Fra) and went on to win. Veikko Karvonen (Fin), in his third marathon, finished swiftly, overtaking the Soviet champion and record holder Feodosiy Vanin towards the finish. Gailly could only manage eighth.

1	Jack Holden (GB)	2:32:13.2
2	Veikko Karvonen (Fin)	2:32:45
3	Feodosiy Vanin (Sov)	2:33:47

1954 Berne 25 August

Two Soviet runners Boris Grishayev and Ivan Filin led for the greater part of the race except for a period around 20 km when the Swede Gustaf Jans-

(sixth at 30 km) had to be content with the silver medal for the second year running.

1	Jim Hogan (GB)	2:20:04.6
2	Aurele Vandendriessche (Bel)	2:21:43.6
3	Gyula Toth (Hun)	2:22:02

1969 Athens 21 September

For the first time since 1906 the classical course from Marathon to Athens was used for a major championship race. Conditions were vastly different from those in April when Bill Adcocks (GB) set a record 2:11:07.2. It was very much warmer as Gaston Roelants (Bel) opened a lead as the road climbed to 30 km, having overhauled Nedo Farcic (Yug) in the process. The Belgian star was still in front at 40 km but as he neared the stadium so he was caught by Ron Hill (GB). Roelants' brave gamble had only just failed. Adcocks had to retire due to a foot injury.

1	Ron Hill (GB)	2:16:47.8
2	Gaston Roelants (Bel)	2:17:22.2
3	Jim Alder (GB)	2:19:05.8

1971 Helsinki 15 August

The Helsinki marathon, held on a much cooler day, attracted a record entry of 52 runners, 41 of whom finished. A large group were together until 25 km when Roelants, Kael Lismont (Bel) and Trevor Wright (GB) broke away from Ron Hill and Colin Kirkham (GB). Lismont, competing in his third marathon, had a 12-second advantage over Wright at 35 km which he gradually increased to the finish. Both Hill and Kirkham overtook Roelants in the last five kilometres, as runners from Britain and Belgium shared the top five positions.

1	Karel Lismont (Bel)	2:13:09
2	Trevor Wright (GB)	2:13:59.6
3	Ron Hill (GB)	2:14:34.8

1974 Rome 8 September

At the time of the start of the marathon in late afternoon the conditions were still very hot. Ian Thompson (GB), running his fourth marathon in the space of eleven months and still unbeaten, was up with the leaders from the start. Soon after half-way he left Roelants, Eckhard Lesse (GDR) and Lismont to finish a clear winner, ahead of Lesse and Roelants, as Lismont was forced to abandon the race. Once again British and Belgian runners dominated the top five places with only Lesse breaking their monopoly.

1	Ian Thompson (GB)	2:13:18.8
2	Eckhard Lesse (GDR)	2:14:57.4
3	Gaston Roelants (Bel)	2:16:29.6

1978 Prague 3 September

A record 21 nations were represented at Prague

with the course to Lidice and back flat and open once the city was left. The race, held in cool weather, did not come alive until Massimo Magnani (Ita) made an effort at 35 km to go clear for the first time. Although Magnani was soon caught and dropped, there were still five in contention at 40 km as Lismont led. Waldemar Cierpinski (GDR) and Catalin Andreica (Rom) fell behind leaving Lismont and two Soviet runners to fight it out. Moseyev and Penzin entered the Strahov stadium together and in a sprint finish Moseyev proved the stronger winning by one and a half seconds, the closest margin in a major championship race.

1	Leonid Moseyev (Sov)	2:11:57.5
2	Nikolay Penzin (Sov)	2:11:59
3	Karel Lismont (Bel)	2:12:07.4

1982 Athens 12 September

The heat and the tough course caused the favourites, in particular the vaunted Soviet trio, a lot of trouble. For the first time women raced and they started 15 minutes after the men. The European record holder Gerard Nijboer (Hol) broke away at 27 km and, although he looked to be tiring towards the end, he hung on for a fine win. It was the first time that the Netherlands had won a major championship marathon. In finishing in second and third places, Belgian runners captured their seventh and eighth medals in the last seven European championship marathons.

1	Gerard Nijboer (Hol)	2:15:16
2	Armand Parmentier (Bel)	2:15:51
3	Karel Lismont (Bel)	2:16:04

Rosa Mota running her first marathon was a surprise winner in the women's division and won Portugal's first ever medal at any event in the European championships. The best Soviet finisher, champion Zoya Ivanova, was only eighth, and the German record holder and fastest on paper, Charlotte Teske, could manage no better than 12th.

1	Rosa Mota (Por)	2:36:04
2	Laura Fogli (Ita)	2:36:29
3	Ingrid Kristiansen (Nor)	2:36:39

Rosa Mota. (All Sport)

Commonwealth Games

1930 Hamilton 21 August

Although the idea of an Empire Games was first mooted in 1891, the first definite moves came from the Canadians after the 1928 Olympic Games. With Hamilton the venue, it was natural that the local hero Johnny Miles, twice winner at Boston, was one of the favourites. English hopes had suffered as record holder Harry Payne had been knocked down by a car whilst training on the eve of the race, and Sam Ferris had defied doctor's orders not to compete in the AAA event before leaving for Canada. Duncan McLeod Wright had won this last event and was a convincing winner at Hamilton, beating Ferris by half a mile, having been in front from ten miles.

1	Duncan McLeod Wright (Sco)	2:43:43
2	Sam Ferris (Eng)	no time
3	Johnny Miles (Can)	no time

1934 London 7 August

Having won the AAA title for the third successive year Donald McNab Robertson was favourite for the London race. However, from 12 miles one of the top Canadian runners Harold Webster, ironically English-born, took control of the race and won by over four minutes. Robertson and Wright moved into the medal positions in the latter stages ahead of Harold Wood, the first Englishman to finish.

1	Harold Webster (Can)	2:40:36
2	Donald McNab Robertson (Sco)	2:45:08
3	Duncan McLeod Wright (Sco)	2:56:20

1938 Sydney 7 February

Only runners from Canada, Newfoundland and the British Isles had competed in the first two Empire Games' marathons, but at Sydney there were entrants from both Australia and South Africa. One of the two Africans, Jackie Gibson, had been the second fastest performer in the world in 1937 with 2:30:45. Indeed it was Gibson and Johannes Coleman (SA) who shared the race work-load until the latter made a move at half-way to win by more than seven minutes in a time just outside Gibson's record. Norris pipped Gibson for the silver medal as Robertson finished a detached fourth.

1	Johannes Coleman (SA)	2:30:49.8
2	Bert Norris (Eng)	2:37:57
3	Jack Gibson (SA)	2:38:20

1950 Auckland 11 February

New Zealand staged the fourth Games after a break of 12 years. There was rain in the air as the 16 marathon runners lined up at the start. The British

champion Jack Holden dominated the race, only running into difficulties in the last ten miles when first he had to discard his shoes and run barefoot, and then in the final two miles fend off an over-friendly dog. Jack Clarke (NZ) took the bronze medal as his nation entered the race for the first time.

1	Jack Holden (Eng)	2:32:57
2	Sidney Luyt (SA)	2:37:02.2
3	Jack Clarke (NZ)	2:39:26.4

1954 Vancouver 7 August

A noon-time start in the heat of a scorching Canadian summer day did not deter the overwhelming favourite Jim Peters (Eng) from running at a fast pace right from the gun. Entering the stadium, Peters' lead was some 20 minutes but like Pietri (astonishingly the Italian family name equivalent of Peters) 46 years before, he found the effects of the heat and change from road to track unsteadying. Off balance and suffering from severe heat exhaustion he stumbled and fell. Unable to pull himself together, Peters continued to scramble his way around the remaining 300 yd of the track, veering from side to side and often falling on all fours. At the finishing line for the track events (but not the marathon) Peters was rescued from further humiliation. Only six of the 12 entrants finished, victory going to Joe McGhee (Sco) who himself had taken a rest by the roadside during the race. The second English runner, Stan Cox, also suffered from sunstroke and ran into a post with two miles to go to the finish. Peters did not gain consciousness until 1.40 am the following day and remained in hospital for a week.

1	Joe McGhee (Sco)	2:39:36
2	Jack Meckler (SA)	2:40:57
3	Johannes Barnard (SA)	2:51:49.8

1958 Cardiff 24 July

Dave Power (Aus) took the title and with it the first medal won by Australia in the Commonwealth marathon. He had earlier won the six mile track title. Power dominated the race over a tough course once the turn had been reached but he had to work hard to keep ahead of Barnard in the closing stages. The South African thus took his second medal in consecutive Games. England had her best overall result in the Games to date with third, fourth and sixth places.

1	Dave Power (Aus)	2:22:45.6
2	Johannes Barnard (SA)	2:22:57.4
3	Peter Wilkinson (Eng)	2:24:42

1962 Perth 29 November

The Games returned to the southern hemisphere, the marathon being held on a showery afternoon.

Dave Power (Aus) wins the 1958 Commonwealth title in his marathon debut. (Popperfoto)

The race turned into a straight England–Australia confrontation with the host nation having their best Games' marathon ever. Brian Kilby, already British and European champion in 1962, came through from 19 miles to edge out Power, whose silver medal position was the best yet achieved by a defending champion. Australian champion Keith Ollerenshaw finished fourth.

1	Brian Kilby (Eng)	2:21:17
2	Dave Power (Aus)	2:22:15.4
3	Rod Bonella (Aus)	2:24:07

1966 Kingston 11 August

For the first time a major Games was held in the Caribbean and Jamaica had the honour of staging them. Due to the intense heat the marathon started at 5.30 am but already it was very hot and humid. From 20 miles the British pair of Jim Alder (Sco) and Bill Adcocks (Eng) began to draw away from the field and on the approaches to the stadium Alder opened up a lead. Having been mis-directed, Alder found himself to be behind Adcocks on the stadium track but luckily had enough in reserve to regain the lead and deservedly take the gold medal.

1	Jim Alder (Sco)	2:22:07.8
2	Bill Adcocks (Eng)	2:22:13
3	Mike Ryan (NZ)	2:27:59

1970 Edinburgh 23 July

The thirty strong field assembled for the marathon was by far the finest in the history of the Commonwealth Games, and produced equally brilliant results. After Jerome Drayton (Can) had set the pace with sub-five minute miling, Ron Hill streaked through the half-way point in 1:02:35.2, still the fastest ever recorded in a completed major marathon. As both Drayton and world record holder Derek Clayton (Aus) dropped out, so Hill powered on to a British and European record time, winning by two and a half minutes. Twelve runners bettered 2:20 as England had another successful marathon, with the third member Bill Adcocks taking sixth place.

1	Ron Hill (Eng)	2:09:28
2	Jim Alder (Sco)	2:12:04
3	Don Faircloth (Eng)	2:12:19

1974 Christchurch 31 January

No one took advantage of the cool conditions until Ian Thompson (Eng), running only his second marathon, opened a lead at 30 km over the New Zealand veteran Jack Foster, fourth finisher in 1970. The pace was brisk and in third was the surprising Richard Mabuza (Swa). Positions were unchanged at the finish with Thompson clipping 16 seconds off Hill's record as the latter could finish no better than 18th, one place behind Jerome Drayton (Can). It was appropriate that New Zealand should have their best ever marathon as behind Foster, Terry Manners (fourth) and John Robinson (tenth) performed solidly.

1	Ian Thompson (Eng)	2:09:12
2	Jack Foster (NZ)	2:11:18.6
3	Richard Mabuza (Swa)	2:12:54.4

1978 Edmonton 11 August

The final outcome of the marathon appeared to be cut and dried when Jerome Drayton moved in front of fellow Canadian Paul Bannon, with just over two

Jim Alder (5) and Bill Adcocks battle for the 1966 Commonwealth title, Alder winning with Adcocks second. (AP)

kilometres remaining. It appeared that at last the enigmatic Drayton would win a major title. Drama occurred outside the stadium when unknown Gidamis Shahanga (Tan), who had made up 37 seconds between 35 km and 40 km, pulled back yet another 13 seconds and passed Drayton in seemingly effortless style. For the first time an African nation had won a Commonwealth marathon title.

1	Gidamis Shahanga (Tan)	2:15:39.8
2	Jerome Drayton (Can)	2:16:13.5
3	Paul Bannon (Can)	2:16:51.6

1982 Brisbane 8 October

On a hot sunny morning defending champion Shahanga and another Tanzanian find, Juma Ikangaa, sped over the first half of the tough Brisbane course in an amazing 1:03:50. Shortly afterwards Ikangaa shook off his team-mate and continued solo. The Australian favourite Rob de Castella had conserved his energy and timing his move to perfection caught the African champion at 38 km. After a short, absorbing tussle, during which time each runner passed the other twice, de Castella stormed away to win by 12 seconds. Ikangaa became the first African to better 2:10 and Mike Gratton in third took England's first medal in a major competition since 1974. A record 17 nations were represented at the 6 am start.

1	Rob de Castella (Aus)	2:09:18
2	Juma Ikangaa (Tan)	2:09:30
3	Mike Gratton (Eng)	2:12:06

Radames Gonzalez wins the 1979 Pan American title for Cuba. (Popperfoto)

Pan American Games

The first Pan American Games were staged in Buenos Aires in 1951 and like the Olympic Games were to be held quadrennially. With the unfavourable climatic conditions of the southern American nations and little consideration being given to the marathon runners, the marathon was never a great success in the early years. In addition, half-marathons were the vogue in the Americas outside the United States and Canada and the number of competitors invariably small.

It was appropriate that in the Argentinian capital the star of the marathon should be the 1948 Olympic champion Delfo Cabrera who was also the current South American half-marathon title holder. His winning margin of only a fraction under ten minutes is still the biggest in a major Games' marathon. Runner-up Reinaldo Gorno just held off the Central American champion Velazquez for the silver medal, but there were no United States or Canadian athletes in the field. They did make their appearance four years later at Mexico City when the first ever Games were held at altitude. Inexperience in distance running at altitude, then a comparatively unknown factor, forced early leader John Kelley (USA) to abandon the race. Doroteo Flores (Gua), who had won at Boston three years earlier, was the only finisher to better three hours. Kelley made up for this defeat when the Games were held in Chicago in 1959. Despite hot, stifling weather Kelley, already four times national champion, won with a fine solo performance. By taking first, second and fourth places this remains the best United States Pan-American team effort.

It was the turn of a Mexican to succeed at Sao Paulo,

venue of the fourth celebrations, when in very humid conditions Fidel Negrete won in a new national record time. He further improved the record in finishing 21st in the 1964 Olympics. Conditions at Winnipeg in 1967 were probably the best as far as the marathon runners were concerned in the short history of the Games. The course was flat, the weather not too demanding and Andy Boychuk (Can) won impressively. His win meant that there had been a different winning nation in each of the first six marathons. United States became the first to repeat when Frank Shorter won at Cali in a time which remained a championship record until 1983. The US champion Kenny Moore was forced to retire after being with the leaders early in the race.

The Games returned to Mexico City in 1975 but once again the marathon runners had to contend with the problems of altitude. For two thirds of the race Chuck Smead (USA) and Tom Howard (Can) led but in the end Rigoberto Mendoza came through to capture the gold and Cuba's first medal in the event. Cuba became the first country to retain the title at San Juan in 1979 when the race was again held in very hot weather, even with the start at 4 pm. Fifteen of the 19 runners finished as Colombia, one of the best of the South American marathon nations, had their best result with second and fourth places. Bearded Jorge Gonzalez (PR) set a new Games record winning the 1983 race held at Caracas on a humid afternoon by a near record margin of 7 min 47 sec as the expected North American challenge failed to materialise.

1951 Buenos Aires 6 March

1	Delfo Cabrera (Arg)	2:35:00.2
2	Reinaldo Gorno (Arg)	2:45:00
3	Luis Velazquez (Gua)	2:46:02.8

1955 Mexico City 19 March

1	Doroteo Flores (Gua)	2:59:09.2
2	Onesimo Rodriguez (Mex)	3:02:25.6
3	Luis Velazquez (Gua)	3:05:25.2

1959 Chicago 2 September

1	John J Kelley (USA)	2:27:54.2
2	Jim Green (USA)	2:32:16.9
3	Gordon Dickson (Can)	2:36:18.6

1963 Sao Paulo 4 May

1	Fidel Negrete (Mex)	2:27:55.6
2	Gordon McKenzie (USA)	2:31:17.2
3	Peter McArdle (USA)	2:34:14

1967 Winnipeg 4 August

1	Andy Boychuk (Can)	2:23:02.4
2	Agustin Calle (Col)	2:25:50.2
3	Alfredo Penaloza (Mex)	2:27:48.2

1971 Cali 5 August

1	Frank Shorter (USA)	2:22:40
2	Jose Gaspar (Mex)	2:26:30
3	Hernan Barreneche (Col)	2:27:19

1975 Mexico City 20 October

1	Rigoberto Mendoza (Cub)	2:25:02.9
2	Chuck Smead (USA)	2:25:31.6
3	Tom Howard (Can)	2:25:45.5

1979 San Juan 14 July

1	Radames Gonzalez (Cub)	2:24:09
2	Luis Barbosa (Col)	2:24:44
3	Rick Hughson (Can)	2:25:34

1983 Caracas 28 August

1	Jorge Gonzalez (PR)	2:12:42
2	Cesar Mercado (PR)	2:20:29
3	Miguel Cruz (Mex)	2:21:11

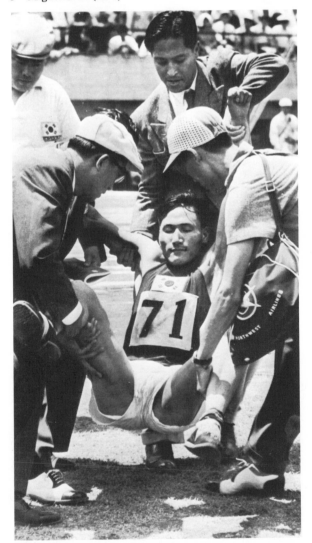

1958 Asian Games champion Lee Chang Hoon (Kor) carried off at the finish. (Popperfoto)

Asian Games

In the same month and year that the Pan American Games were inaugurated, so the Asian version got under way in India. The marathon at New Delhi came just five days after the Argentinian event. In the Indian race the national champion Chhota Singh survived the hot, dusty route to win by a handsome margin as conditions for the runners were as bad as those for their American counterparts. After a break of three years the second Games were held in Manila, but without the marathon. From then on the Games were held every four years and at Tokyo in 1958 the favoured Japanese could only salvage the bronze medal as Lee Chang Hoon (Kor), fourth in the 1956 Olympics, led from start to finish to record a big nine-minute winning margin. Four years later, at Jakarta, there were just eight runners at the start, only four of whom were to survive the sweltering heat. Gurnam Singh (Ind) led for 30 km but the conditions proved too much for him and he retired, leaving Masayuki Nagata (Jap) to take the gold medal.

Bangkok hosted both the 1966 and 1970 Games and on both occasions the Japanese took first and second, with Kenji Kimihara becoming the first champion to successfully defend his title. In 1966 he turned back the challenge of the world record holder Morio Shigematsu, and then in 1970 had a battle with Harnek Singh (Ind), the early leader, before finishing ahead of Yoshiro Mifune. With no marathon being run at Teheran in 1974, it was the turn of Bangkok yet again to stage the eighth Games (and sixth marathon) in 1978. By this time the North Koreans had become a dominant force in the marathon and after Shivnath Singh (Ind) dropped back, the race became a Japanese–Korean duel with Mineteru Sakamoto causing an upset with the second Japanese Susumu Sato fourth. In 1982 the Games returned to New Delhi and once again the North Korean challenge failed. The marathon was held in the middle of the day in extreme heat but this did not deter the young South Korean Yang Kon Kim from scoring a well deserved, though upset, win.

1951 New Delhi 11 March

1	Chhota Singh (Ind)	2:42:58.6
2	Katsuo Nishida (Jap)	2:49:03
3	Surat Singh (Ind)	2:53:49.3

1958 Tokyo 29 May

1	Lee Chang Hoon (Kor)	2:32:55
2	Myitung Naw (Bur)	2:42:46
3	Nobuyoshi Sadanaga (Jap)	2:43:44

1962 Jakarta 29 August

1	Masayuki Nagata (Jap)	2:34:54.2

| 2 | Mohamed Jousef (Pak) | 2:43:02 |
| 3 | Myitung Naw (Bur) | 2:49:37.1 |

1966 Bangkok 15 December

1	Kenji Kimihara (Jap)	2:33:22.8
2	Morio Shigematsu (Jap)	2:35:04.2
3	Lee Sang Hoon (Kor)	2:40:56

1970 Bangkok 15 December

1	Kenji Kimihara (Jap)	2:21:03
2	Yoshiro Mifune (Jap)	2:24:20.8
3	Kang Myung Kwang (Kor)	2:26:47.8

1978 Bangkok 17 December

1	Mineteru Sakamoto (Jap)	2:15:29.7
2	Chang Sop Choe (PRK)	2:15:57.4
3	Chun Son Goe (PRK)	2:16:10.3

1982 New Delhi 2 December

1	Yang Kon Kim (Kor)	2:22:21
2	Fumiaki Abe (Jap)	2:24:09
3	Seetharama Kukkappa (Ind)	2:25:07

African Games

Brazzaville was the venue for the first African Games in 1965 but the marathon was excluded from the programme. Not until 1973 was the next edition held and at Lagos the 1968 Olympic champion Mamo Wolde, who had won the longest track event at Brazzaville (5000 m), and his colleague Lengissa Bedane dominated the race. The Swaziland runners were well behind in third and fourth. These two nations renewed rivalry in 1978 at Algiers when the Games were revived after a break of five and a half years. Richard Mabuza, third in both the Lagos and Christchurch marathons, took revenge in taking the gold medal ahead of the Ethiopians. The Lesotho champion Gabashane Rakabaele, who had recorded a time of 2:12:33 in 1977, could do no better than eleventh. Although Ghana and Nigeria, who featured in the 1973 race, did not enter, there were still eleven nations who provided 17 finishers in under three hours, a commendable achievement in the conditions.

1973 Lagos 14 January

1	Mamo Wolde (Eth)	2:27:32
2	Lengissa Bedane (Eth)	2:28:16
3	Richard Mabuza (Swa)	2:34:17.7

1978 Algiers 27 July

1	Richard Mabuza (Swa)	2:21:53
2	Dereje Nedi (Eth)	2:23:08
3	Gebru Gurmu (Eth)	2:27:35

The
International
Races

Asahi

The Asahi sponsored marathon, first held in 1947 to encourage post-war Japanese activity has, over the ensuing years, developed into an international race of the highest calibre. Popularly known as the Fukuoka marathon, that city now being its permanent site, the annual December event has become the Mecca for the marathon elite with the year's top runners all being invited. It was not until 1954, when the race was held over a hilly course at Kamakura, that there was any overseas participation. With the arrival of runners from Argentina (who provided the winner Reinaldo Gorno), Finland, Korea and New Zealand, this was the first ever international marathon held in Japan. From 1955 to 1966 the event became known as the Asahi International marathon and although a system of alternating venues was in operation, it was somewhat appropriate, in view of what lay ahead, that Fukuoka hosted the first such race. Veikko Karvonen, the European champion and second the previous year, was the victor, and it was five years before a visiting athlete would mount the victor's rostrum again. In finishing second behind Karvonen, Kurao Hiroshima low-

ered Kitei Son's twenty-year-old national record to 2:23:51, and equalled his 1953 placing. He further improved his time in winning the 1957 race and in 1959 became the first to score two wins in the event.

Fukuoka became the permanent venue from 1959 onwards, except in 1963 when the Asahi event was staged over the forthcoming Olympic course in Tokyo. The course at Fukuoka is basically very flat and on leaving the Heiwadai stadium it skirts Hakata Bay (the ancient name for Fukuoka) to Gannosu where the runners turn and make their way back to the finish along the same road. The Olympic bronze medallist Barry Magee (NZ) won in 1960 and became the first to break 2:20 at this venue, and the following year Dr Pavel Kantorek (Cze) won, thus culminating a fine series of runs after four successive years finishing fourth or better. In 1963 another New Zealand athlete, Jeff Julian, scored an upset in turning back the Japanese Olympic hopefuls at Tokyo, but Toru Terasawa, winner in 1962, made amends for his disappointing Olympic run by winning the 1964 race in an Asian record time.

In 1966 the race title was changed to that of the

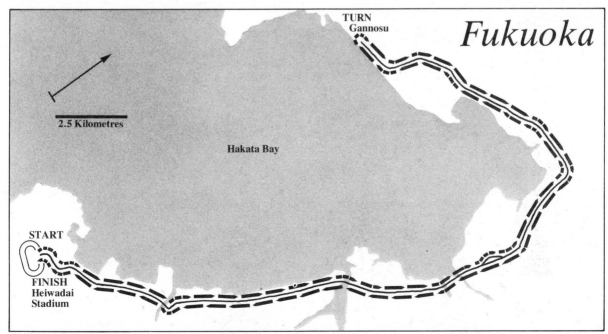

Fukuoka

TURN
Gannosu

Hakata Bay

2.5 Kilometres

START
FINISH
Heiwadai
Stadium

International Open Championship and eight nations were invited to send runners. In a most thrilling finish Mike Ryan (NZ) held off the 1965 winner Hidekuni Hiroshima, by just six tenths of a second, the narrowest win in the history of the Asahi marathon. Ryan was responsible for an extraordinarily fast opening pace the next year, which resulted in the one and only world record to be set at this venue. As the New Zealand star paid for his overzealous start so Derek Clayton (Aus) became

the first to better 2:10 with a superb 2:09:36.4, with runner-up Seiichiro Sasaki setting a new Asian record of 2:11:17. Conditions were unusually warm in 1968 as Bill Adcocks won with a European and British record of 2:10:47.8, a time only beaten by

Mike Ryan (NZ) finishes ahead of Hidekuni Hiroshima (Jap) in closest ever Fukuoka marathon, 1966.
Inset:
Ron Hill (GB) and Hayami Tanimura (Jap) fight for second place in Fukuoka, 1969. (Both Asahi Shimbun)

Clayton, whilst in 1969 Jerome Drayton (Can) literally ran away from the opposition in pouring rain, recording a new North American record in the process. The newly named series had got off to a most auspicious start and fully deserved its tag of the unofficial world marathon championship. Akio Usami stopped the rot in 1970 to give the organising country their first victory since 1965 and with it some hope of success at the 1972 Olympics. By the end of 1970, 22 of the top 50 world fastest times had been set at Fukuoka.

Frank Shorter dominated the next four editions in a truly awesome manner, regardless of the opposition or the conditions. In 1971 he won against a strong wind and three years later was equally dominant on the coldest race day yet encountered. His winning margin of 1 min 59.6 sec in 1973 is still the widest since the inauguration of the championship event in 1966. North American runners continued to triumph in the next three marathons as first Jerome Drayton added to his 1969 success with wins in 1975 and 1976, and Bill Rodgers (USA) after being third in 1975, won in 1977. In fourth position that year, and first Japanese, was the young Toshihiko Seko. Winning in 1978-9-80, the last two with devastating sprints off the final bend, Seko looked all set to equal Shorter's four wins in a row, but much to the consternation of his followers failed to race in 1981. Although the standard of the top finishers was not quite so high in 1981 (there had been eleven runners under 2:12 in 1980) an event record of 40 athletes bettered 2:20, as Rob de Castella (Aus) missed Salazar's newly set world record by just five seconds, but his time of 2:08:18 was the fastest ever recorded over a standard out and back course. In 1982 Paul Ballinger (NZ) took advantage of near perfect weather to set a new national record of 2:10:15, although it was a pity that the field was deplete of many star runners.

The Japanese Olympic trial was staged at Fukuoka in 1983. Toshihiko Seko equalled Shorter's achievement of four wins, overtaking Ikangaa in the home straight as the latter took 35 seconds off his own African record.

WINNERS (JAPANESE UNLESS STATED): FIRST THREE FROM 1966

1947		Toshikazu Wada	2:45:45
1948		Saburo Yamada	2:37:25
1949		Shinzo Koga	2:40:26
1950		Shunji Koyanagi	2:30:47
1951		Hiroyoshi Haigo	2:30:13
1952		Katsuo Nishida	2:27:59
1953		Hideo Hamamura	2:27:26
1954		Reinaldo Gorno (Arg)	2:24:55
1955		Veikko Karvonen (Fin)	2:23:16
1956		Keizo Yamada	2:25:15
1957		Kurao Hiroshima	2:21:40
1958		Nobuyoshi Sadanaga	2:24:01
1959		Kurao Hiroshima	2:29:34
1960		Barry Magee (NZ)	2:19:04
1961		Pavel Kantorek (Cze)	2:22:05
1962		Toru Terasawa	2:16:18.4
1963		Jeff Julian (NZ)	2:18:00.6
1964		Toru Terasawa	2:14:48.2
1965		Hidekuni Hiroshima	2:18:35.8
1966	1	Mike Ryan (NZ)	2:14:04.8
	2	Hidekuni Hiroshima	2:14:05.2
	3	Hirokazu Okabe	2:15:09.2
1967	1	Derek Clayton (Aus)	2:09:36.4
	2	Seiichiro Sasaki	2:11:17
	3	Dave McKenzie (NZ)	2:12:25.8
1968	1	Bill Adcocks (GB)	2:10:47.8
	2	Yoshiaki Unetani	2:12:40.6
	3	Tadaaki Ueoka	2:13:37.6
1969	1	Jerome Drayton (Can)	2:11:12.8
	2	Ron Hill (GB)	2:11:54.4
	3	Hayami Tanimura	2:12:03.4
1970	1	Akio Usami	2:10:37.8
	2	Kenny Moore (USA)	2:11:35.8
	3	Yoshiaki Unetani	2:12:12
1971	1	Frank Shorter (USA)	2:12:50.4
	2	Akio Usami	2:13:22.8
	3	Jack Foster (NZ)	2:13:42.4
1972	1	Frank Shorter (USA)	2:10:30
	2	John Farrington (Aus)	2:12:00.4
	3	Kenichi Otsuki	2:14:00.6
1973	1	Frank Shorter (USA)	2:11:45
	2	Brian Armstrong (Can)	2:13:43.4
	3	Eckhard Lesse (GDR)	2:13:53.8
1974	1	Frank Shorter (USA)	2:11:31.2
	2	Eckhard Lesse (GDR)	2:12:02.4
	3	Pekka Päivärinta (Fin)	2:13:09
1975	1	Jerome Drayton (Can)	2:10:08.4
	2	Dave Chettle (Aus)	2:10:20
	3	Bill Rodgers (USA)	2:11:26.4
1976	1	Jerome Drayton (Can)	2:12:35
	2	Ian Thompson (GB)	2:12:54.2
	3	Waldemar Cierpinski (GDR)	2:14:56
1977	1	Bill Rodgers (USA)	2:10:55.3
	2	Leonid Moseyev (Sov)	2:11:57
	3	Massimo Magnani (Ita)	2:13:04
1978	1	Toshihiko Seko	2:10:21
	2	Hideki Kita	2:11:05
	3	Shigeru Soh	2:11:41.2
1979	1	Toshihiko Seko	2:10:35
	2	Shigeru Soh	2:10:37
	3	Takeshi Soh	2:10:40
1980	1	Toshihiko Seko	2:09:45
	2	Takeshi Soh	2:09:49
	3	Kunimitsu Itoh	2:10:05
1981	1	Rob de Castella (Aus)	2:08:18
	2	Kunimitsu Itoh	2:09:37
	3	Shigeru Soh	2:10:19
1982	1	Paul Ballinger (NZ)	2:10:15
	2	Hideki Kita	2:11:09
	3	Bruno Lafranchi (Swz)	2:11:12
1983	1	Toshihiko Seko	2:08:52
	2	Juma Ikangaa (Tan)	2:08:55
	3	Shigeru Soh	2:09:11

Race venues: 1947 Kumamoto; 1948 Takamatsu; 1949 Shizuoka; 1950 Hiroshima; 1951 Fukuoka; 1952 Ube; 1953 Nagoya; 1954 Kamakura; 1955 Fukuoka; 1956 Nagoya; 1957 Fukuoka; 1958 Utsunomiya. With the exception of 1963 (Tokyo) the remaining races have been held at Fukuoka.

Athens

It was not until 1955 that the Greek Athletic Board (SEGAS) decided to stage an international marathon over the original Olympic course from Marathon to Athens. Indeed, apart from the Balkan Games no other international marathon had been held in Greece since the Intermediary Games of 1906. Even then it was decided to hold the event, named the International Classical Marathon, biennially. The course record was lowered gradually over the first five events, despite the demanding nature of the point to point route. Beginning at the village of Marathon, the runners turn off to the left at about 5 km (3 miles) to circle the tomb of the warriors slain in the battle of Marathon. There they toss the olive twigs, given to them at the start, on to the base of the monument. The road is fairly flat to 20 km (12½ miles) but from 20 km to 32 km (20 miles) the course climbs some 65 m (200 ft). From the summit the runners race downhill to the finish at the marble Panathenaic stadium, rebuilt for the 1896 celebrations, on a site used for training and exercising by the ancient Greeks since about 329 BC.

The first Classical marathon attracted runners from six nations but there was little opposition for Veikko Karvonen (Fin) who won by 11 min 32 sec, and in 1959 the Finnish squad was again dominant taking first, third and fourth places. In 1961 Olympic champion Abebe Bikila (Eth) won barefooted as the race month was shifted from October to May, and two years later 'Buddy' Edelen (USA) triumphed only weeks before setting a new world record in England, as runners from ten countries took part. Conditions in 1965 were extremely hot and the field was faced with a stiff head wind. Jozsef

Suto (Hun), fifth in the Tokyo Olympics with a time of 2:17:55.8, was slowed to a time outside 2:30 yet he still won by a massive 18 min 26 sec from Ivailo Charankov (Bul), a record margin in a race of this calibre.

In 1969 the date was again changed, this time to April, and the weather was dramatically different, being much cooler at the 4 pm start and with a slight following breeze. It was without doubt the finest field yet assembled as the first five in the Mexico Olympics were rematched. Olympic bronze medallist Mike Ryan (NZ) set the pace for the first 20 km. As Ryan faded, so Kenji Kimihara (Jap) and Bill Adcocks (GB), second and fifth respectively in Mexico, led to the top of the long climb, whereupon the British runner sped away unchallenged to the finish. His winning time of 2:11:07.2 remains one of the finest achievements of all time, taking into consideration this most trying course. Even though the month of April was considered most favourable for the marathon, the weather was still fickle. Akio Usami (Jap) led from start to finish in 1971, combating heat and wind all the way, yet in 1974 conditions were overcast and heavy as Ian Thompson (GB) won comfortably from colleague Max Coleby in the then second fastest time recorded at this venue. From 1975 the weather has not been at all conducive to good performances and in addition the quality of the fields assembled has dropped off, possibly because of the many sponsored races now being staged in more attractive locations and over less demanding courses. In the majority of races, the runners have been faced with very warm weather and a troublesome wind, but the Greeks were able to rejoice in 1977 as their champion Theopanis Tsimigatos overtook the 1975 winner Yuriy Lap-

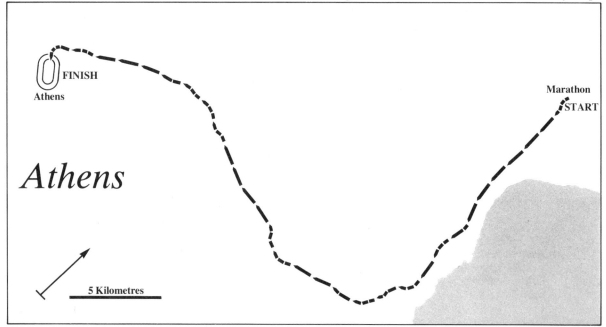

Athens

FINISH
Athens

Marathon
START

5 Kilometres

Bill Adcocks (GB, 5), Demissie Wolde (Eth), Huseyin Aktas (Tur), Kenji Kimihara (Jap) and Gyula Toth (Hun) at 28 km in 1969 Marathon to Athens race. (AP)

tyev (Sov) in the closing stages, to record Greece's first win. The closest ever finish occurred in 1979 when the Turkish record holder Veli Balli out-sprinted Anatoliy Aryukov (Sov) to win by a mere two tenths of a second.

Since 1976 a 'Popular' marathon has been held each October, recently drawing fields in excess of 1000 runners, but only in 1977 has a fast time been recorded. That year, Kebede Balcha (Eth) beat two of his colleagues in 2:14:40.8 as since then winning times have been in the region of 2:27 to 2:34.

CLASSICAL WINNERS

Year	Winner	Time
1955	Veikko Karvonen (Fin)	2:27:30
1957	Franjo Mihalic (Yug)	2:26:27.8
1959	Eino Oksanen (Fin)	2:26:30
1961	Abebe Bikila (Eth)	2:23:44.6
1963	Buddy Edelen (USA)	2:23:06.8
1965	Jozsef Suto (Hun)	2:30:40.4
1967	Jürgen Busch (GDR)	2:20:40
1969	Bill Adcocks (GB)	2:11:07.2
1971	Akio Usami (Jap)	2:19:25
1973	Colin Kirkham (GB)	2:16:45.4
1974	Ian Thompson (GB)	2:13:50.2
1975	Yuriy Laptyev (Sov)	2:25:27
1976	Mircea Damian (Rom)	2:27:33
1977	Theopanis Tsimigatos (Gre)	2:39:36.4
1978	Nikolay Penzin (Sov)	2:21:40
1979	Veli Balli (Tur)	2:28:04.4
1980	Vladimir Pontokov (Sov)	2:20:52
1982	Rodolfo Gomez (Mex)	2:11:49

Veli Balli (Tur) holds off Anatoliy Aryukov (Sov) by two tenths of a second at Athens, 1979. (Popperfoto)

Boston

The Boston Athletic Association, founded on 15 March 1887, has staged the most venerable of all marathons annually on Patriots Day, or the nearest Monday thereto, since 1897. Only once, in 1918, was the event not held, a ten-man military team race taking its place. Except for changes at the start and finish, the course has remained the same throughout the 86-year-old history of the run. Since 1907, when the race started on the Hopkinton Road, the route passes through Ashland (scene of the start from 1897 to 1906) and Framingham to Natick. So far the road is slightly downhill, but from Natick it drops appreciably through Wellesley to Newton Lower Falls. Then commences a five-mile climb to the summit of Heartbreak Hill before the final downward route via Lake Street and Coolidge Corner to the finish at the Prudential Tower in Boston. The first two finishes were at the Irvington Street Oval, but from then until 1965 it was on Exeter Street at the BAA clubhouse. The race currently starts at Hopkinton Green.

No course is easy. Running the marathon distance itself is an achievement. Just because the Boston course is in the main downhill has not meant that it is always easy to negotiate. Perfect spring weather has not always prevailed on race day and competitors have had to contend with a variety of climes over the years. In 1909 and 1976 temperatures soared towards 100°F (38°C), melting the road surface into the bargain, and on at least another dozen occasions records show that the day in question was extremely hot. Bitingly cold easterly winds, in 1933 particu-

larly, have often hit the runners head on. Sleet and slush (1912), steady, driving rain (1929 and 1955), snow flurries (1908 and 1935) and intense cold (1942) have all, at one time or another, made the race an uncomfortably severe one. Even a dust storm, generated by high winds, blinded the gallant runners in 1903. These are but a few of the years when conditions have been at their most trying.

1897 to 1914

These were the formative years. Boston had the previous September been upstaged by New York in being the first to hold a marathon in the New World. It was appropriate that the winner at New York, John McDermott should triumph at Boston. His winning margin of 6 min 52 sec remains to this day the widest in the history of the race.

The Canadians first put in an official appearance in 1900 and led by James Caffrey swept the first three places. Caffrey returned the following year to successfully defend his title; not until the era of DeMar would there be a repeat winner. Sammy Mellor, third in 1901, won the 1902 event as Caffrey withdrew through illness, and although not winning, he set the pace in each of the next four races before succumbing in the final stages. Fred Lorz who had been disqualified in the 1904 Olympic Games marathon was soon allowed to compete again and won in 1905, whilst the winner the following year, Tim Ford, is the youngest ever Boston champion at 18 years of age.

Throughout the history of the pre-war Boston races, Indians competed with a great deal of success. Among the tribes represented were the Mohawk, Hopi, Penobscot, Missassaja, Narraganset and

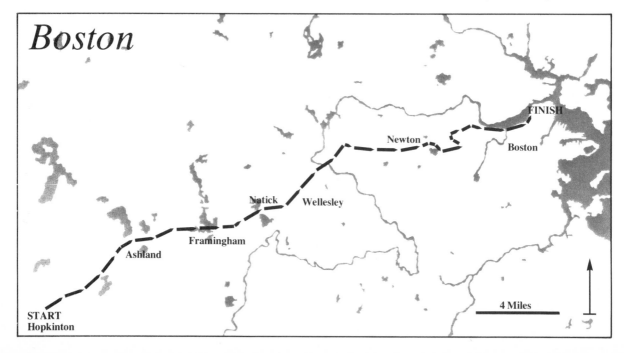

Onondaga. Tom Longboat originated from the latter, and he won the 1907 race in record time through driving sleet. It is a strange phenomenon that no Olympic champion has ever won at Boston. In 1908, three months before his London triumph, John Hayes took second, thus equalling the feat of the 1904 Olympic champion Tom Hicks. Albin Stenroos in 1926 also managed the runner-up position. In 1912 Mike Ryan won with a time which lasted nine years as a short course record, whilst the 1919 winner Carl Linder, also an accomplished javelin thrower and decathlete, had been rejected for military service because of having flat feet!

1920 to 1939

The 1920 race was also one of the United States Olympic trials, and in an upset overseas-born runners finished in the first three places. In 1921 Frank Zuna became the first to better 2:20 for the 24½ mile course, but the following year Clarence DeMar improved the time with the first of three consecutive

wins. In each race he defeated the opposition convincingly. Upset by Canadian Johnny Miles in 1926, DeMar came back to take another two victories before giving second best to Miles again in 1929.

Jimmy Henigan won the 1931 race at his tenth try (and only the second time he had lasted the distance) for a popular result, whilst the German ex-sailor Paul de Bruyn, resident in New York, gained Olympic selection by winning in 1932. Leslie Pawson scored the first of three wins that he would achieve over a period of eight years in 1933. His winning time lasted six years as a record for the course which had been full distance since 1926. Although equalled by John J Kelley (1957–62) no one has held the full course record longer. A second Indian tribe from Rhode Island, the Narraganset, provided the champion in Ellison 'Tarzan' Brown in

First three at 1958 Boston, from left: John J Kelley (USA), second, Franjo Mihalic (Yug), first, and Eino Pulkkinen (Fin), third. (AP)

1936, and the impoverished redskin won again three years later, when, in freezing rain, he became the first to run the full Boston course in under 2:30.

1940 to 1959
At 6 ft 2 in (1.88 m) the 1942 winner Bernard Joseph Smith, a milkman by profession, is still the tallest ever Boston champion, although he very nearly did not run due to a heavy cold. In 1945 John Adelbert Kelley took his second win ten years after his first, yet on seven occasions he was runner-up and he finished in the top ten 18 times. Kelley ran his 50th Boston marathon in 1981 at the age of 73 by which time he had completed over 100 marathons, and of those at Boston he only failed to finish the course in 1928, 1932 and 1956.

The European record fell to Stylianos Kyriakidis of Greece in 1946, and the world record the following year to 5 ft 1 in (1.55 m) Yun Bok Suh (Kor), the **Eino Oksanen (Fin) wins his third Boston marathon, 1962. (AP)**

shortest winner of all, despite being bowled over by a dog en route. Foreign runners continued to triumph and in 1948 Gérard Côté scored his fourth and final success, but only after a somewhat acrimonious duel with Ted Vogel. Only DeMar with seven victories had more wins than the Canadian at Boston. It was then the turn of the Orient to dominate and in 1950 the Koreans, under the guidance of the 1936 Olympic champion Kitei Son, took the first

Left:
Japanese dominate Boston 1965. From left: Aurele Vandendriessche (Bel), Morio Shigematsu, winner, Hideaki Shishido and Takayuki Nakao (all Jap). (Hideaki Miyagi)

Boston 1966. Japanese stars Kenji Kimihara (3), Seiichiro Sasaki (5), Toru Terasawa (1) and Hirokazu Okabe (3) finish in the first four places. (Hideaki Miyagi)

Joan Benoit (USA), setting a new world record at Boston, 1983. (Popperfoto)

three places. This was the first overseas sweep of the medals for exactly 50 years.

In 1951, 1953 and 1955 the Japanese won and impressed with their depth, whilst in between Guatemala (first and third in 1952) and Finland provided the champions. The 1954 race was termed 'the battle of the giants' because of the quality of the field. Jim Peters, the world's fastest, was overtaken at 18 miles by the European champion elect Veikko Karvonen, and had to be content with second place. The 1948 Olympic champion Delfo Cabrera retired during the duel which was waged in near eighty degree heat. John J Kelley (no relation to the older John A Kelley) became the first American to win since 1945, when he held off a challenge by Karvonen in 1957, but overseas domination continued with Franjo Mihalic succeeding in 1958.

1960 to 1983

Eino Oksanen, a Finnish detective, won in 1961 and 1962, thus adding to his victory in 1959 and upholding his country's fine record of recent years. Since 1954 Finland had provided winners in six of the nine races. There was another top rate field in 1963 but a bitter east wind affected Ethiopians Abebe Bikila and Mamo Wolde, on record schedule pace, and the consistent Belgian champion Aurele Vandendriessche won. His time was the first under 2:20 for the full distance at Boston, as Brian Kilby, the 1962 European champion, and Oksanen finished third and fourth.

The Japanese triumphed in 1965 as Vandendriessche (he had won again in 1964) prevented them from taking all the first six places, and in 1966 they were equally dominant in taking the first four positions. History was made that year as Roberta Gibb, disguising herself in a hooded sweatshirt, became the first woman to run at Boston, albeit unofficially. Her finishing time was 3:21:40.

The mid-sixties saw the start of the running boom in the United States. This was emphasised no better than by the number of starters at Boston. From the 15 runners who toed the line drawn in the dirt in 1897, the numbers gradually climbed as the years passed, particularly after the Second World War. The explosion began in 1967 when more than 600 athletes started and within two years the number had exceeded 1000, doubling by 1975. Although since 1978 the field has been swollen by as many as two to three thousand unofficial runners, the official number of starters and finishers (the latter determined by a closing time between three and a half and four hours after the start) since 1976 has been:

	Starters	Finishers	Closing time
1976	1942	1161	3:30
1977	2766	2329	4:00
1978	4391	4071	4:00
1979	7910	5958	3:35
1980	5471	3665	3:37
1981	6881	5590	4:01
1982	5939	4562	3:35
1983	6070	5388	3:58

Taken from the official results book.

Ron Hill took a record 3 min 19 sec off the best time set by Yoshiaki Unetani in 1969, when he mastered the cold and damp conditions prevailing in 1970, and two years later women were officially accepted into the event. Nina Kuscsik who had made her debut in the 1969 race became the first recognised winner in 3:10:21, after two consecutive runner-up placings behind Sarah Berman in 1970 and 1971. Berman, a mother of two, had also finished first in 1969.

For the first time 2:10 was bettered in the race by Bill Rodgers in 1975, his finishing performance being a new North American record. Although dropping out in 1977 Rodgers returned to triumph in three consecutive years from 1978 through 1980, the first of these being the closest ever finish at Boston as Jeff Wells was only two seconds behind at the tape.

Toshihiko Seko, second in 1979, put an end to Rodgers' winning streak the following year, but only after a fine duel with cross-country champion Craig Virgin, as Rodgers finished third. In 1982 the new world record holder, Cuban-born Alberto Salazar, was involved in yet another tight finale as for the first time in history two runners bettered 2:09, two seconds separating him and Dick Beardsley. The race incorporated the trials for the World Championship in 1983 and in the absence of Salazar, Greg Meyer took full advantage of the favourable conditions to win in a time of 2:09:01. But the highlight of the 87th Boston was reserved for the women and Joan Benoit in particular. Running the first half of the race at sub 2:20 pace Benoit decimated the world record by no less than 2 min 46 sec, only the third time that a world record had been beaten at this venue, and the second by a woman.

WINNERS *(US UNLESS STATED)*: FIRST THREE FROM 1976

1897	John McDermott	2:55:10
1898	Ron McDonald	2:42:00
1899	Lawrence Brignolia	2:54:38
1900	Jim Caffrey (Can)	2:39:44.4
1901	Jim Caffrey (Can)	2:29:23.6
1902	Sam Mellor	2:43:12
1903	John Lorden	2:41:29.8
1904	Mike Spring	2:38:04.4
1905	Fred Lorz	2:38:25.4
1906	Tim Ford	2:45:45
1907	Tom Longboat (Can)	2:24:24
1908	Tom Morrissey	2:25:43.2
1909	Henri Renaud	2:53:36.8
1910	Fred Cameron (Can)	2:28:52.4
1911	Clarence DeMar	2:21:39.6
1912	Mike Ryan	2:21:18.2
1913	Fritz Carlson	2:25:14.8
1914	Jim Duffy (Can)	2:25:01.2
1915	Edouard Fabre (Can)	2:31:41.2
1916	Arthur Roth	2:27:16.4

1917		Bill Kennedy	2:28:37.2
1918		marathon not held	
1919		Carl Linder	2:29:13.4
1920		Peter Trivoulidas (Gre)	2:29:31
1921		Frank Zuna	2:18:57.6
1922		Clarence DeMar	2:18:10
1923		Clarence DeMar	2:23:37.4
1924		Clarence DeMar	2:29:40.2
1925		Charles Mellor	2:33:00.6
1926		John Miles (Can)	2:25:40.4
1927		Clarence DeMar	2:40:22.2
1928		Clarence DeMar	2:37:07.8
1929		John Miles (Can)	2:33:08.6
1930		Clarence DeMar	2:34:48.2
1931		Jim Henigan	2:46:45.8
1932		Paul de Bruyn (Ger)	2:33:36.4
1933		Leslie Pawson	2:31:01.6
1934		Dave Komonen (Can)	2:32:53.8
1935		John A Kelley	2:32:07.4
1936		Ellison Brown	2:33:40.8
1937		Walter Young (Can)	2:33:20
1938		Leslie Pawson	2:35:34.8
1939		Ellison Brown	2:28:51.8
1940		Gérard Côté (Can)	2:28:28.6
1941		Leslie Pawson	2:30:38
1942		Joe Smith	2:26:51.2
1943		Gérard Côté (Can)	2:28:25.8
1944		Gérard Côté (Can)	2:31:50.4
1945		John A Kelley	2:30:40.2
1946		Stylianos Kyriakidis (Gre)	2:29:27
1947		Yun Bok Suh (Kor)	2:25:39
1948		Gérard Côté (Can)	2:31:02
1949		Gösta Leandersson (Swe)	2:31:50.8
1950		Kee Yong Ham (Kor)	2:32:39
1951		Shigeki Tanaka (Jap)	2:27:45
1952		Doroteo Flores (Gua)	2:31:53
1953		Keizo Yamada (Jap)	2:18:51
1954		Veikko Karvonen (Fin)	2:20:39
1955		Hideo Hamamura (Jap)	2:18:22
1956		Antti Viskari (Fin)	2:14:14
1957		John J Kelley	2:20:05
1958		Franjo Mihalic (Yug)	2:25:54
1959		Eino Oksanen (Fin)	2:22:42
1960		Paavo Kotila (Fin)	2:20:54
1961		Eino Oksanen (Fin)	2:23:39
1962		Eino Oksanen (Fin)	2:23:48
1963		Aurele Vandendriessche (Bel)	2:18:58
1964		Aurele Vandendriessche (Bel)	2:19:59
1965		Morio Shigematsu (Jap)	2:16:33
1966		Kenji Kimihara (Jap)	2:17:11
1967		Dave McKenzie (NZ)	2:15:45
1968		Amby Burfoot	2:22:17
1969		Yoshiaki Unetani (Jap)	2:13:49
1970		Ron Hill (GB)	2:10:30
1971		Alvaro Mejia (Col)	2:18:45
1972		Olavi Suomalainen (Fin)	2:15:39
1973		Jon Anderson	2:16:03
1974		Neil Cusack (Ire)	2:13:39
1975		Bill Rodgers	2:09:55
1976	1	Jack Fultz	2:20:19
	2	Mario Cuevas (Mex)	2:21:13
	3	Jose de Jesus (PR)	2:22:10
1977	1	Jerome Drayton (Can)	2:14:46
	2	Veli Balli (Tur)	2:15:44
	3	Brian Maxwell (Can)	2:17:21

1978	1	Bill Rodgers	2:10:13
	2	Jeff Wells	2:10:15
	3	Esa Tikkanen (Fin)	2:11:15
1979	1	Bill Rodgers	2:09:27
	2	Toshihiko Seko (Jap)	2:10:12
	3	Bob Hodge	2:12:30
1980	1	Bill Rodgers	2:12:11
	2	Marco Marchei (Ita)	2:13:20
	3	Ron Tabb	2:14:48
1981	1	Toshihiko Seko (Jap)	2:09:26
	2	Craig Virgin	2:10:26
	3	Bill Rodgers	2:10:34
1982	1	Alberto Salazar	2:08:51
	2	Dick Beardsley	2:08:53
	3	John Lodwick	2:12:01
1983	1	Greg Meyer	2:09:01
	2	Ron Tabb	2:09:32
	3	Benji Durden	2:09:58

Course distances: 1897–1923 24 miles 1232 yd (39 km); 1924–6 26 miles 209 yd (41.9 km); 1927–50 26 miles 385 yd (42.195 km); 1951–6 25 miles 938 yd (40.5 km); 1957–83 26 miles 385 yd (42.195 km).

WOMEN

1972		Nina Kuscsik	3:08:58
1973		Jackie Hansen	3:05:59
1974		Miki Gorman	2:47:11
1975		Liane Winter (GFR)	2:42:24
1976	1	Kim Merritt	2:47:10
	2	Miki Gorman	2:52:27
	3	Dorothy Doolittle	2:56:26
1977	1	Miki Gorman	2:48:33
	2	Marilyn Bevans	2:51:12
	3	Lisa Lorrain	2:56:04
1978	1	Gayle Barron	2:44:52
	2	Penny De Moss	2:45:36
	3	Jane Killion	2:47:23
1979	1	Joan Benoit	2:35:15
	2	Patti Lyons	2:38:22
	3	Sue Krenn	2:38:50
1980	1	Jacqueline Gareau (Can)	2:34:28
	2	Patti Lyons	2:35:08
	3	Gillian Adams (GB)	2:39:17
1981	1	Allison Roe (NZ)	2:26:46
	2	Patti Catalano	2:27:51
	3	Joan Benoit	2:30:16
1982	1	Charlotte Teske (GFR)	2:29:33
	2	Jacqueline Gareau (Can)	2:36:09
	3	Eileen Claugus	2:38:48
1983	1	Joan Benoit	2:22:43
	2	Jacqueline Gareau (Can)	2:29:28
	3	Mary Shea	2:33:24

1983 times in the official results book are one second faster than those shown above which were corrected by Boston officials.

Enschede

The idea of staging an international marathon in the Netherlands was formulated, not as one would have expected in that country but in Norway. The occasion was the IAAF meeting held at Oslo in August 1946 and those responsible were a member of the Dutch Federation and one from Czecho-slovakia who happened to be a founder member of

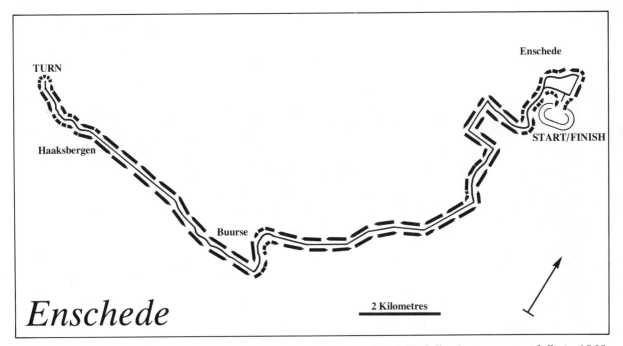

Enschede

the Kosice marathon. At this conference a track meet between the two nations was arranged to take part in Enschede the following July and it was decided to hold a marathon race on the first day, and from then to be held biennially. A field of 51 lined up for the first race which resulted in an unknown Finnish runner Eero Riikonen winning by less than a minute from John Systad (Nor).

For some unknown reason the course distance in 1949 was only 40 km and the British champion Jack Holden was a clear first. The first three races to be held in the 1950s each had some feature to write them into the history of the event. The Finnish champion Veikko Karvonen won with a record margin of 6 min 28 sec in 1951, still the biggest victory. Two years later Jim Peters set a world record for an out and back course winning by over five minutes from colleague Stan Cox. And in 1955 Reinaldo Gorno (Arg) survived a heavy cloudburst at the mid-point to edge out Osvaldo Suarez, also from Argentina, by a single second in the closest finish ever. In 1957 the race started from the newly completed Diekman stadium and the route used is basically the same as at present. From Enschede the road goes through Buurse to the turn at Haaksbergen and back over the same flat road to the finish at the stadium. Pavel Kantorek (Cze), winner in 1959, had come close to being the first to win twice when in 1963 he was overtaken by his compatriot Vaclav Chudomel in the final stages and had to be content with second.

The tenth marathon in 1965 attracted over one hundred runners for the first time and was won by the consistent Belgian Aurele Vandendriessche. Japan made their race entry an auspicious one by winning in 1967, following up successfully in 1969, the first time that a single nation had provided the winner in following races. But the record was not to last long as the next three races were all won by British athletes. With over two hundred and fifty starters in 1971, it was fitting that Peters' record should fall to another British runner, Bernie Allen, who, leading from 15 km, won in fine style. Olympic champion Mamo Wolde finished a poor 20th, whilst Abebe Bikila was an interested onlooker. In 1975 Enschede celebrated its 650th anniversary and the 1973 winner Ron Hill became the first to repeat a victory when despite the intense heat he set a course record. Bill Rodgers (USA) and Neil Cusack (Ire), winner at Boston in 1974, both dropped out of the race much to the disappointment of the organisers. No less than 23 countries were represented in 1977 and the North American continent furnished a winner for the first time when Brian Maxwell (Can) shook off a Japanese challenge at 35 km to win. Two years later Kirk Pfeffer (USA) dominated the race in record time from a field of 370. After a bright, sunny start the weather turned to cloud, then back to sun, as Pfeffer went clear after the turn and heavy showers developed. As the rain became heavier, the American went faster to be timed in 2:11:50 at the finish, pulling a record number of ten to under 2:20. The largest field to date (over four hundred) gathered at the Diekman stadium in 1981 on a warm, humid day. Cor Vriend became the first Netherlands runner to win since 1957, as for the first time in the history of the race there was a women's division, won by Jane Wipf (USA) in 2:38:21. Wipf's time was improved in 1983 by Priscilla Welch (GB) who recorded 2:36:32, and in winning the men's race Kevin Forster made it a British

Jim Peters (GB) wins at Enschede in 1953 with a world record for an out and back course. (AP)

double. It is a refreshing fact that, despite newly formed annual races at Amsterdam and Rotterdam, the Enschede event is still a most popular biennial attraction, particularly to the regular British contingent.

WINNERS *(NETHERLANDS UNLESS STATED)*

1947	Eero Riikonen (Fin)	2:44:13
1949	Jack Holden (GB)	2:20:52
1951	Veikko Karvonen (Fin)	2:29:02
1953	Jim Peters (GB)	2:19:22
1955	Reinaldo Gorno (Arg)	2:26:33
1957	Piet Bleeker	2:32:39
1959	Pavel Kantorek (Cze)	2:26:48
1961	Peter Wilkinson (GB)	2:24:11
1963	Vaclav Chudomel (Cze)	2:25:10.4
1965	Aurele Vandendriessche (Bel)	2:21:16
1967	Yoshiro Mifune (Jap)	2:20:53.8
1969	Kazuo Matsubara (Jap)	2:19:29.8
1971	Bernie Allen (GB)	2:16:54.2
1973	Ron Hill (GB)	2:18:06.2
1975	Ron Hill (GB)	2:15:59.2
1977	Brian Maxwell (Can)	2:15:14
1979	Kirk Pfeffer (USA)	2:11:50
1981	Cor Vriend	2:15:54
1983	Kevin Forster (GB)	2:14:19

Karl Marx Stadt

As a result of a joint venture by local track and field authorities and the national federation, an international marathon was first staged at Karl Marx Stadt (formerly Chemnitz) in April 1967. The course, in the town park, is unusual in that only about 40% is of tarmacadam, the remainder, except for a stretch of cobble, being of cinder and packed earth. In 1979 the current course of eight laps of

The first three winners at Karl Marx Stadt. From left: Jürgen Busch (1967), Bill Adcocks (1968) and Tim Johnston (1969).

4.9 km (3 miles) plus the extra three kilometres at the finish, was brought into use. Seventy-eight runners from six European nations were at the start of the first race as Jürgen Busch won by less than six seconds in a GDR record time. In 1968 the number of countries sending athletes doubled and on an overcast, showery day Bill Adcocks (GB) took the lead from 33 km (20½ miles) to set a new European record of 2:12:16.8. Runners from the GDR, Romania, Hungary, Finland and Switzerland all set national records, whilst Britain took the team prize through Adcocks and Jim Alder (fourth).

The next year the time of the start changed from

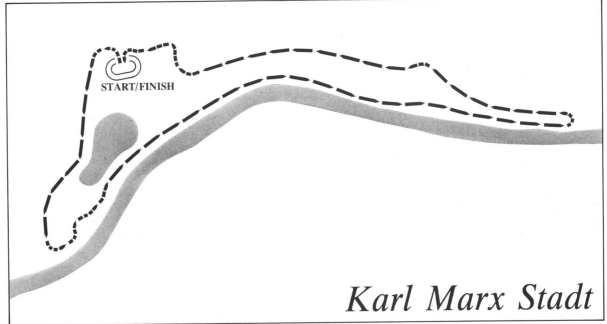

START/FINISH

Karl Marx Stadt

9 am to 5 pm and Britain repeated its success of 1968 as Tim Johnston triumphed. Third was Jürgen Busch and he dominated in 1970 from start to finish, winning by a record margin of 3 min 53 sec. He also carried off the honours the following year but by only 4.6 sec on a day when a cold wind, rain and snow hampered the runners, and as he had also taken third place in 1968 his event record was most impressive. There were a record 104 starters from 13 countries in 1972 as Eckhard Lesse, making his marathon debut, lowered the national record in winning. He defended his title the following April, overtaking the early leader Bernie Allen (GB) at 25 km on a day when the temperature soared into the high seventies. Such were the conditions that 64 of the 97 starters dropped out. Lesse did not take part in 1974 but equalled Busch's three wins the next year in cold, icy weather. Waldemar Cierpinski's debut at Karl Marx Stadt in 1976 was a positive one as he turned back the challenge of Günter Mielke (GFR), whilst in 1977 Pekka Päivärinta (Fin) became the first visiting athlete to succeed since 1969. After a 12-month break, two races were held in 1979 as first Jürgen Eberding overtook Jukka Toivola (Fin) at 35 km, thus regaining the host nation's winning ways, and then on 1 September Cierpinski triumphed in a four nation international. The Olympic champion was timed in 2:15:50 and led the GDR to victory from Great Britain, the Soviet Union and Poland, who finished in that order.

The following year Cierpinski bettered the 12-year-old course record, breaking the challenge of Oyvind Dahl (Nor) in the final two kilometres on a sunny day, when a record 25 were timed in under 2:20. Jürgen Eberding joined the ranks of Busch, Lesse and Cierpinski as a double winner in 1981

Karl Marx Stadt, 1980. From left: Oyvind Dahl (Nor) second, Waldemar Cierpinski (GDR) winner, and Hans-Joachim Truppel (GDR) third.

which was notable for the first female runner to take part. The Hungarian Jozsefne Babinyecz was timed in 2:51:02. In 1982 it was the turn of Hans-Joachim Truppel to win, 13 years after running at Karl Marx Stadt for the first time when he finished 14th. Since then he had never been lower than eighth, completing every race except 1976, and had been runner-up in 1971 and third on another four occasions.

WINNERS *(GDR UNLESS STATED)*

1967	Jürgen Busch	2:16:09.2
1968	Bill Adcocks (GB)	2:12:16.8
1969	Tim Johnston (GB)	2:15:31.2
1970	Jürgen Busch	2:14:41.2
1971	Jürgen Busch	2:17:30
1972	Eckhard Lesse	2:13:19.4
1973	Eckhard Lesse	2:17:36.2
1974	Gerald Umbach	2:15:59.8
1975	Eckhard Lesse	2:14:49.6
1976	Waldemar Cierpinski	2:13:57.2
1977	Pekka Päivärinta (Fin)	2:13:32.4
1979	Jürgen Eberding	2:14:52.1
1980	Waldemar Cierpinski	2:11:17
1981	Jürgen Eberding	2:15:25
1982	Hans-Joachim Truppel	2:15:48
1983	Jorg Peter	2:15:34

WOMEN

1981	Jozsefne Babinyecz (Hun)	2:51:02
1982	Antonia Ladanyine (Hun)	2:41:07
1983	Katrin Dörre	2:37:41

Kosice

The Kosice marathon was conceived by a group of Czech officials, attending the 1924 Olympic Games in Paris. During a subsequent meeting of the East Slovakian sub-Carpathian district of the Czech federation in August that year, the first marathon was scheduled for October. For this inaugural event the course stretched from Turna to Kosice, but from then on, except for variations in 1925 (Kosice–Cana–Haniska–Kosice) and 1952 (Presov–Kosice) the route has been from Kosice to Sena and back. Eight runners, all from Czechoslovakia, were the pioneers of the first race, and seven finished, but the next year the Hungarians were invited and their five athletes all finished in the first eight. Hungarian Pal Kiraly's winning time of 2:41:55 was not bettered until 1931. Although from 1925 until the last pre-war race in 1937 the number of those starting did not exceed fifty, foreign nations sent runners every year. After Hungary, Germany and Austria were first represented in 1926, Yugoslavia (1927), Poland and Latvia (1930), Argentina (1933), Finland (1934), Romania (1935), France and Sweden (1937) followed in quick succession. In 1937 more than half the 41 starters were from a record seven invited countries.

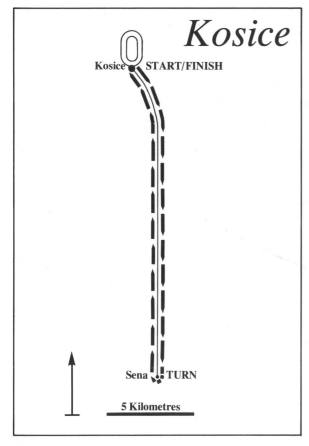

Kosice

Kosice START/FINISH

Sena TURN

5 Kilometres

Kosice 1932. From left: Willi Boss (Ger), Arturs Motmillers (Lat) and winner Jozsef Galambos (Hun) in lead. (Kosice)

Gösta Leandersson (Swe) won in 1948 and 1950, whilst Erkki Puolakka (Fin), the first to better 2:30 for the course, was successful in 1952 and 1954. The Soviet Union sent a team for the first time in 1957 and placed five in the first seven including the winner Ivan Filin, as British runners took second and sixth. Two years later the Soviet European champion Sergey Popov won in a record 2:17:45.2, the first time that 2:20 had been beaten at Kosice, and led his team to another victory over Great Britain. In 1958 Pavel Kantorek became the first Czech to win an international version of the race since Sulc, and went on to win again in 1962 and 1964, but the record equalling fourth win eluded him. Olympic champion Abebe Bikila, now racing in shoes, won in

Medal winners at Kosice 1965. From left: Bill Adcocks (GB, second), Aurele Vandendriessche (Bel, first) and Brian Kilby (GB, third). (Hideaki Miyagi)

By 1931 there had already been two double winners, Jozsef Galambos (Hun) and Paul Hempel (Ger) but the star attraction that year was the newly crowned 30 km track world record holder Juan Zabala (Arg). Making his marathon debut in the pouring rain, Zabala ran away from the opposition, setting a record time and beating second place Galambos by no less than 14 min 37 sec. The Hungarian returned to win again in 1932–3 and his four wins in the event have not been equalled. In addition to his second place in 1931 he was also runner-up in 1934, when for the first time since 1924 the host nation provided the champion in Josef Sulc. Another consistent visitor to Kosice in the pre-war era was the Latvian Arturs Motmillers who, in winning in 1935, became his country's one and only winner of an international marathon. His best time of 2:41:38.2 set in 1933 lasted as a national record until 1954.

After the war there was a dramatic increase in the number of participants in the race, now named the International Peace Marathon. Twelve nations, including the United States for the first time, sent runners in 1947 and 1948, whilst in 1950 the number of those starting exceeded the one hundred mark for the first time. Nordic countries excelled from 1946 to 1956, winning all except 1947, 1951 and 1953, the last two being all-Czech races only.

'Buddy' Edelen (USA), after winning Kosice race in 1963, in a time which lasted as an event record for 16 years. (Kosice)

1961 whilst the world record holder 'Buddy' Edelen beat the course record holder Sergey Popov with an even faster time of 2:15:09.6 in 1963.

Seventeen nations sent runners in 1965 and a record 130 athletes were at the start the following year. From 1965 through 1970 the races were won by runners from six different countries, as in 1969 Demissie Wolde (Eth) came within half a minute of Edelen's record. The 40th race in 1970 gathered together a field of 278 but the star attraction Derek Clayton (Aus), the world record holder, could only manage fifth place. In 1971 Gyula Toth (Hun) added his name to the illustrious few who had managed to win the event at least twice, whilst the 50th anniversary run in 1974 was held on one of the worst days in the history of the Kosice marathon, as a bitterly cold wind and driving rain harassed the runners. The next year the North Koreans Chang Sop Choe and Chun Son Goe crossed the line in an intended tie but the judges gave Choi first place, even though their times were identical. Goe soon took revenge, beating his colleague in both 1977 and 1978, also taking the scalp of Olympic champion Waldemar Cierpinski in 1977. In between, there occurred the closest ever finish (other than the staged finale in 1975) when Takeshi Soh (Jap) edged out the British champion Barry Watson by seven and a half seconds, in the absence of the Koreans. As well as being the 750th anniversary of the founding of Kosice, 1980 was the year of the 50th marathon and over one thousand runners participated including, for the first time, women. An upset occurred when Aleksey Lyagushev (Sov) beat the favoured European champion Leonid Moseyev (Sov), as Cierpinski was never a threat, due to illness which forced him to retire.

WINNERS *(CZECH UNLESS STATED)*

1924	Karol Halla	3:01:35
1925	Pal Kiraly (Hun)	2:41:55
1926	Paul Hempel (Ger)	2:57:02
1927	Jozsef Galambos (Hun)	2:48:25.2
1928	Jozsef Galambos (Hun)	2:55:45
1929	Paul Hempel (Ger)	2:51:31
1930	Istvan Zelenka (Hun)	2:50:58.2
1931	Juan Zabala (Arg)	2:33:19
1932	Jozsef Galambos (Hun)	2:43:14.4
1933	Jozsef Galambos (Hun)	2:37:53.2
1934	Josef Sulc	2:41:26.3
1935	Arturs Motmillers (Lat)	2:44:57.2
1936	Gyorgy Balaban (Aut)	2:41:08
1937	Desiré Leriche (Fra)	2:43:41.7
1945	Antonin Spiroch	2:47:21.8
1946	Mikko Hietanen (Fin)	2:35:02.4
1947	Charles Heirendt (Lux)	2:36:06
1948	Gösta Leandersson (Swe)	2:34:46.4
1949	Martti Urpalainen (Fin)	2:33:45.6
1950	Gösta Leandersson (Swe)	2:31:20.2
1951	Jaroslav Strupp	2:41:07.8
1952	Erkki Puolakka (Fin)	2:29:10
1953	Walter Bednar	2:53:32.8
1954	Erkki Puolakka (Fin)	2:27:21
1955	Evert Nyberg (Swe)	2:25:40
1956	Thomas Nilsson (Swe)	2:22:05.4
1957	Ivan Filin (Sov)	2:23:57.8
1958	Pavel Kantorek	2:29:37.2
1959	Sergey Popov (Sov)	2:17:45.2
1960	Sam Hardicker (GB)	2:26:46.8
1961	Abebe Bikila (Eth)	2:20:12
1962	Pavel Kantorek	2:28:29.8
1963	Buddy Edelen (USA)	2:15:09.6
1964	Pavel Kantorek	2:25:55.4
1965	Aurele Vandendriessche (Bel)	2:23:47
1966	Gyula Toth (Hun)	2:19:11.2
1967	Nedo Farcic (Yug)	2:20:53.8
1968	Vaclav Chudomel	2:26:28.4
1969	Demissie Wolde (Eth)	2:15:37
1970	Mikhail Gorelov (Sov)	2:16:26.2
1971	Gyula Toth (Hun)	2:21:43.6
1972	John Farrington (Aus)	2:17:34.4
1973	Vladimir Moseyev (Sov)	2:19:01.2
1974	Keith Angus (GB)	2:20:09
1975	Chang Sop Choe (PRK)	2:15:47.8
1976	Takeshi Soh (Jap)	2:18:42.4
1977	Chun Son Goe (PRK)	2:15:19.4
1978	Chun Son Goe (PRK)	2:13:34.5
1979	Jouni Kortelainen (Fin)	2:15:12
1980	Aleksey Lyagushev (Sov)	2:15:25
1981	Hans-Joachim Truppel (GDR)	2:16:58
1982	Gyorgy Sinko (Hun)	2:18:48
1983	Frantisek Visnicky (Cze)	2:16:52

WOMEN

1980	Sarka Balcarova	2:50:15
1981	Christa Vahlensieck (GFR)	2:37:46
1982	Gillian Burley (GB)	2:43:26
1983	Raisa Sadreydinova (Sov)	2:34:41

London

Although throughout the years the Polytechnic Harriers' marathon had terminated in the western suburbs of London, no such race had ever been staged in or around the centre of London. The 1908 Olympic marathon finished at the White City in Shepherds Bush, and 40 years later the Olympic race was held to the north-west of London, in Middlesex, with the finish in Wembley. A London marathon staged by the Highgate Harriers was held from 1968 to 1975 and was run in the Hendon area of north-west London. In 1980 Kathrine Switzer and her Avon entourage proved that it was possible to stage a marathon in the centre of the capital when they successfully held their third Avon international race which started in Battersea Park and finished outside the Guildhall in the City. With generous sponsorship from Gillette, the backing of other firms and the assistance of the Greater London Council, the first London marathon materialised in March 1981. Race director Chris Brasher, the 1956 Olympic steeplechase gold medallist, ably assisted by his Olympic colleague, John Disley, devised a route primarily based on that used by the women the year before.

It is worth describing the present course briefly. Starting in Greenwich Park the route goes east to Woolwich Arsenal before turning back through Lewisham and Southwark, to cross the River Thames via Tower Bridge. Once across the river the runners turn east for a loop around the Isle of Dogs before returning to pass the Tower of London. Through the City, the runners then follow the Victoria Embankment, across Westminster Bridge to

the finish. However, in 1981 the course finished on Constitution Hill. For the most part the road is flat and the surface good. For the inaugural event, the field was limited to 8000 yet over 21 000 applications were received and in the end 7055 runners faced the starter on an overcast, rainy morning. Two overseas visitors Dick Beardsley (USA) and Inge Simonsen (Nor) raced alone from 16 miles and joining hands on the approach to the finish, broke the tape together. Their winning time of 2:11:48 was the fastest ever recorded in England, whilst in 138th place Joyce Smith set a new British and Commonwealth women's record of 2:29:57.

In 1982 the world's biggest ever marathon field of 16 350 assembled on a very much warmer day and, for the first time in Great Britain, the marathon was televised throughout in entirety. Members of Parliament as well as the media celebrities, were all attracted to this mammoth run after the phenomenal success of the opening race, as were other sports personalities and Charity Fund raisers. Hugh Jones, running his ninth marathon, took the lead early on and finished in a new British All-Comers record of 2:09:24, only 12 seconds outside the British record set by Ian Thompson in 1974. In registering his fourth marathon victory, he left the American trio of Jeff Wells, Kevin McCarey and Phil Coppess well beaten in fourth to sixth places. Joyce Smith repeated her 1981 win with another British record time but more impressive was her complete domination of the previously unbeaten Lorraine Moller (NZ), twice Avon champion. Wet and cool conditions prevailed for a record 16 500 runners the following year. Commonwealth bronze medallist Mike Gratton shook off Gerry Helme at

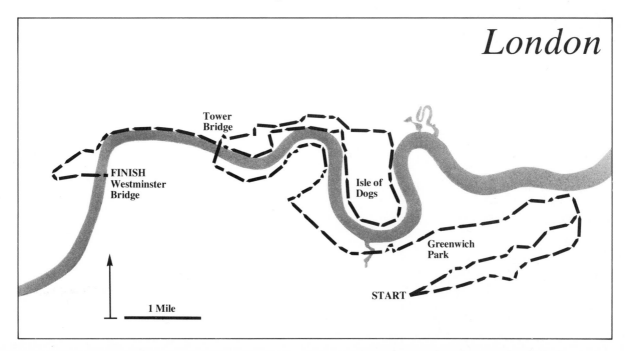

London

Tower Bridge

FINISH Westminster Bridge

Isle of Dogs

Greenwich Park

START

1 Mile

22 miles to win in 2:09:43 and became the fifth fastest British runner of all time. Once more, world records tumbled as 29 athletes bettered 2:15, 93 were under 2:20, 298 below 2:30 and a massive 1991 under 3:00, whilst 15 776 (95.6%) of the starters completed the course. In the absence of Joyce Smith, Grete Waitz (Nor) overcame an attack of cramp to set a world record of 2:25:28.7, a tenth better than Allison Roe's mark at New York in 1981, although both were rounded up to 2:25:29 as per IAAF rules. In second place Mary O'Connor, running her second marathon, became the third New Zealand girl to better 2:30.

RESULTS *(BRITISH UNLESS STATED)*

1981	1	Dick Beardsley (USA)	(tie)	2:11:48
	1	Inge Simonsen (Nor)		2:11:48
	3	Trevor Wright		2:12:53
1982	1	Hugh Jones		2:09:24
	2	Oyvind Dahl (Nor)		2:12:21
	3	Mike Gratton		2:12:30
1983	1	Mike Gratton		2:09:43
	2	Gerry Helme		2:10:12
	3	Henrik Jorgensen (Den)		2:10:47

WOMEN

1981	1	Joyce Smith	2:29:57
	2	Gillian Drake (NZ)	2:37:12
	3	Gillian Horowitz	2:40:44
1982	1	Joyce Smith	2:29:43
	2	Lorraine Moller (NZ)	2:36:15
	3	Judith Hine (NZ)	2:41:49
1983	1	Grete Waitz (Nor)	2:25:28.7
	2	Mary O'Connor (NZ)	2:28:20
	3	Glynis Penny	2:36:21

	Starters	Finishers
1981	7 055	6 418
1982	16 350	15 758
1983	16 500	15 776

In 1983 a record 19 735 entries were accepted but of these approximately 3000 withdrew and thus the starting number is also approximate although in excess of 1982.

Montreal

In 1979 Montreal staged the second World Cup track and field meet and although not part of the event, two marathons took place under the presidency of Serge Arsenault. The elite race was held the day after the popular mass event which attracted over 8500 runners. Starting on the Jacques Cartier Bridge, the course crossed to the south shore before turning west to cross the Champlain Bridge. The route then turned east, reaching the mid-point on the Concorde Bridge and on to Notre Dame Island, before circling St Helen's Island where the race finished in the park.

Ian Thompson (GB) led a field of 58 as far as the half-way stage in the first race before being overtaken, as Kebede Balcha (Eth) proved stronger than Dave Chettle (Aus), beating him by six seconds at the finish. Balcha's time was a new African record and he revelled in the conditions which were too hot for one of the pre-race favourites Bill Rodgers (USA), whilst Commonwealth champion Gidamis Shahanga (Tan) did not finish. The following year (1980) a strong breeze as well as the inevitable heat hindered the runners, but again there was a close finish as Dave Cannon (GB) only moved ahead of

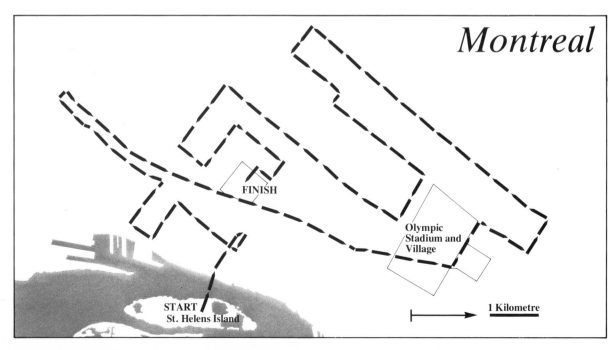

Montreal

FINISH

Olympic
Stadium and
Village

START
St. Helens Island

1 Kilometre

another Australian Garry Henry in the last three kilometres to win by 15 seconds. The women's race was also close as Patti Catalano (USA) outran the 1979 winner Jacqueline Gareau (Can) in the final stages. Kebede Balcha returned to win for a second time in 1981, lowering the record once more as runner-up Domingo Tibaduiza (Col) set a new South American record of 2:12:22.7. In the women's division Linda Staudt had little opposition, winning by nearly 13 minutes. In order to fit in with the fast expanding international calendar, the fourth race was brought forward from September to May but despite the usual 9.30 am start the temperature was still in the region of 30°C (86°F) and the humidity was very high. With the popular and elite fields combined, the starters numbered a record 11 000 but due to the heat 3500 of these did not complete the race. In spite of the conditions, the winner Benji Durden, who led from 30 km, still recorded a good time, although the slowest so far in this series which doubtless will continue to add much to the world of marathon racing. In 1983 Kebede Balcha scored his third win in convincing style, lowering the Ethiopian record in the process, as colleague Miruts Yifter failed to finish in his marathon debut. A new course was used which crossed the Jacques Cartier bridge into the city and finished at the Parc Lafontaine.

RESULTS *(CANADIAN UNLESS STATED)*

1979	1	Kebede Balcha (Eth)	2:11:35
	2	Dave Chettle (Aus)	2:11:41
	3	Chris Wardlaw (Aus)	2:13:52
1980	1	Dave Cannon (GB)	2:11:21.8
	2	Garry Henry (Aus)	2:11:36.8
	3	Gary Fanelli (USA)	2:14:16.3
1981	1	Kebede Balcha (Eth)	2:11:10.4
	2	Domingo Tibaduiza (Col)	2:12:22.7
	3	Dennis Rinde (USA)	2:13:37.8
1982	1	Benji Durden (USA)	2:13:22
	2	Ryszard Kopijasz (Pol)	2:14:50.2
	3	Gian-Paolo Messina (Ita)	2:15:05.4
1983	1	Kebede Balcha (Eth)	2:10:03
	2	Pete Pfitzinger (USA)	2:12:33
	3	Jacky Boxberger (Fra)	2:12:55

WOMEN

1979	1	Jacqueline Gareau	2:40:56
	2	Helene Rochefort	2:46:30
	3	Sissel Grottenberg (Nor)	2:54:28
1980	1	Patti Catalano (USA)	2:30:57.1
	2	Jacqueline Gareau	2:31:41.8
	3	Sylviane Fouache (Fra)	2:43:14.2
1981	1	Linda Staudt	2:33:32.8
	2	Janice Arenz (USA)	2:46:31.8
	3	Sylviane Puntous	2:49:40.5
1982	1	Annick Lebreton (Fra)	2:36:05.5
	2	Cindy Hamilton	2:39:01.7
	3	Jacqueline Gareau	2:41:19.3
1983	1	Lizanne Bussieres	2:36:05
	2	Annick Loir (Fra)	2:36:09
	3	Anne Hird (USA)	2:39:39

New York

The 'Big Apple', as New York is popularly known by its residents, had been the very first city in the New World to stage a marathon in 1896, the same year as the inaugural Olympic Games. Only Boston (first held in 1897) and Yonkers (1907) then made any long-term attempt to uphold the American marathon tradition. That is until Fred Lebow came onto the scene. Holding a marathon within the confines of Central Park was his brainchild, and it came to fruition in the autumn of 1970, attracting 126 runners. The field had to negotiate one lap of 1.7 miles (2.75 km) and four of 5.9 miles (9.5 km) to complete the distance.

There was nothing too significant in the following two years, other than a steady increase in the number of those starting which rose to nearly 300, and Beth Bonner, one of five female entrants in 1971, setting an American record. However, in 1973 Lebow persuaded Olympic Airways to sponsor the race, as a result of which the number of entrants rose dramatically to the five hundred mark within two seasons. Tom Fleming, winner in 1973, repeated in 1975 as Olympic Airways withdrew their support and the onus fell on the New York RRC to keep the series alive. Their enthusiasm helped persuade the AAU to give the women's race championship status the next year. 1976 was Bi-Centennial year and an extravagant idea of running the race through the five Metropolitan boroughs was discussed by Ted Corbitt of the RRC and publicity director George Spitz. Lebow would be the race director and the Rudin family, whose late father had been a known area distance runner, the first guarantor.

The initial concept of the route crossing all five districts, meant that through necessity the course would be of the point to point variety, and thus would pass through the many ethnic communities on the way to the finish. The start in Fort Wadsworth on Staten Island is unique, as on crossing the Verrazano Bridge the runners are on the upper level. Once into Brooklyn the routes converge, as both the out- and in-bound roads are used, necessitating a course separation on Fourth Avenue and the competitors pass through the Scandinavian and Italian Bay Ridge area. Shortly past the ten mile point, the field reaches the Hassidic Jewish and Hispanic communities of Williamsburg, before coming to Greenpoint and the eastern European settlements. The half-way point is on the slope of the Pulaski Bridge which enters the third borough, Queens. Soon the course reaches Queensboro Bridge, carpeted to assist the runners, which crosses East River into Manhattan. Along First Avenue into the Bronx, the field proceeds by Yorkville (of German origin), then Spanish Harlem, home of the Caribbean immi-

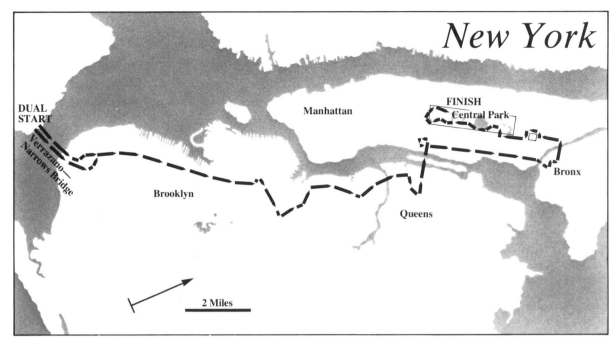

New York

DUAL START

Verrazano Narrows Bridge

Brooklyn

Manhattan

FINISH Central Park

Queens

Bronx

2 Miles

grants, then back through black Harlem on to Fifth Avenue. The final three miles are in Central Park and the finish at the Tavern on the Green, but for the most part, although relatively flat, the road is poorly surfaced and there is an abundance of pot holes.

Pekka Päivärinta, the Finnish jack-of-all-trades, made the early running in the 1976 race on an overcast morning. At the half-way point, Bill Rodgers took over and won with three minutes to spare from Olympic champion of 1972, Frank Shorter. There were over two thousand starters but the following year the number had more than doubled.

Rodgers's main opposition came from Gary Bjorklund once Shorter dropped out, and they stayed within close contact for 25 km before Rodgers pulled away. Bjorklund repeated these tactics in 1978 but once more Rodgers got the upper hand and secured his third consecutive win. In the women's division, Grete Waitz won her marathon debut in world record time, as the previous fastest Christa Vahlensieck retired at 18 miles.

With temperatures reaching 74°F (23°C) the 1979 race was the warmest to date with a high humidity. Kirk Pfeffer, running for the first time at New York, shot through the mid-point in 1:03:51 and held on until caught by Rodgers at 23 miles. Waitz set another record in her second marathon and finished 69th overall. Rodgers's successful run came to an end in 1980. A cold, windy day saw a record 14 012 runners at the start. Alberto Salazar in his marathon debut shook off the attention of Rodolfo Gomez at 21 miles for a 33-second winning margin and the fastest ever first marathon run. Top contenders Dick Beardsley and Bill Rodgers collided at 14 miles, the

latter losing 100 yd as he fell and with it any chance of a top position. Once more Waitz led the women's section from the start to record her third world record in as many races.

In 1981 for the first time in the history of the event, two world records were set on the same day at the same venue and in the same race. Taking full advantage of ideal weather (cool, overcast and a light breeze) Salazar ran alone from 17 miles to set an undisputed record. Waitz, threatened by the American Julie Brown, was forced to retire with shin splints as Allison Roe then went ahead of Brown at 15½ miles setting a record in the process.

Conditions were much warmer in 1982 and there was a head wind. Once again Gomez was the main opposition for Salazar and only lost in the final 200 yd, the margin at the tape being a mere four seconds. In the absence of an injured Roe, Waitz returned to comfortably win her fourth New York marathon.

Rod Dixon (NZ) became the first non-American winner in 1983 when over a rain-swept course he overtook Geoff Smith (GB) in the final quarter of a mile. Both runners were rewarded with national records whilst Grete Waitz had little difficulty winning the women's division.

WINNERS *(US UNLESS STATED):* **FIRST THREE FROM 1976**

1970	Gary Muhrcke	2:31:38.2
1971	Norman Higgins	2:22:54.2
1972	Sheldon Karlin	2:27:52.8
1973	Tom Fleming	2:21:54.8
1974	Norbert Sander	2:26:30.2
1975	Tom Fleming	2:19:27

1976	1	Bill Rodgers	2:10:09.6
	2	Frank Shorter	2:13:12
	3	Chris Stewart (GB)	2:13:21
1977	1	Bill Rodgers	2:11:28.2
	2	Jerome Drayton (Can)	2:13:52.2
	3	Chris Stewart (GB)	2:13:56.8
1978	1	Bill Rodgers	2:12:11.6
	2	Ian Thompson (GB)	2:14:12
	3	Trevor Wright (GB)	2:14:35.3
1979	1	Bill Rodgers	2:11:42
	2	Kirk Pfeffer	2:13:08.4
	3	Steve Kenyon (GB)	2:13:29.1
1980	1	Alberto Salazar	2:09:41
	2	Rodolfo Gomez (Mex)	2:10:13
	3	John Graham (GB)	2:11:46
1981	1	Alberto Salazar	2:08:12.7
	2	Jukka Toivola (Fin)	2:10:52
	3	Hugh Jones (GB)	2:10:59
1982	1	Alberto Salazar	2:09:29
	2	Rodolfo Gomez (Mex)	2:09:33
	3	Daniel Schlesinger	2:11:54
1983	1	Rod Dixon (NZ)	2:08:59
	2	Geoff Smith (GB)	2:09:08
	3	Ron Tabb	2:10:46

WOMEN

1971		Beth Bonner	2:55:22
1972		Nina Kuscsik	3:08:41.6
1973		Nina Kuscsik	2:57:07.2
1974		Kathy Switzer	3:07:29
1975		Kim Merritt	2:46:14.8
1976	1	Miki Gorman	2:39:11
	2	Doris Brown	2:53:02
	3	Toshiko D'Ellia	3:08:17
1977	1	Miki Gorman	2:43:10
	2	Kim Merritt	2:46:03.1
	3	Gayle Barron	2:52:19
1978	1	Grete Waitz (Nor)	2:32:29.8
	2	Martha Cooksey	2:41:50
	3	Sue Petersen	2:44:44
1979	1	Grete Waitz (Nor)	2:27:32.6
	2	Gillian Adams (GB)	2:38:32.2
	3	Jacqueline Gareau (Can)	2:39:05.7
1980	1	Grete Waitz (Nor)	2:25:41
	2	Patti Catalano	2:29:33
	3	Ingrid Kristiansen (Nor)	2:34:24
1981	1	Allison Roe (NZ)	2:25:28.8
	2	Ingrid Kristiansen (Nor)	2:30:08
	3	Julie Shea	2:30:11
1982	1	Grete Waitz (Nor)	2:27:14
	2	Julie Brown	2:28:33
	3	Charlotte Teske (GFR)	2:31:53
1983	1	Grete Waitz (Nor)	2:27:00
	2	Laura Fogli (Ita)	2:31:49
	3	Priscilla Welch (GB)	2:32:31

	Starters	Finishers
1976	2 090	1 549
1977	4 823	3 885
1978	9 875	8 588
1979	11 503	10 477
1980	14 012	12 512
1981	14 496	13 223
1982	14 308	13 599
1983	15 193	14 471

Alberto Salazar (USA), breaking away from Rodolfo Gomez (Mex) in 1980 New York win. (AP)

Polytechnic Harriers

Had the British marathon team performed more creditably at the 1908 Olympics then the *Sporting Life* newspaper might never have deemed it necessary to award a marathon trophy, and the Polytechnic Harriers may never have featured so prominently in the history of the event. However, twelfth place, the best that the squad could manage, was a great disappointment to all concerned. The *Sporting Life* offered a £500 silver trophy to be competed for, and awarded to the winner of an annually held road race of not less than 25 miles. The Polytechnic Harriers had staged one of the pre-Olympic trials and it was they who arranged the first marathon in conjunction with the paper in 1909. The origins of the Harriers date back to 1873 when the Hannover Athletic Club was formed. The Harriers, which as the name implies was the running section, followed ten years later. A cross-country race was held in October 1883 and the first club championship in that particular event followed the next year.

The inaugural marathon drew 68 runners to the start in the grounds of Windsor Castle. The route went

Polytechnic Harriers

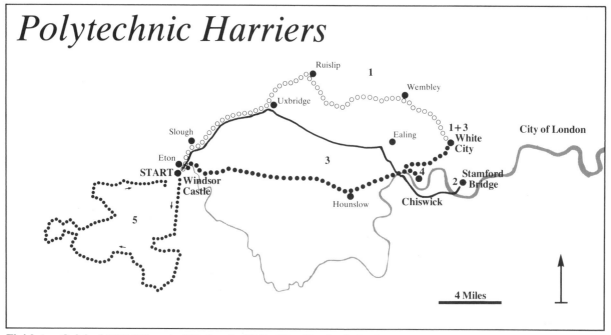

Finish 1.   Original 1908 OG route, Windsor to White City, Shepherds Bush
Finish 2.   Polytechnic Harriers marathon 1909–32, Windsor to Stamford Bridge
Finish 3.   Polytechnic Harriers marathon 1933–7, Windsor to White City
Finish 4.   Polytechnic Harriers marathon 1938–9 and 1946–72, Windsor to Chiswick
Finish 5.   Polytechnic Harriers marathon since 1973, Windsor circuit.

via Eton, Slough, Uxbridge, Southall and Kew Bridge to the stadium at Stamford Bridge, a distance of 26 miles 385 yd. Despite dusty conditions and a head wind Henry Frederick ('Harry') Barrett of the organising club, was a fine winner in a world record time. It was indeed a most promising start. From then until the start of the First World War the races were full of excitement, although no marathon was staged in 1910 due to the death of the King. In 1911 Henry ('Harry') Green won and at 5 ft 3 in (1.60 m) he is the smallest ever winner, whilst in 1912 a wrong turn on entering the stadium deprived the winner Jim Corkery (Can) of a new world record as the finishers all ran 360 yd (579 m) short of the requisite distance. Overseas competitors dominated in 1913, there being only one British name in the first seven, Fred Lord, who was fifth. Alexis Ahlgren led a strong Swedish contingent (first, fourth and seventh) with an undisputed world record of 2:36:06.6 which lasted as an event record for 19 years. In the last race before the war Ahlgren was forced to retire with stomach trouble at 19 miles as on a sultry day Ahmed Djebellia, a French Algerian, delighted the spectators by exercising vigorously on the grass infield after breaking the tape, 50 years before Abebe Bikila did the same at Tokyo.

On resumption of the series in 1919 there was a much depleted field and Djebellia returned but he had suffered considerably in the French Army and did not last the distance. Another war combatant Arthur Robert ('Bobby') Mills, a farmer who had never exceeded 14 miles at a time previously, entered in 1920 and not only won in his marathon debut but set a British record in the process. He won by seven minutes, a margin of superiority which he retained in 1921–2 as he defended his title. A severe attack of stitch at 17 miles prevented him from adding to his wins in 1923, but even this could not detract from the achievement of the winner Axel Jensen who won by a record margin of 13 min 9 sec, his time lasting as a Danish record until 1946. Eighty runners lined up for the start in 1924, the most since the first race. Duncan McLeod Wright held off a fast finishing young Air Force runner Sam Ferris, who like Wright was taking part in his first full marathon.

Harry Barrett wins the first Polytechnic Harriers' race in 1909. (Polytechnic Harriers)

The *Sporting Life* trophy presented to the winner of the Poly until 1962. (H W Neale)

The 1925 race also incorporated the first official national championship, even though the Poly, as it was popularly known, had long been so regarded unofficially. Ferris won by two minutes in the first of no less than five consecutive wins. He employed similar tactics in each of his races, starting cautiously and never taking the lead before 12 miles (1928) or in the case of his 1926 win as late as 21 miles. In 1928 there was a record number of 95 starters and Ferris was at his most brilliant best winning by more than nine minutes, but he was forced to miss the 1930 race through an injury sustained in the RAF cross-country championships. He won again in 1931–2 both with clear margins and in 1933 took part in his last marathon as the race finished at the White City stadium, Shepherds Bush, for the first time. Ferris won but his advantage of 70 seconds was the narrowest in his eight Poly wins.

Duncan Wright took the 1934 race, held in extreme heat, ten years after his first success, but Bert Norris of the organising club captured the next three. Norris was a late starter in the marathon event yet his winning time in 1936 lasted 14 years as a Poly record. He missed the 1938 race, won by the Swedish champion Henry Palmé, but finished second to the Swede the next year when for the first time the race finished at the new Polytechnic stadium at Chiswick. The marathon, though understandably small in entrants, continued through the war years, Leslie Griffiths winning three of the six races to be held between 1940 and 1945. In 1941 the winner Gerry Humphreys was aged 19 years, the youngest ever champion in the Poly. The 1948 race also included the national championship and the trial for the forthcoming Olympics and attracted a record 145 runners. Jack Holden, already defending champion and favourite, won the first of three successive races but unfortunately did not finish the Olympic

Axel Jensen (Den) wins the 1923 Poly. In his career, Jensen won 111 of 169 races at all distances.

event, and in 1950 became the oldest winner at the age of 43 years 96 days. Holden ran his last marathon in 1951 in a race won by Jim Peters who set a national record in his debut as Holden was forced to retire. Peters won the next three Polys, taking his tally to four, with new world record times in each and it took another such record nine years later to finally deprive him of the course record.

After his retirement later in 1954, a great void was left on the British marathon scene. No runner remotely approached his times during the next eight years and although there were some most able performers they were still a class apart from Peters. In 1962 the *Sporting Life* no longer considered themselves to be sufficiently associated with athletics to justify their continuation with the Poly, and so Callard and Bowser stepped into the breach. The following year saw the staging of the 50th race and the first of three consecutive world records was set by the popular American 'Buddy' Edelen, who broke away from the 1962 winner Ron Hill at 21 miles and from then on was never troubled. Hill was again in with a strong chance of winning in 1964 and at the finish was just 17 seconds behind Basil Heat-

Morio Shigematsu (Jap) wins the 1965 Poly in a world record 2:12:00 which is still the event record. (Keystone)

ley's new record of 2:13:55 in the closest finish to a Poly marathon yet. Edelen returned to do battle with the visiting Japanese in 1965 when on an overcast, misty day Morio Shigematsu, recent winner at Boston, powered away from Toru Terasawa (Jap) and Edelen to win in 2:12:00. Shigematsu's time remains an event record to this day and without doubt the mid-sixties were never-to-be-forgotten years in the history of the Poly and would never be repeated. In 1966 the race included the British championship for the first time since 1952 but with the advent of the Manchester Maxol marathon in 1969 and the staging of championships and trials at other venues, the field became more and more depleted of stars.

In 1973 the Windsor to Chiswick course was finally abandoned as increasing traffic and the accompanying marshalling difficulties was making it a most hazardous task. The race was held in Windsor Park and surrounding roads and attracted only 63 athletes to the start, a measure of the declining importance attached to the event. In addition it was under distance, whereas the previous year the wrong course had been taken and the runners ran far in excess of that required. The AAA event was staged at Windsor in 1974, but only at the last moment, and victory went overseas to Akio Usami of Japan. Since 1958 this was only the third time that this race had held the championship in conjunction with its own event. For the first time since 1910 a race was not held in 1975 through lack of support, but Goldenlay Eggs came to the rescue in 1976 to ensure the continuation of the Poly. Despite its unfortunate demise in recent years, no marathon record would be complete without including the Poly. Any race which in its time had been started by so many members of the Royal Family, including three reigning monarchs, and on whose courses no less than eight world records, more than at any other single venue, had been set, is worthy of such high esteem.

WINNERS (BRITISH UNLESS STATED)

1909	Harry Barrett	2:42:31
1911	Harry Green	2:46:29.8
1912*	Jim Corkery (Can)	2:36:55.4
1913	Alexis Ahlgren (Swe)	2:36:06.6
1914	Ahmed Djebellia (Fra)	2:46:30.8
1919	E Woolston	2:52:30.2
1920	Bobby Mills	2:37:40.4
1921	Bobby Mills	2:51:41.4
1922	Bobby Mills	2:47:30.4
1923	Axel Jensen (Den)	2:40:46.8
1924	Duncan McLeod Wright	2:53:17.4
1925	Sam Ferris	2:35:58.2
1926	Sam Ferris	2:42:24.2
1927	Sam Ferris	2:40:32.2
1928	Sam Ferris	2:41:02.2
1929	Sam Ferris	2:40:47.4
1930	Stan Smith	2:41:55
1931	Sam Ferris	2:35:31.8
1932	Sam Ferris	2:36:32.4
1933	Sam Ferris	2:42:24.2
1934	Duncan McLeod Wright	2:56:30
1935	Bert Norris	2:48:37.8
1936	Bert Norris	2:35:20
1937	Bert Norris	2:48:40
1938	Henry Palmé (Swe)	2:42:00
1939	Henry Palmé (Swe)	2:36:56
1940	Leslie Griffiths	2:53:41.6
1941	Gerry Humphreys	3:12:36
1942	Leslie Griffiths	2:53:56.4
1943	Leslie Griffiths	2:54:44
1944	Tom Richards	2:56:39
1945	Tom Richards	2:48:45.6
1946	Harry Oliver	2:38:12
1947	Cecil Ballard	2:36:52.4
1948	Jack Holden	2:36:44.6
1949	Jack Holden	2:42:52
1950	Jack Holden	2:33:07
1951	Jim Peters	2:29:24
1952	Jim Peters	2:20:42.2
1953	Jim Peters	2:18:40.2
1954	Jim Peters	2:17:39.4
1955	Bob McMinnis	2:36:23
1956	Ron Clark	2:20:15.8
1957	Eddie Kirkup	2:27:04.4
1958	Colin Kemball	2:22:27.4
1959	Dennis O'Gorman	2:25:11.2
1960	Arthur Keily	2:19:06
1961	Peter Wilkinson	2:20:25
1962	Ron Hill	2:20:59
1963	Buddy Edelen (USA)	2:14:26
1964	Basil Heatley	2:13:55
1965	Morio Shigematsu (Jap)	2:12:00
1966	Graham Taylor	2:19:04
1967	Fergus Murray	2:19:06
1968	Kenji Kimihara (Jap)	2:15:15
1969	Phil Hampton	2:25:22
1970	Don Faircloth	2:18:15
1971	Phil Hampton	2:18:31
1972	Don Faircloth	2:31:52
1973*	Bob Sercombe	2:19:48
1974	Akio Usami (Jap)	2:15:16
1975	not held	
1976	Bernie Plain	2:15:43
1977	Ian Thompson	2:14:32
1978	David Francis	2:19:05
1979	Mike Gratton	2:19:53
1980	Tony Byrne	2:22:23
1981	Bernie Plain	2:24:07
1982	Graham Ellis	2:23:28
1983	Alan McGee	2:22:55

WOMEN

1978	Gillian Adams	2:54:11
1979	Jane Davies	3:21:23
1980	Gillian Adams	2:45:11
1981	Caroline Rodgers	2:51:03
1982	Kath Binns	2:36:12
1983	Valerie Howe	3:05:40

* denotes short course.

From 1909 to 1932 the course was from Windsor to Stamford Bridge; 1933 to 1937 Windsor to White City; 1938–9 Windsor to Chiswick; 1940 Windsor Great Park; 1941 to 1945 Chiswick; 1946 to 1972 Windsor to Chiswick; from 1973 Windsor.

World Championships

Conditions for the men in Helsinki on 14 August 1983 were considerably cooler than that for the women, although the final stages of the rolling course were made more difficult by a head-wind. A large group at the front, which still numbered 16 at 30 km, together with a number of tight turns, made the going difficult for the leaders. It was not until just prior to 35 km that Rob de Castella and Kebede Balcha made the first real break. On a hill at 37.5 km de Castella made a move to which Balcha could not respond and by 40 km the Australian led by 12 seconds, a margin he increased to 24 seconds over the Ethiopian by the finish. Olympic champion Waldemar Cierpinski overtook Kjell-Erik Stahl (Swe) just before the tape to take the bronze medal, leaving Stahl with the consolation of setting a new national record of 2:10:38. Agapius Masong (Tan), fifth, and Armand Parmentier (Bel), sixth, also bettered 2:11 with times of 2:10:42 and 2:10:57 respectively as 63 of 82 starters finished.

RESULT

1	Rob de Castella (Aus)	2:10:03
2	Kebede Balcha (Eth)	2:10:27
3	Waldemar Cierpinski (GDR)	2:10:37

For the women 7 August was very hot and sunny and initial breaks were made by Jacqueline Gareau (Can) at 11 km and then Regina Joyce (Ire), who led by 30 seconds at 25 km. Grete Waitz (Nor), closely shadowed by Julie Brown (USA) caught Joyce soon after 30 km and by 35 km Waitz had an advantage of 25 seconds which she increased to 2 min 22 sec by 40 km with a 5 km split of 16:22 the fastest of the entire race. The Norwegian won by exactly three minutes in the fine time of 2:28:09, as in an exciting battle for the silver medal Marianne Dickerson (USA), running only her third marathon, overtook Raisa Smekhnova (Sov) on the final bend to capture second place. Previously unbeaten European champion Rosa Mota (Por), who had been eighth at 30 km, finished fourth ahead of Gareau in 2:31:50.

RESULT

1	Grete Waitz (Nor)	2:28:09
2	Marianne Dickerson (USA)	2:31:09
3	Raisa Smekhnova (Sov)	2:31:13

IAAF/Citizen Golden Marathon

The first Golden marathon in 1982 attracted only 38 starters and was held over the traditional course

Rodolfo Gomez (Mex, 3) and Kunimitsu Itoh (Jap, 1) battle for the first IAAF Golden marathon won by Gomez. (Popperfoto)

from Marathon to Athens. Rodolfo Gomez (Mex) moved to the fore at 20 km as heavy rain began to fall, and was quickly joined by Kunimitsu Itoh (Jap). They accelerated away spread-eagling the field in the process and on the downhill stretch to the finish Gomez went ahead to win in the second best time ever recorded over the route. Vladimir Kotov (Sov), third for most of the race, finished second as Itoh faded to ninth of the 30 finishers.

RESULT

1	Rodolfo Gomez (Mex)	2:11:49
2	Vladimir Kotov (Sov)	2:13:34
3	Greg Meyer (USA)	2:14:07

European Nations Cup

At the first European Nations Cup marathon at Agen (Fra) in 1981, a total of 19 nations were represented in the race which took place on a hot, cloudless day over flat country roads. Massimo Magnani (Ita) broke clear just before 30 km and won comfortably, leading Italy to an easy team title. Laredo (Spa) staged the second edition in 1983 two months before the World Championship race on which most runners had set their sights and many had already been selected. In a sprint finish, Waldemar Cierpinski and Jürgen Eberding (GDR) held off the Italian challenge and thus improved the team position of the previous year. In both years an unofficial women's race was held.

RESULTS

1981

Agen			
	1	Massimo Magnani (Ita)	2:13:29
	2	Waldemar Cierpinski (GDR)	2:15:44
	3	Tommy Persson (Swe)	2:15:45

1983

Laredo			
	1	Waldemar Cierpinski (GDR)	2:12:26
	2	Jürgen Eberding (GDR)	2:12:26
	3	Gianni Poli (Ita)	2:12:28

TEAM

1981			
	1	Italy	30 points
	2	Soviet Union	72
	3	Poland	80
1983	1	GDR	22
	2	Italy	28
	3	Spain	45

WOMEN

1981			
	1	Zoya Ivanova (Sov)	2:38:58
	2	Charlotte Teske (GFR)	2:41:04
	3	Nadyezhda Gumerova (Sov)	2:44:49
1983	1	Nadyezhda Gumerova (Sov)	2:38:36
	2	Tamara Surotsyeva (Sov)	2:39:17
	3	Raisa Sadryedinova (Sov)	2:40:22

Avon

This series of all-women marathon races was the brainchild of Kathrine Switzer, an employee of Avon Products Inc., herself a marathon runner. In 1967 she entered the Boston race as K V Switzer, thus acquiring an official starting number even though women were not officially allowed to enter. Switzer incurred the wrath of Boston official 'Jock' Semple who tried to force her out of the race on discovering her sex but to no avail.

Atlanta hosted the first Avon international race in 1978, with 184 runners tackling a tough course on a hot day. Julie Brown (USA) broke away at the half-way stage, only to be caught within three miles of the finish by Martha Cooksey. Cooksey, a Californian vegetarian with one win in her five pre-Avon marathons, went on to win comfortably as Brown dropped out. It was fitting that the second marathon should be held in the home town of Dr Ernst van Aaken, a German physician and woman marathon trainer who had lost his legs as a result of a road accident whilst training. At Waldniel (GFR), on a bright autumn afternoon, Karen Doppes (USA) was the early leader of the 262 runners, representing 24 nations. Joyce Smith (GB) took over the lead from 25 km to finish first in a new Commonwealth record, as Kim Merritt (USA) finished strongly to take second. Thirty-six of the 188 finishers were inside 3:00 as British, Swiss, Belgian, and Argentinian national records were broken.

London staged the marathon in 1980, the first time that a marathon had been held in the very centre of the capital. On a warm, sunny morning the first break occurred at 25 km when Nancy Conz (USA), running her second marathon, moved to the front. Lorraine Moller (NZ) a school teacher, in fifth place at that point, started a drive which took her to Conz's shoulder by 30 km and on to finish first at the Guildhall. Canadian debutante Linda Staudt came through to take third but former world record holder Christa Vahlensieck (GFR) was among the non finishers. The fourth Avon race over a picturesque Ottawa course attracted a record 670 starters. Nancy Conz led from the gun, held off a brief challenge from Linda Staudt and then turned back a late rush by Joan Benoit to win in style. The United States dominated the race as Midde Hamrin (Swe) in seventh was the first non-US finisher with only 58% of the field finishing on yet another very warm day.

A further large American dominated field crossed the Golden Gate Bridge in bright sun shortly after 7 am, as San Francisco played host to the 1982 Avon. At the half-way stage there were just three in contention, including 1980-champion Lorraine Moller who in winning became the first to take the title on two occasions. For the first time in a women's marathon, over one thousand runners took part in the 1983 edition, held over much of the relatively flat 1984 Olympic course in Los Angeles. Julie Brown led from the start to the finish to record the fastest time ever set in an all women's marathon, with a record series winning margin of 6 min 56 sec. On a cool, cloudy day a record number of 934 athletes completed the race.

RESULTS

1978 Atlanta			
	1	Martha Cooksey (USA)	2:46:15
	2	Sarolta Monspart (Hun)	2:51:40
	3	Manuela Angenvoorth (GFR)	2:51:53

1979 Waldniel			
	1	Joyce Smith (GB)	2:36:27
	2	Kim Merritt (USA)	2:39:43
	3	Carol Gould (GB)	2:40:37

1980 London			
	1	Lorraine Moller (NZ)	2:35:11
	2	Nancy Conz (USA)	2:36:02
	3	Linda Staudt (Can)	2:37:39

1981 Ottawa			
	1	Nancy Conz (USA)	2:36:45.9
	2	Joan Benoit (USA)	2:37:24
	3	Julie Isphording (USA)	2:38:25.9

1982 San Francisco			
	1	Lorraine Moller (NZ)	2:36:13
	2	Carey May (Ire)	2:38:32
	3	Laurie Binder (USA)	2:38:46

1983 Los Angeles			
	1	Julie Brown (USA)	2:26:26
	2	Christa Vahlensieck (GFR)	2:33:22
	3	Marianne Dickerson (USA)	2:33:44

The
International
Runners

Dorando Pietri

Ninety-thousand spectators roared their acclaim as a small olive skinned Italian was the first runner to enter the White City stadium at the end of the gruelling 1908 Olympic marathon. Losing momentum, brought about by negotiating the downward ramp on to the cinder track and being re-directed to the left as against the right as he had thought, Dorando Pietri stumbled and fell. After collapsing for a fifth time in the space of 250 m, when opposite the Royal Box, Pietri was helped across the finishing line, his legs unable to carry him a step further. Inevitably, disqualification followed and victory went to the American Johnny Hayes.

Dorando Pietri (Ita) leads in the 1908 Olympic marathon. (Hulton Picture Library)

Pietri was born in Mandrio (Ita) on 16 October 1885 and began his sporting career in 1904—on a bicycle! This enthusiasm lasted just two races before he turned to what proved to be his true vocation, running. The very next year he won his first national title over 25 km and later, in his overseas debut, took the Paris 30 km race. He was forced to retire from the 1906 Athens marathon due to abdominal pains, when leading by five minutes at 24 km, and a similar disaster occurred when he competed in the inaugural Italian marathon championship two years later. He eventually gained Olympic selection by virtue of setting a 40 km track record 17 days before the London event. After the Olympic race, Pietri went to the United States and in November turned professional, easily beating Hayes in his first such race before losing to Tom Longboat (Can) three weeks later. Pietri lost again to Longboat over 25 miles early in 1909, and twice to Alfred Shrubb (GB) in 12 and 15 miles events. Whilst usually holding his own in head-to-head encounters, he was well beaten in two international marathons, held at the New York Polo Grounds in 1909. The next year Pietri again beat Hayes, but only in the final 385 yd, and took revenge over Henri St Yves (Fra) at 15 miles (twice) and Longboat (20 km), before visiting South America for the first time. Between May and July he was unbeaten in ten competitions (including two victories against horse ridden opponents) and ran his fastest ever marathon in Buenos Aires. This proved to be his last such race and he retired in 1911, after exchanging wins over 20 km with Gösta Ljungström in Sweden during October. In an extraordinarily well documented career Pietri won 38 of 59 amateur races, and 50 of 69 as a professional. He eventually moved to San Remo where he died on 7 February 1942.

CAREER RECORD *(42.195 KM UNLESS STATED)*

2 Apr 1906 Rome (42 km)	2:42:00.6	(1)
1 May 1906 Athens (41.86 km)	d n f	(–)
26 Aug 1906 Arona (41.09 km)	d n f	(–)
3 Jun 1908 Rome NC (40 km)	d n f	(–)
7 Jul 1908 Carpi (40 km)	2:38:00	(1)
24 Jul 1908 White City OG disq	2:54:46.4	(–)
25 Nov 1908 New York (Madison Square G)	2:44:20.4	(1)
15 Dec 1908 New York (Madison Square G)	d n f	(–)

2 Jan	1909 Buffalo (25 miles)	d n f	(–)
11 Jan	1909 St Louis	2:44:32.4	(1)
22 Jan	1909 Chicago	2:56:00.4	(1)
12 Feb	1909 Orlando	2:59:30	(1)
15 Mar	1909 New York (Madison Square G)	2:48:08	(1)
3 Apr	1909 New York (Polo Grounds)	2:45:37	(2)
9 May	1909 New York (Polo Grounds)	2:58:19	(6)
18 Dec	1909 London (Royal Albert Hall)	d n f	(–)
30 Jan	1910 San Francisco	2:41:35	(1)
24 May	1910 Buenos Aires (42.4 km)	2:38:48.2	(1)

Hannes Kolehmainen

Less than 13 seconds separated the first two runners to cross the finishing line in the 1920 race at Antwerp. To this day it remains the closest finish in an Olympic marathon. The winner, Hannes Kolehmainen, was one of the greatest of a long line of Finnish distance aces, and had already won three gold medals at the 1912 celebrations. In addition he had set world records at distances ranging from 2 km to 30 km, in a career stretching over 20 years. Kolehmainen's winning time at Antwerp of 2:32:35.8 was the fastest recorded in the history of the event and was made all the more remarkable in view of the distance negotiated, which was 42.750 km.

Hannes, whose full name was Johannes Petter Kolehmainen, was born on 9 December 1889 at Kuopio (Fin) and was the youngest and most accomplished of three distance running brothers. He had made his marathon debut in 1907, at the tender age of 17 and by the end of 1909 had taken part in eight such races. From then until 1920, by which time Kolehmainen was resident in the United States, he had only one more marathon outing, at Boston in 1917. He gained selection for the Finnish Olympic squad by winning one of the American trials, held over a long course in warm weather at New York, in impressive style. After his memorable Belgian victory, Hannes ran only two more marathons, failing to finish in both of them. He had returned to live in his native Finland in 1920 and died on 11 January 1966.

CAREER RECORD *(42.195 KM UNLESS STATED)*

16 Jun	1907 Viipuri (40.2 km)		3:06:19	(3)
2 Sep	1907 Helsinki (40.2 km)		2:57:25.4	(3)
21 Jun	1908 Viipuri (40.2 km)		2:52:36	(4)
13 Jun	1909 Helsinki	track	3:05:22	(2)
4 Jul	1909 Helsinki		3:12:19.3	(4)
31 Aug	1909 Stockholm	track	3:09:19	(5)
5 Sep	1909 Gothenburg (40.2 km)	track	2:42:59	(3)
19 Sep	1909 Hanko	track	3:10:31.4	(1)
19 Apr	1917 Boston (24.5 miles)		2:31:58.6	(4)
5 Jun	1920 New York (26.5 miles)		2:47:49.4	(1)
22 Aug	1920 Antwerp (42.750 km)	OG	2:32:35.8	(1)
13 Jul	1924 Paris	OG	d n f	(–)
17 Jun	1928 Kauhava	OT	d n f	(–)

Hannes Kolehmainen (Fin), after winning the 1920 Olympic marathon title.

Clarence DeMar

DeMar won a record seven Boston marathons, yet after his first win in 1911, partly due to a suspected heart murmur and an increasing time-consuming interest in religion, it was 1917 before he commenced training again and once more raced at Boston. What honours the 23-year-old Clarence De Mar might have achieved in the five years following the 1912 Olympics, is a matter for pure conjecture.

DeMar was born in Madeira, Ohio, on 7 June 1888, and by the time he was ten years old he was fatherless and working on a farm for his keep. He began running when at Vermont University, where he coached himself, as he did throughout his long career. A three-year spell in the Army further disrupted his running career but he kept in good shape with regular road runs. Although missing the 1920 Olympic Games (he had finished 12th at Stockholm eight years earlier) his renewed enthusiasm, plus the security of a steady job as a printer, led him to winning again at Boston, eleven years after his initial success. So began some nine years of major achievements for DeMar, with only an Olympic gold medal eluding him. Five more victories at Boston followed, three national title wins in 1926–7–8, major firsts at Baltimore, Philadelphia and Port Chester, as well as many triumphs in minor New England events. After 1930 the wins became scarcer, although that particular year had been one of his best, but he did manage to get into the top ten finishers at Boston on three more occasions in 1931 (fifth), 1933 (eighth) and 1938 (seventh) for a grand total of 15 such placings. DeMar continued to compete at that venue up to 1954, by which time his marathons had surpassed the one-hundred mark. He died on 10 July 1958 from cancer, and not the heart ailment which had been so wrongly diagnosed some 50 years earlier.

Clarence DeMar (USA), winning his record seventh and final Boston marathon, 1930. (AP)

CAREER HIGHLIGHTS (1910 TO 1938)

1910 2:29:52.6 (2nd, Boston); 1911 2:21:39.6 (1st, Boston); 1912 2:50:46.6 (12th, Olympics); 1913–16 did not compete; 1917 2:24:04.2 (1st, Brockton, MA); 1918–21 did not compete; 1922 2:18:10 (1st, Boston); 1923 2:23:37.4 (1st, Boston).

All 24.7 miles except 1912 and 1917, 25 miles.

8 Mar 1924	Baltimore		2:50:23.4	(3)
19 Apr 1924	Boston (26.1 miles)		2:29:40.2	(1)
13 Jul 1924	Paris	OG	2:48:14	(3)
19 Apr 1925	Boston (26.1 miles)	AAU	2:33:37	(2)
12 Oct 1925	Port Chester		2:31:07.8	(2)
19 Apr 1926	Boston (26.1 miles)		2:32:15	(3)
15 May 1926	Baltimore	AAU	2:45:05.2	(1)
2 Jun 1926	Philadelphia		2:42:00	(1)
12 Oct 1926	Port Chester		2:38:30.6	(1)
26 Mar 1927	Baltimore	AAU	2:43:40.8	(1)
19 Apr 1927	Boston		2:40:22.2	(1)
30 May 1927	Buffalo		2:40:34	(2)
8 Oct 1927	Port Chester		2:41:21.4	(4)
19 Apr 1928	Boston	AAU	2:37:07.8	(1)
19 May 1928	Long Beach, CA		no time	(7)
5 Aug 1928	Amsterdam	OG	2:50:42	(27)
12 Dec 1928	Port Chester		3:01:40.4	(2)
19 Apr 1929	Boston	AAU	2:43:47	(9)
15 Jun 1929	Los Angeles		3:10:00	(2)
12 Oct 1929	Port Chester		2:39:14	(2)
7 Nov 1929	Halifax		2:50:00	(1)
19 Apr 1930	Boston		2:34:48.2	(1)
18 May 1930	Pawtucket, RI		2:41:00	(1)
14 Jun 1930	Los Angeles		2:34:45	(1)
21 Sep 1930	Hamilton		2:43:30	(3)
13 Oct 1930	Port Chester		2:46:15	(1)

1931 2:51:59 (5th, Port Chester); 1932 2:46:15 (18th, Boston); 1933 2:43:18.6 (8th, Boston); 1934 2:36:15 (1st, Manchester, MA); 1935 2:52:49 (11th, Yonkers); 1936 2:49:08 (16th, Boston); 1937 2:47:18 (4th, Washington, DC); 1938 2:43:30.4 (7th, Boston).

Kee-Chung Sohn (Kitei Son)

Born in Sinuiju, Korea, on 29 August 1914, Kee-Chung Sohn's first successes were on the track over 1500 m and 5000 m during the autumn of 1932. The following October, prompted by success in an eight-mile race, the longest ever that he had attempted, he entered and won his first marathon, albeit over a short course. More track wins followed in August 1934 and in early 1935 Sohn ventured to Tokyo for the first time to compete in a marathon. It was ironical that a fine win was marred again by another short course and when defeat did present itself to Sohn, it was over the regular distance for the first time in five marathons! On that occasion Yasuo Ikenaka set a new world record, with Sohn a distant third.

Competing on the track in both Seoul and Tokyo during the summer of 1935, Sohn reduced his best 10000 m time to 32:54.0, as well as running three more marathons in his native Korea. In November Sohn contested the Japanese marathon championship for the first time and taking advantage of ideal weather, took complete control of the race in the second half to win in a world record 2:26:42.

Kitei Son (Jap) leads Ernie Harper (GB) in the 1936 Olympic marathon. (Asahi Shimbun)

There was no doubt about the distance as the race took place over the newly certified Rokugo course. Sohn moved to Tokyo to prepare for the 1936 Olympics but had to settle for second in the final trial behind fellow Korean Sun Yong Nam. At Berlin, Sohn was content to let the defending champion Juan Zabala set a suicidal pace for the first 20 km, before moving to the front eight kilometres later to win comfortably. After the Games he retired from competition and at the end of the war returned to Korea and concentrated on training the newly formed national marathon squad.

CAREER RECORD

10 Oct 1933	Seoul*			2:29:34.4	(1)
22 Apr 1934	Seoul*			2:24:51.2	(1)
8 Oct 1934	Seoul*			2:32:19.8	(1)
21 Mar 1935	Tokyo*			2:26:14	(1)
4 Apr 1935	Tokyo			2:39:24	(3)
18 May 1935	Seoul*			2:24:28	(1)
29 Sep 1935	Seoul			2:42:02	(1)
8 Oct 1935	Seoul			2:33:39	(2)
3 Nov 1935	Tokyo			2:26:42	(1)
18 Apr 1936	Tokyo	OT		2:28:32	(1)
21 May 1936	Tokyo	FOT		2:38:03	(2)
9 Aug 1936	Berlin	OG		2:29:19.2	(1)

denotes a known short course.

Gérard Côté

Gérard Côté's first love was boxing, but he was also more than adept at baseball, ice hockey, snowshoeing and roller hockey, until one Pete Gavuzzi took him under his wing. Gavuzzi, a British citizen of Italian extraction who had run the two epic Trans-America races of 1928–9, losing the latter by just 2 min 47 sec after 79 days, planned a training routine which soon had Côté running ten-mile road runs effortlessly.

One of eleven children, Côté was born in St Barnabé, Quebec, on 26 July 1913 and four years later moved to St Hyacinthe, in which region he has lived ever since. In 1936 Côté ran his first Boston marathon. It was not surprising that he dropped out before the finish, as only two days earlier he had run the course in training. Thus began a marathon career which but for the intervening war years would have seen Côté as a prime contender for Olympic honours in both 1940 and 1944, had the celebrations gone ahead. Starting with the Yonkers race in the autumn of 1936, Côté produced a string of class performances there and at Boston in the ensuing 12 years. Only missing Boston in 1945 and Yonkers in 1944 and 1945 due to Army service, he never finished below eighth at Boston, which he won four times, whilst at Yonkers the lowest place he dropped to was fourth. His three wins there also included the AAU titles and in addition he won the Canadian Championship races in 1942–3–8 and 1954.

The Canadian, who enjoyed a cigar and beer after his road exertions, mainly for the benefit of the reporters, had to be content with a lowly 17th (2:48:31) in his one Olympic marathon in 1948. Somewhat of an extrovert, he gained considerable publicity in his final Boston win, after a close waged duel with Ted Vogel, when tempers became raised between the two runners during the race.

RECORD AT BOSTON AND YONKERS, 1936 TO 1949

19 Apr 1936	Boston			d n f	(–)
3 Nov 1936	Yonkers			2:42:23	(2)
19 Apr 1937	Boston			2:46:46	(7)
7 Nov 1937	Yonkers			2:43:40	(2)
19 Apr 1938	Boston			2:44:01.4	(8)
6 Nov 1938	Yonkers			2:43:40	(2)
19 Apr 1939	Boston			2:37:43	(8)
12 Nov 1939	Yonkers			2:35:33	(2)
19 Apr 1940	Boston			2:28:28.6	(1)
10 Nov 1940	Yonkers	AAU		2:34:06.2	(1)
19 Apr 1941	Boston			2:37:59	(4)
9 Nov 1941	Yonkers			2:45:59	(4)
19 Apr 1942	Boston			2:39:59	(6)
8 Nov 1942	Yonkers			2:43:59	(3)
19 Apr 1943	Boston			2:28:25.8	(1)
7 Nov 1943	Yonkers	AAU		2:38:35.3	(1)
19 Apr 1944	Boston			2:31:50.4	(1)
20 Apr 1946	Boston			2:36:34	(3)

Gérard Côté (Can) wins his fourth Boston marathon, 1948. (AP)

27 Oct 1946	Yonkers	AAU	2:47:53.6	(1)
19 Apr 1947	Boston		2:32:11	(4)
26 Oct 1947	Yonkers		2:44:31	(4)
19 Apr 1948	Boston		2:31:02	(1)
19 Apr 1949	Boston		2:42:55	(6)
15 May 1949	Yonkers		2:42:38.5	(4)

Year best performances not set in the above races:

1938 2:37:16 (2nd, Canadian Champs.); 1941 2:33:42 (2nd, Salisbury, MA); 1945 2:54:06 (4th, Poly).

The Yonkers race was not held in 1948.

Jim Peters

Without a shadow of a doubt Jim Peters was responsible for the transformation of the marathon with a series of record breaking times over a three-year period in the early 1950s. James Henry Peters, born in Homerton, London, on 24 October 1918, was an able track performer, winning the AAA 6-mile and 10-mile titles before placing ninth in the 1948 Olympic 10000 m final. Following the Olympics, Peters did little running but in 1951 made a serious comeback and, advised by Albert 'Johnny' Johnston, began to tackle the marathon. As a result of daily training, with an emphasis on speed, his debut in the Poly that year was a memorable one as he became the first British runner to better 2:30. Peters continued his winning ways in taking the British titles in 1951 and 1952. In the latter, which also incorporated the Olympic trial, he set a new world record of 2:20:42.2, which made him one of the favourites at Helsinki.

Failure there did not dishearten Peters and he competed successfully in cross-country, road and track events, before becoming the first to break the magic 2:20 barrier the following June. That year (1953) he took part in four marathons and in each set world records for both point to point and out and back courses. In the AAA race, when he bettered

Jim Peters setting his third and final world record in the Poly, 1954. (Keystone)

heat. Peters entered the stadium with a lead of some 20 minutes and there followed an even more horrific repetition of the Pietri saga which had taken place 46 years previously in London. Suffering from the heat and resultant dehydration, Peters finally collapsed into the arms of a British official before the marathon finish line was reached. He never raced again.

CAREER RECORD

16 Jun	1951	Windsor to Chiswick	Pol	2:29:24	(1)
21 Jul	1951	Perry Barr	AAA	2:31:42	(1)
14 Jun	1952	Windsor to Chiswick	AAA	2:20:42.2	(1)
27 Jul	1952	Helsinki	OG	d n f	(–)
13 Jun	1953	Windsor to Chiswick	Pol	2:18:40.2	(1)
25 Jul	1953	Cardiff	AAA	2:22:29	(1)
12 Sep	1953	Enschede		2:19:22	(1)
4 Oct	1953	Turku		2:18:34.8	(1)
19 Apr	1954	Boston		2:22:40	(2)
26 Jun	1954	Windsor to Chiswick	AAA	2:17:39.4	(1)
7 Aug	1954	Vancouver	EG	d n f	(–)

Abebe Bikila

Spectators lining the Appian Way cheered as the barefooted runner, wearing Ethiopian colours, padded confidently towards the finish of the 1960 Olympic marathon in Rome. Even the experts knew very little about the new champion, whose winning time shaved eight tenths of a second off the recognised world record.

Abebe Bikila was born at Mout on 7 August 1932

Olympic champion Abebe Bikila (Eth) leads Vaclav Chudomel (Cze) at Kosice, 1961. (Kosice)

Zatopek's Olympic time, he twice encountered a herd of cows on the course. A trip to Boston in April 1954 met with defeat at the hands of Veikko Karvonen (Fin), who thus took ample revenge for the heavy loss he had suffered at the hands of Peters the previous October at Turku. On his return, Peters, maintaining more than 100 miles a week in training, lowered the world record to 2:17:39.4 over the favourable Windsor to Chiswick route. Jim Peters' last race was a tragic one. The occasion was the Empire Games event at Vancouver held in extreme and was a member of the Imperial Bodyguard, having joined the Army at the age of nineteen. He had trained at a special camp, set up by a Swedish sports adviser Onni Niskanen, who held a government post at Addis Ababa. The Olympic event was Bikila's third marathon in 1960 and was quite probably only the third he had ever run over the classic distance. In 1961 he was successful in three major international races in Europe and Japan, and in 1962 lowered his best 10000 m track time to 29:00.8 at Berlin, which ranked him fourth in the world. In 1963 he ran his next marathon at Boston, where he was on record schedule until a savage combination of a bitter wind and the notorious hills cost him the race and his first known defeat. Once more Boston had proved the *bête noire* for Olympic champions, as no one had ever won there.

An operation for appendicitis left Bikila just six weeks to recover in time to defend his title at Tokyo. In the Japanese capital he became the first marathon runner to do so successfully and in so doing chopped a minute and a half from the existing world record. The recurrence of an injury, sustained in Spain in the summer of 1967, forced him to retire from the 1968 Olympic race in Mexico City. In 1969 Bikila was involved in a car accident, as a result of which he sustained a broken neck and almost complete paralysis. Despite intensive treatment at the Stoke Mandeville (GB) hospital, he gained little relief and died on 25 October 1973 after a severe haemorrhage. Vast crowds attended his funeral which followed in Addis Ababa.

CAREER RECORD

Jul	1960	Addis Ababa		2:39:50	(1)
Aug	1960	Addis Ababa		2:21:23	(1)
10 Sep	1960	Rome	OG	2:15:16.2	(1)
7 May	1961	Athens		2:23:44.6	(1)
25 Jun	1961	Osaka		2:29:27	(1)
8 Oct	1961	Kosice		2:20:12	(1)
19 Apr	1963	Boston		2:24:43	(5)
31 May	1964	Addis Ababa		2:23:14.4	(1)
3 Aug	1964	Addis Ababa		2:16:18.8	(1)
21 Oct	1964	Tokyo	OG	2:12:11.2	(1)
9 May	1965	Otsu		2:22:58.8	(1)
24 Jul	1966	Zarauz		2:20:28.8	(1)
30 Oct	1966	Seoul		2:17:04	(1)
30 Jul	1967	Zarauz		d n f	(–)
20 Oct	1968	Mexico City	OG	d n f	(–)

Derek Clayton

Clayton was born in Barrow-on-Furness, Lancashire, on 17 November 1942, eventually settling in Australia 21 years later via Belfast where he had lived for a time. Taking up marathon running in 1965, he won his first race which was the Victorian state championship event. Only three races later Clayton, already Australian national champion,

became the first runner to better 2:10 for the marathon distance. Making the most of favourable conditions over the fast, certified Fukuoka course, he won the second Japanese International Open championship in 2:09:36.4, after an epic battle with the diminutive Seiichiro Sasaki.

Never one to shirk hard, fast training, the 6 ft 2 in (1.88 m) Clayton devised his own punishing programme, consistently running in excess of 140 miles (225 km) a week and on occasions reaching 200 miles (322 km) in training alone. Such mileage no doubt contributed greatly to the succession of injuries to the tendons and cartilages of both legs, which needed frequent surgery in the years that followed. Only two months before competing in his first Olympic Games, the Melbourne-based runner developed an ailment to his right knee. This, plus the unfavourable Mexico City altitude, prevented Clayton from finishing higher than a creditable seventh. At home, a post-race operation was successful and in May 1969, during a European tour, he once more lowered the world record, on this

Derek Clayton (Aus), setting a world record at Fukuoka in 1967, with runner-up Seiichiro Sasaki (Jap). (Asahi Shimbun)

occasion to 2:08:33.6. Despite oft repeated allegations that the course at Antwerp was under distance, this was never categorically proven beyond doubt and the clocking remained unbeaten until 1981. It is arguable whether Clayton ever fully recovered from the monumental effort put into this one particular race and the devastating physical after effects. More operations followed and successes in Australia were outweighed by defeats at two Commonwealth Games, as well as the 1972 Olympic event.

CAREER RECORD

21 Oct	1965	Melbourne		2:22:12	(1)
21 May	1966	Melbourne		d n f	(–)
12 Aug	1967	Tyabb		2:18:28	(1)
9 Sep	1967	Adelaide	NC	2:21:58	(1)
3 Dec	1967	Fukuoka		2:09:36.4	(1)
25 May	1968	Hobart	NC	2:14:47.8	(1)
20 Oct	1968	Mexico City	OG	2:27:23.8	(7)
19 May	1969	Ankara		2:17:26	(1)
30 May	1969	Antwerp		2:08:33.6	(1)
20 Jul	1969	Manchester	AAA	2:15:40	(2)
6 Jun	1970	Tralagon		2:13:39	(1)
23 Jul	1970	Edinburgh	CG	d n f	(–)
4 Oct	1970	Kosice		2:21:10.2	(5)
29 Aug	1971	Morwell		2:24:40	(1)
25 Sep	1971	Hobart	NC	2:11:08.8	(1)
24 Jun	1972	Tyabb		2:20:25	(1)
22 Jul	1972	Euroa		2:16:19	(1)
10 Sep	1972	Munich	OG	2:19:49.6	(13)
9 Dec	1972	Fukuoka		d n f	(–)
11 Aug	1973	Ballarat		2:17:23	(1)
8 Sep	1973	Perth	NC	2:12:07.6	(1)
31 Jan	1974	Christchurch	CG	d n f	(–)

Ron Hill

Ron Hill's marathon breakthrough eventually arrived after eight years and 14 races over the distance by which time he held or had held world track records at 10 miles, 15 miles and 25 km, plus British records at 6 miles, 20 km, and one hour. Since his debut in 1961 he had worn the British vest in major marathons at the European Championships in 1962 and 1966, and the 1964 Olympic Games, but the results were poor. The first Manchester Maxol event in 1969 attracted a fine international field and Hill brought off a superb win with his then fastest time of 2:13:42 and with it his first national marathon title.

Two months later Hill won the European championship over the testing Marathon to Athens route, and then failed in a desperate late bid to catch Jerome Drayton (Can) at Fukuoka. In April 1970 he sped over the Boston course in a record 2:10:30, which eclipsed the British and European record set by Bill Adcocks two years before. At Edinburgh that July, Hill won the Commonwealth Games in 2:09:28, the fastest undisputed time ever run, but the following year he had to be content with the bronze medal in the European race. It was his fourth appearance in those championship marathons—a

Ron Hill (GB) wins the 1970 Boston marathon in European record time. (AP)

record. By the time of the Munich Olympics, Hill had won five of his nine races in three years. It is debatable whether he was over-trained or over-prepared for that particular race, but there was no doubt that his sixth position was a great disappointment, both to himself and his public. By the end of 1975, a year which produced his last major victories, Hill had won 16 out of 38 marathons, recording sub 2:20 times in 21 of them, a total which he increased to 29 by the end of 1979, then a world record. He has continued to run with success throughout the world and was timed in 2:20:57 in the 1982 London race when 43.

Born in Accrington, Lancashire, on 25 September 1938, Hill became a textile chemist on graduating

Frank Shorter (USA) after his first Fukuoka win. (Asahi Shimbun)

from Manchester University before moving into the sporting goods trade. Besides being a world class athlete, he has been instrumental in the introduction of carbohydrate loading as a preparation strategy for competitive racing, has experimented with high altitude training and has designed a complete new range of running equipment.

CAREER HIGHLIGHTS

1961 2:24:22 (1st, Liverpool); **1962** 2:21:59 (1st, Poly); **1963** 2:18:06 (2nd, Poly); **1964** 2:14:12 (2nd, Poly); **1965** 2:26:33 (1st, Beverley); **1966** 2:20:55 (3rd, Poly); **1967** 2:23:43 (2nd, Enschede); **1968** 2:17:11 (4th, AAA).

20 Jul 1969	Manchester	AAA	2:13:42	(1)
21 Sep 1969	Athens	EC	2:16:47.8	(1)
7 Dec 1969	Fukuoka		2:11:54.4	(2)
20 Apr 1970	Boston		2:10:30	(1)
23 Jul 1970	Edinburgh	CG	2:09:28	(1)
6 Dec 1970	Fukuoka		2:15:27	(9)
13 Jun 1971	Manchester	AAA	2:12:39	(1)
15 Aug 1971	Helsinki	EC	2:14:34.8	(3)
4 Jun 1972	Manchester	AAA	2:12:51	(2)
10 Sep 1972	Munich	OG	2:16:30.6	(6)
6 Apr 1973	Athens		2:21:29	(5)
21 Jul 1973	Szeged		2:23:02	(1)
1 Sep 1973	Enschede		2:18:06.2	(1)
27 Oct 1973	Harlow	AAA	2:13:22	(2)
31 Jan 1974	Christchurch	CG	2:30:24	(18)
15 Jun 1974	Windsor	AAA	2:21:36	(6)
20 Jul 1974	Szeged		2:19:27.8	(1)
6 Oct 1974	Kosice		2:28:30	(28)
30 Nov 1974	Baltimore		2:17:23	(1)
21 Apr 1975	Boston		2:13:28	(5)
19 May 1975	Ankara		2:21:36	(1)
15 Jun 1975	Debno		2:12:34.2	(1)
2 Aug 1975	Montreal		2:26:01	(3)
30 Aug 1975	Enschede		2:15:59.2	(1)
7 Dec 1975	Baltimore		2:17:06	(2)

1976 2:16:59 (4th, AAA); **1977** 2:16:37 (2nd, Poly); **1978** 2:19:37 (4th Huntsville, AL); **1979** 2:15:46 (3rd, Metairie, LA); **1980** 2:27:28 (12th, Miami); **1981** 2:22:55 (15th, Miami); **1982** 2:20:57 (39th, London); **1983** 2:23:45 (159th, London).

At the end of 1983 Ron Hill had competed in 72 marathons, winning 20.

Frank Shorter

Already established as a versatile top class performer over cross-country and track with six AAU and NCAA titles in two years, it was something of a surprise when Frank Shorter decided to enter the 1971 AAU marathon. He held his own in the illustrious company of Kenny Moore, until hitting the wall at 20 miles, eventually losing by 56 seconds. That second place guaranteed him a trip to altitude Cali (1971 m, 3172 ft) for the Pan-American Games and he promptly captured both the 10000 m and the marathon. So began a five-year period of near invincibility in the latter event.

Born in Munich on 31 October 1947, it was to that venue he returned in 1972 to take part in the Olympic Games. Although outside Abebe Bikila's record, Shorter was a convincing winner in 2:12:19.8, the fastest time that he had so far recorded, after finishing fifth in the 10000 m. He was even quicker at Fukuoka (2:10:30) in taking the first of four successive wins in that top event. In the 12 marathons that he contested after his 1971 defeat up to the Montreal Olympics, Shorter lost only two minor races, in 1973 and 1974, when suffering from untimely injuries. He was only just unsuccessful in his attempt to retain the Olympic title in Canada and had to settle for the silver medal. Early in 1977 Shorter suffered an injury to his left foot, which later required surgery, and dropped out of his one marathon at New York. Thereafter he was subjected to recurring set-backs and whilst never recapturing his old form, remained a tough competitor on the road, particularly over the shorter distances. After graduating from Yale University, Shorter qualified in Law at the University of Florida, before returning to Boulder, where he now lives in close

Ian Thompson (GB) on his way to winning 1974 Commonwealth gold medal in record time. (Mark Shearman)

proximity to one of his running stores. He is a respected commentator and writer on the sport.

CAREER RECORD *(TO THE END OF 1976)*

18 Aug	1968	Alamosa, CO	OT	d n f	(–)
6 Jun	1971	Eugene	AAU	2:17:44.6	(2)
5 Aug	1971	Cali	PAG	2:22:40	(1)
5 Dec	1971	Fukuoka		2:12:50.4	(1)
9 Jul	1972	Eugene	OT	2:15:57.8	(1) eq
10 Sep	1972	Munich	OG	2:12:19.8	(1)
3 Dec	1972	Fukuoka		2:10:30	(1)
18 Mar	1973	Otsu		2:12:03	(1)
20 May	1973	Korso		d n f	(–)
2 Dec	1973	Fukuoka		2:11:45	(1)
8 Dec	1974	Fukuoka		2:11:31.2	(1)
15 Dec	1974	Honolulu		2:33:32	(4)
4 Oct	1975	Crowley, LA		2:16:29	(1)
22 May	1976	Eugene	OT	2:11:51	(1)
31 Jul	1976	Montreal	OG	2:10:45.7	(2)
24 Oct	1976	New York		2:13:12	(2)

YEAR BESTS (1977 TO 1983)

1977 did not complete a marathon; 1978 2:18:15 (23rd, Boston); 1979 2:16:14.8 (7th, New York); 1980 2:20:11 (4th, Honolulu); 1981 2:17:27.7 (3rd, Chicago); 1982 2:22:16.5 (5th, Honolulu).

Ian Thompson

The 43rd British marathon championship, held at Harlow on 27 October 1973, attracted a field of over 370 of the country's best runners. Among the entrants, the elite of which had their sights on selection for the forthcoming Commonwealth Games, was a clubman from Luton United Athletic Club, Ian Thompson. Thompson, who had the same month celebrated his 24th birthday (he was born at Birkenhead (GB) on 16 October 1949) was making his first attempt at the distance. With track bests of 14:05.4 (5000 m) and 30:10 (10000 m) Thompson, a dedicated runner, was just another number at the start. At the finish he had astounded the experts by winning in 2:12:40, then the fastest ever debut marathon and only a second outside the championship record set by Ron Hill two years earlier. Hill, the favourite, had to be content with second place.

In his next marathon at Christchurch, Thompson won with 2:09:12, a time bettered only by Derek Clayton in 1969, and a British record, and followed up with a win in Greece nine weeks later. Thompson had won his first three marathons in impressive style. He extended his winning streak to four in taking the European title in an oppressively hot Rome and then won at Korso the next year. Thompson's sixth race was the Olympic trial in the spring of 1976, but cramping up at 19 miles, he could only finish seventh and therefore missed selection.

Despite a fine second at Fukuoka that December (ahead of the Olympic champion Waldemar Cierpinski) and wins in the 1977 Poly and the 1980 Centenary AAA title race, Thompson never fully recovered the sparkling form of his first marathon year. His one Olympic race at Moscow in 1980 ended in retirement, along with the other two British team members.

CAREER RECORD (1973 TO 1980)

Date	Venue		Time	
27 Oct 1973	Harlow	AAA	2:12:40	(1)
31 Jan 1974	Christchurch	CG	2:09:12	(1)
6 Apr 1974	Marathon to Athens		2:13:50.2	(1)
8 Sep 1974	Rome	EC	2:13:18.8	(1)
26 Oct 1975	Korso		2:24:30	(1)
8 May 1976	Rotherham	AAA/OT	2:19:07	(7)
24 Oct 1976	New York		2:26:26	(22)
5 Dec 1976	Fukuoka		2:12:54.2	(2)
21 May 1977	Amsterdam		2:17:47.4	(4)
11 Jun 1977	Windsor		2:14:32	(1)
23 Oct 1977	New York		2:17:46	(13)
13 Nov 1977	Auckland	39.7 km	2:03:31	(3)
4 Dec 1977	Fukuoka		2:33:41	(44)
7 May 1978	Sandbach	AAA	2:20:21	(28)
16 Jul 1978	Oyarzun		2:21:00	(1)
22 Oct 1978	New York		2:14:12	(2)
12 Nov 1978	Auckland		2:13:49	(1)
30 Dec 1978	Ginnosar		2:19:50	(5)
28 Jan 1979	Hamilton		2:21:48	(2)
26 Aug 1979	Montreal		2:15:24	(6)
21 Oct 1979	New York		2:13:42.2	(4)
3 Feb 1980	Auckland		2:20:17	(10)
3 May 1980	Milton Keynes	AAA	2:14:00	(1)
1 Aug 1980	Moscow	OG	d n f	(–)
23 Aug 1980	Stockholm		2:19:25	(3)
21 Sep 1980	Rotherham		2:18:59	(1)
7 Dec 1980	Fukuoka		2:18:14	(32)

YEAR BESTS (1981 TO 1983)

1981 2:13:50 (1st, Birmingham); 1982 2:14:07 (1st, Paris); 1983 2:18:09 (1st, Bolton).

At the end of 1983 Thompson had won 17 of his 39 marathons.

1977 Fukuoka marathon. From left: Mineteru Sakamoto (Jap), Bill Rodgers (USA) winner, Takeshi Soh (Jap) and Leonid Moseyev (Sov) in the lead. (Popperfoto)

Bill Rodgers

At the end of 1981, Bill Rodgers had amassed 21 victories from 33 marathons since his first race at Boston in 1973, one of the most consistent records in modern times. Scoring major wins in every continent except Africa, he has bettered 2:12 on no less than 12 occasions. Despite these accomplishments Rodgers will go down in marathon history as one of the many outstanding athletes who were unfortunate enough to peak in non-Olympic years, as his record in 1977–8 clearly shows. He was unlucky enough to be suffering from a foot injury at Montreal in 1976, whilst politics prevented him from competing four years later.

Graduating in sociology from Wesleyan College in 1970, William Henry Rodgers (born Newington, CT, on 23 December 1947) only began running seriously in late 1972, after a three-year-break from the sport. Having lasted 20 miles in his first Boston, he joined the Greater Boston Track Club and so his marathon career took off. Following a third place in the 1975 world cross-country championships, Rodgers won the first of four Boston races and went on to set American track records from 15 km to 30 km, as well as a world record at 25 km. In addition he was successful in four consecutive New York marathons. Rodgers is a runner who has never excelled in over-warm conditions and his defeats at Enschede (1975), Boston (1977) and Montreal (1979) came about in such conditions; and although absent, similar temperatures prevailed at Moscow in 1980. Now the owner of a successful running shop, situated on the Boston race route, his outstanding career over the marathon distance is recorded in full below.

CAREER RECORD

16 Apr	1973	Boston		d n f	(–)
28 Oct	1973	Framingham, MA		2:28:12	(1)
15 Apr	1974	Boston		2:19:34	(14)
29 Sep	1974	New York		2:35:59	(5)
1 Dec	1974	Philadelphia		2:21:57	(1)
21 Apr	1975	Boston		2:09:55	(1)
30 Aug	1975	Enschede		d n f	(–)
7 Dec	1975	Fukuoka		2:11:26.4	(3)
22 May	1976	Eugene	OT	2:11:58	(2)
31 Jul	1976	Montreal	OG	2:25:14	(40)
24 Oct	1976	New York		2:10:09.6	(1)
7 Nov	1976	Sado*		2:08:23	(1)
5 Dec	1976	Baltimore		2:14:22	(1)
13 Feb	1977	Kyoto		2:14:26.2	(1)
18 Apr	1977	Boston		d n f	(–)
21 May	1977	Amsterdam		2:12:46.6	(1)
8 Oct	1977	Waynesboro, VA		2:25:17	(1)
23 Oct	1977	New York		2:11:28.2	(1)
4 Dec	1977	Fukuoka		2:10:55.3	(1)
17 Apr	1978	Boston		2:10:13	(1)
22 Oct	1978	New York		2:12:11.6	(1)
3 Dec	1978	Fukuoka		2:12:51.3	(6)
16 Apr	1979	Boston		2:09:27	(1)
26 Aug	1979	Montreal		2:22:12	(18)
21 Oct	1979	New York		2:11:42	(1)
21 Apr	1980	Boston		2:12:11	(1)
5 Oct	1980	Toronto		2:14:46.8	(1)
26 Oct	1980	New York		2:13:20.3	(5)
10 Jan	1981	Houston		2:12:19.6	(1)
20 Apr	1981	Boston		2:10:34	(3)
1 Aug	1981	Rio de Janeiro		2:14:13	(1)
15 Aug	1981	Stockholm		2:13:26	(1)
11 Oct	1981	Columbus		2:17:28	(7)
24 Jan	1982	Houston		2:14:51	(5)
31 Jan	1982	Tokyo		2:24:41	(37)
28 Mar	1982	Seoul		2:28:34	(34)
19 Apr	1982	Boston		2:12:38	(4)
7 Aug	1982	Rio de Janeiro		d n f	(–)
17 Oct	1982	Melbourne		2:11:08	(1)
22 Jan	1983	Miami*		2:15:08	(1)
18 Apr	1983	Boston		2:11:59	(10)
25 Sep	1983	Beijing		d n f	(–)
16 Oct	1983	Chicago		2:21:40	(30)

* denotes short course.

Waldemar Cierpinski

Early success as a steeplechaser more or less came to an end when Waldemar Cierpinski finished a creditable third in the Kosice marathon of 1974. He returned the following autumn and ran three minutes faster, yet such was the quality of the field, his finishing position was only seventh.

Born in Neugattersleben (GDR) on 3 August 1950, Cierpinski won the national steeplechase title in 1972 but then further honours over the distance eluded him. He by-passed the marathon in 1975 but

renewed his efforts the next year with the Olympic Games in mind. Although something of a surprise winner at Karl Marx Stadt, Cierpinski showed it to be no fluke when six weeks later he carried off the national title in the second fastest time ever achieved by a GDR marathon runner.

At Montreal he was his country's sole representative in the event. Defending champion Frank Shorter showed at the front early on but Cierpinski was never far behind and when he made his charge late in the race no one could hold him. His winning time of 2:09:55 demolished Bikila's Olympic record and was a surprise to all except the GDR squad. Favourite for the 1978 European race in Prague, Cierpinski was shunted out of the medals in a tight finish, and two poor results at Fukuoka in 1978 and 1979 could have done little for his confidence. However, Cierpinski trained hard for the defence of his Olympic crown and picked up the national 10000 m titles in 1979 and 1980. Cierpinski was a comfortable winner at Moscow and thus equalled Bikila's feat of the 1960s in carrying off two Olympic marathon titles. Since then his record has been patchy but he showed a welcome return to form in early 1983, in winning the European Cup race at Laredo, leading the GDR team to a convincing win in the process. He followed up with a fine third in the World Championship race in his third fastest ever time and was first European finisher.

CAREER RECORD

6 Oct	1974	Kosice		2:20:28.4	(3)
5 Oct	1975	Kosice		2:17:30.4	(7)
17 Apr	1976	Karl Marx Stadt		2:13:57.2	(1)
30 May	1976	Wittenberg	NC	2:12:21.2	(1)
31 Jul	1976	Montreal	OG	2:09:55	(1)
5 Dec	1976	Fukuoka		2:14:56	(3)
2 Oct	1977	Kosice		2:16:00.3	(3)
8 May	1978	Prague		2:14:51	(1)
24 Jun	1978	Boxberg	OT	2:14:57.4	(1)
3 Sep	1978	Prague	EC	2:12:20	(4)
3 Dec	1978	Fukuoka		2:22:49	(32)
1 Sep	1979	Karl Marx Stadt		2:15:50	(1)
2 Dec	1979	Fukuoka		d n f	(–)
3 May	1980	Karl Marx Stadt		2:11:17	(1)
1 Aug	1980	Moscow	OG	2:11:03	(1)
5 Oct	1980	Kosice		d n f	(–)
7 Dec	1980	Fukuoka		2:10:24	(6)
13 Sep	1981	Agen	E Cup	2:15:44	(2)
6 Dec	1981	Fukuoka		d n f	(–)
31 Jan	1982	Manila		2:14:27	(1)
30 Jun	1982	Dresden	NC	2:13:59	(1)
12 Sep	1982	Athens	EC	2:17:50	(6)
13 Feb	1983	Tokyo		2:12:40	(7)
19 Jun	1983	Laredo	E Cup	2:12:26	(1)
14 Aug	1983	Helsinki	WC	2:10:37	(3)
4 Dec	1983	Fukuoka		2:15:13	(15)

Gerard Nijboer

Nijboer was already the Netherlands 25 km cham-

Waldemar Cierpinski (GDR) wins the first Manila marathon, 1982. (AP)

pion when he ran his first marathon at Enschede in August 1979. In taking fifth place in a respectable 2:16:48 as first home athlete to finish, he took the national title in the process. Only eight seconds slower at New York two months later, Nijboer showed himself already to be a consistent performer but few would have guessed the in-roads he was to make the following April. Taking full advantage of a bright spring day and a flat Amsterdam course, Nijboer sped over the distance in a brilliant new European best time of 2:09:01. Even with such a time to his credit he was not expected to be a force to be reckoned with at Moscow, yet he fought all the way only to succumb to Cierpinski in the closing stages. Cramp at 18 miles forced him to retire from the New York event and thereafter he became prone to knee injuries. He did not run the event again until the European Championships two years later. On the demanding road from Marathon to Athens, Nijboer

Gerard Nijboer (Hol) wins the 1982 European gold medal. (AP)

struck out to the front at 27 km to carry off the gold medal. Nijboer was born at Uffelte (Hol) on 18 August 1955.

CAREER RECORD

Date		Location		Time	
25 Aug	1979	Enschede		2:16:48	(5)
21 Oct	1979	New York		2:16:56.6	(11)
26 Apr	1980	Amsterdam		2:09:01	(1)
1 Aug	1980	Moscow	OG	2:11:20	(2)
26 Oct	1980	New York		d n f	(–)
12 Sep	1982	Athens	EC	2:15:16	(1)
9 Apr	1983	Rotterdam		2:15:23	(15)
14 Aug	1983	Helsinki	WC	2:16:59	(29)

Toshihiko Seko

After a cautious and erratic start in his first three marathon races, Toshihiko Seko has graduated into one of the world's top exponents at the distance. Winning five out of his last six marathons, Seko's victory at Tokyo in 1983 culminated in an Asian record of 2:08:38, fifth fastest ever time recorded.

Seko has lived with his Wasuda University coach and Japanese running guru Kiyoshi Nakamura, himself a 1936 Olympian, since 1977 when the latter convinced Seko, already Japanese High School middle distance champion, to turn to the marathon. Following three successive most impressive wins at Fukuoka and world track records at 25 km and 30 km set in New Zealand, a knee injury prevented Seko from running the marathon after his 1981 Boston triumph until 1983.

Seko by-passed Helsinki to prepare for the Olympic trial at Fukuoka. In winning, he extended his win streak to five and secured his Los Angeles berth.

Born in Yokkaiichi City on 15 July 1956, Seko is currently employed by a Tokyo food company, S B Foods Ltd, where he has worked since graduating from Waseda University.

CAREER RECORD

Date		Location		Time	
13 Feb	1977	Kyoto		2:26:00	(10)
4 Dec	1977	Fukuoka	NC	2:15:00.1	(5)
8 Jul	1978	Milton Keynes		2:53:17	(68)
3 Dec	1978	Fukuoka		2:10:21	(1)
16 Apr	1979	Boston		2:10:12	(2)
2 Dec	1979	Fukuoka	NC	2:10:35	(1)
7 Dec	1980	Fukuoka		2:09:45	(1)
20 Apr	1981	Boston		2:09:26	(1)
13 Feb	1983	Tokyo		2:08:38	(1)
4 Dec	1983	Fukuoka		2:08:52	(1)

Alberto Salazar

In the space of four races in the two years between October 1980 and 1982, Alberto Baudrey Salazar had already indelibly inscribed his name into the annals of marathon running. Born in Havana, Cuba, on 7 August 1958, Salazar was brought to the United States in 1960 by his family who took up residence in Florida. Encouraged by his brother, Salazar soon became competent on the track and by the time he was 19 was United States junior champion over 5000 m and 10000 m. By October 1980, Salazar had scored victories in both the AAU and NCAA cross-country championships and had lowered his best 10000 m time to below twenty-eight minutes.

He was all set for his first marathon venture at New York. Salazar predicted a time of 2:10 and he did not disappoint. His winning 2:09:41 was the fastest first marathon ever recorded and he left the strong Mexican Rodolfo Gomez well beaten in second. In the summer of 1981 he took third place in the World Cup 10000 m, before returning to New York for his second marathon, which was even more astonishing than the first. Putting together halves of 1:04:10 and 1:04:02.7, Salazar set an undisputed world record of 2:08:12.7, laying to rest Clayton's 1969 time in the process. April 1982 saw him pull apart the Boston record with 2:08:51, despite being pushed all the way by Dick Beardsley who was only two seconds adrift at the tape. At the finish, Salazar was suffering from hypothermia and acute dehydration and had an intravenous solution of dextrose and glucose administered. Fully recovered, he set two fine new American records over 5000 m and 10000 m on a European summer tour and on return scored a third success at New York in 2:09:29, against a stiff breeze and a strong challenge from Rodolfo Gomez. His winning streak came to an end in early 1983 at Rotterdam, when a much publicised clash with the Commonwealth champion Rob de Castella ended in victory for the Australian and a disappointing fifth for Salazar.

At Fukuoka he was again fifth but ran his fastest time to date over an out and back course.

CAREER RECORD

26 Oct	1980	New York		2:09:41	(1)
25 Oct	1981	New York		2:08:12.7	(1)
19 Apr	1982	Boston		2:08:51	(1)
24 Oct	1982	New York		2:09:29	(1)
9 Apr	1983	Rotterdam		2:10:08	(5)
4 Dec	1983	Fukuoka		2:09:21	(5)

Robert de Castella

Watched over by his Xavier College (Melbourne) coach Pat Clohessy since the age of eleven, Francois Robert de Castella could not have wanted a better tutor as he developed into a world class athlete. De Castella, who maintains a strict non-fat vegetarian diet, was 22 years old when he won both his first two marathons in 1979, the second being the national title race. His first defeat came at the hands of Gerard Barrett in the Olympic trial, for which one of the strongest ever Australian fields had assembled. De Castella took revenge in Moscow, placing tenth overall and third of those from outside Europe to finish. Four months later, de Castella journeyed to Fukuoka, where he lowered his best time to 2:10:44 in eighth place.

A year's lay-off from the marathon meant a gradual, concentrated build up for the 1981 event at the same venue, during which time he averaged around 130 miles (220 km) per week in training. At Fukuoka, de Castella only just missed Salazar's recently-established world record but the Australian's time of 2:08:18 was still the fastest ever run over an out and back course. It was another ten months before he raced the distance again. The occasion was the Commonwealth Games marathon and de Castella was well aware of the rising temperature and near 100% humidity as he allowed the two Tanzanians Ikangaa and Shahanga to build up an early lead. Biding his time, de Castella caught the leader Ikangaa at 38 km to pull away to a fine win. At Rotterdam in April 1983, he had a decisive victory over Salazar to become the undisputed world number one, despite a gallant effort by Carlos Lopes (Por), and further emphasised his superiority with a superb win in the World Championship race.

Born on 27 February 1957, de Castella (popularly known as 'Deke') is a biophysicist with the Australian Institute of Sport at Canberra.

CAREER RECORD

23 Jun	1979	Point Cook			2:14:44	(1)
12 Aug	1979	Herne Hill	NC		2:13:23	(1)
6 Apr	1980	Adelaide	OT		2:12:34	(2)
1 Aug	1980	Moscow	OG		2:14:31	(10)
7 Dec	1980	Fukuoka			2:10:44	(8)
6 Dec	1981	Fukuoka			2:08:18	(1)
8 Oct	1982	Brisbane	CG		2:09:18	(1)
9 Apr	1983	Rotterdam			2:08:37	(1)
14 Aug	1983	Helsinki	WC		2:10:03	(1)

Joyce Smith

By the time Joyce took to the road seriously in 1976, she had been in athletics for no less than 22 years, had been national champion and record holder at 1500 m and 3000 m, won one international and three national cross-country championships and had a bronze medal from the 1974 European 3000 m event.

Born Joyce Byatt at Stoke Newington, London, on 26 October 1937, Smith ran her first marathon at the age of 41 and promptly reduced the national record by a margin of 9 min 17 sec with a time of 2:41:37. In her next race at Waldniel on the occasion of the second Avon championships, her winning 2:36:27 was a Commonwealth record, and she finished her year with yet another victory at Tokyo. In Miami, at the beginning of 1980, Joyce met with defeat for the first time when she was overcome by the heat but she recovered and at Sandbach, in June, further improved her best time to 2:33:32. A bout of chicken-pox and an untimely injury set her back and lack of training meant that she had to be content with seventh in the defence of her Avon title in London. Returning to Japan, Joyce had a tough battle with Jacqueline Gareau (Can), before winning in 2:30:27, then the best ever time recorded by a woman over a non point to point course.

In the first London marathon, four months later, she became only the third woman to better 2:30, which she did with three seconds to spare. Another injury held back Joyce in her preparation for the Osaka race in January 1982, where she finished fifth, but by the time of the London event she had regained fitness and further reduced her best time to a superb 2:29:43. At the age of 44 years 216 days she became the oldest athlete ever to set a British record, and was also the oldest competitor in the first World Championships where she finished a creditable ninth in 2:34:27.

CAREER RECORD

17 Jun	1979	Sandbach	AAA	2:41:37	(1)
22 Sep	1979	Waldniel	Avon	2:36:27	(1)
18 Nov	1979	Tokyo		2:37:48	(1)
12 Jan	1980	Miami		d n f	(–)
22 Jun	1980	Sandbach		2:33:32	(1)
3 Aug	1980	London	AAA/Avon	2:41:22	(7)
16 Nov	1980	Tokyo		2:30:27	(1)
29 Mar	1981	London		2:29:57	(1)

Joyce Smith (GB) and Jacqueline Gareau (Can), Tokyo 1980. (Asahi Shimbun)

24 Jan	1982	Osaka		2:35:34	(5)
9 May	1982	London		2:29:43	(1)
30 Jan	1983	Osaka		2:40:01	(8)
24 Apr	1983	Rome		2:38:04	(3)
5 Jun	1983	Los Angeles	Avon	2:34:39	(5)
7 Aug	1983	Helsinki	WC	2:34:27	(9)
16 Oct	1983	Chicago		2:39:43	(12)

Grete Waitz

The popular Norwegian athlete Grete Waitz had already gained a World Cup success, two world records and a European third place over 3000 m, plus a world cross country title, when she ran her first marathon in October 1978. In that race, at New York, she set the first of three consecutive world records in as many marathons with a time of 2:32:29.8. Running at the same venue in 1979 and 1980 she further reduced the record, first to 2:27:32.6 and then to 2:25:41, before shin soreness forced her out of the 1981 New York marathon at 15 miles. By this time the Scandinavian ace had won her fourth world cross-country championship. Waitz suffered her first ever defeat in this event when she had to be content with the bronze medal at the 1982 championship, and four weeks later was forced out of the Boston marathon in the closing stages due to cramp. Recovering from a stress fracture to her right foot, Grete regained her winning ways in New York in 1982, achieved on only six weeks of training and then in early 1983 regained her cross-country title at

Gateshead. She followed this success by winning her first marathon outside the United States in London with a time of 2:25:28.7, fractionally better than Roe's 1981 New York time, but which was beaten by Joan Benoit at Boston the following day. The World Championship race was the first all-women marathon in which she had competed and never threatened, she was a clear and most deserving winner.

Waitz was born in Oslo on 10 October 1953.

CAREER RECORD

22 Oct	1978	New York		2:32:29.8	(1)
21 Oct	1979	New York		2:27:32.6	(1)
26 Oct	1980	New York		2:25:41	(1)
25 Oct	1981	New York		d n f	(–)
19 Apr	1982	Boston		d n f	(–)
24 Oct	1982	New York		2:27:14	(1)
17 Apr	1983	London		2:25:28.7	(1)
7 Aug	1983	Helsinki	WC	2:28:09	(1)
23 Oct	1983	New York		2:27:00	(1)

Allison Roe

Allison Roe (*née* Deed) was born in Auckland on 30 May 1957 and after early success at tennis turned almost overnight to athletics. Within two years she

Allison Roe (107) leads at the start of the 1980 Tokyo marathon. From left: Julie Brown (USA, 113); Jacqueline Gareau (Can, 102); Gillian Adams (GB) and Joyce Smith (GB, 105). (Asahi Shimbun)

had won the national cross-country championship at the age of eighteen. She made her marathon debut at Auckland in 1980, finishing over two miles behind Joan Benoit (USA), but won a trip to Eugene the following autumn, where she finished a good third behind colleague Lorraine Moller and Marja Wokke (Hol). Two months later, Allison took a fourth place at Tokyo and then won at Auckland again at the beginning of 1981, which was destined to be her greatest year to date. Following a world record over 20 km, Roe gave the world marathon record a scare at Boston with a time of 2:26:46, which made her the second fastest behind Waitz. Then at New York she handed the Norwegian her first defeat and took the world record at the same time with 2:25:28.8. Despite winning at Seoul, Allison was laid low for much of 1982 due to Achilles and other muscle problems, which forced her to withdraw from the Boston marathon at 16 miles.

CAREER RECORD

3 Feb	1980	Auckland	2:51:45	(2)
7 Sep	1980	Eugene	2:34:29	(3)
16 Nov	1980	Tokyo	2:42:24	(4)
7 Feb	1981	Auckland	2:36:16	(1)
20 Apr	1981	Boston	2:26:46	(1)
25 Oct	1981	New York	2:25:28.8	(1)
28 Mar	1982	Seoul	2:43:12	(1)
18 Apr	1983	Boston	d n f	(–)

Joan Benoit

Born in Cape Elizabeth, Maine, on 16 May 1957, Joan took part in a variety of sports at High School, which culminated in track events. She made her marathon debut in Bermuda in 1979, the day after winning the 10 km road race, finishing second to Julie Shea (USA) with whom she had trained briefly at North Carolina State University. The following April she set a US record of 2:35:15 at Boston and was only just outside this time in winning at Eugene in September. In beating Allison Deed (later to become Roe) by 20 min in Auckland, Benoit further reduced the record to 2:31:21 but shortly afterwards underwent an appendicectomy. After finishing fourth in the 1980 Avon and second in the same event a year later, Benoit underwent operations on both Achilles tendons, returning to regain the US record at Eugene in September 1982, her time of 2:26:11 making her third fastest ever. At Boston she passed the half-way in an unbelievable 1:08:23, three minutes faster than at Eugene, was still under 2:20 pace at 20 miles (1:46:44) and finally recorded an amazing world record of 2:22:43.

CAREER RECORD

28 Jan	1979	Hamilton		2:50:54	(2)
16 Apr	1979	Boston		2:35:15	(1)
9 Sep	1979	Eugene		2:35:41	(1)
3 Feb	1980	Auckland		2:31:23	(1)
3 Aug	1980	London	Avon	2:38:42	(4)
20 Apr	1981	Boston		2:30:16	(3)
23 Aug	1981	Ottawa	Avon	2:37:24	(2)
11 Oct	1981	Columbus		2:39:07	(2)
12 Sep	1982	Eugene		2:26:11	(1)
18 Apr	1983	Boston		2:22:43	(1)

Europe

Great Britain

Although the first organised distance race (London to Brighton over 52¼ miles) took place in 1837, it was another 40 years before any runner, amateur or professional, was timed at a distance which can now be related to the modern marathon. By far the best time ever achieved over 25 miles, prior to the 1896 Olympic Games, was 2:33:44 by the amateur George Dunning at Stamford Bridge on 26 December 1881.

The first international marathon to be held, following the Olympics, was the 40 km race from Paris to Conflans on 19 July 1896. It was won handsomely in 2:31:29.8 by the British runner Len Hurst. Hurst became a professional athlete at the age of 15 years, and the following year won no less than 31 races of distances between four and ten miles. He was without doubt the country's first marathon exponent.

Although the French event was not held in 1897, Hurst finished second in the next two editions before resuming his winning ways in 1900 and 1901. In 1900 the course was reversed and Hurst's time that year of 2:26:47.4 was by far the fastest ever recorded. A team of three took part in the 1900 Olympic marathon but as with so many in that ill fated race, none of them finished and it was 1908 before Britain was again represented. In the meantime, despite Hurst's successes at the turn of the century, there were no road races held in the country which exceeded 20 miles.

Of the four major 1908 Olympic marathon trials, the nearest to the intended distance of 26 miles from Windsor to the White City was that organised by Birchfield Harriers at Coventry over 25 miles. This race, on 9 May and won by Jack Price in 2:37:13, can be considered the first true marathon to be held in Britain.

The outcome of the 1908 Olympic race led to the launching of the Polytechnic Harriers event the following year (see The International Races) but this was the only British marathon to be held annually until 1923. That year the *Sporting Chronicle* organised a race at Manchester until 1929, and after a two-year break the *Daily Dispatch* carried on until 1936. Other races had short lives during this period with some, as in the case of Manchester, being revived after the war. Liverpool lasted four years from 1927, Sheffield three years from 1929 and Blackpool six years from 1930, although the latter was staged once more in 1938. The Midland Coun-

Sam Ferris (GB) winning the Olympic silver medal, 1932.

ties Championship flourished from 1932 onwards, as did the Welsh event from 1934. Yet it was the Poly, as it was affectionately known, which continued to thrive and in 1925 the first AAA Championship was awarded to this race. It was won by Sam Ferris, a regular in the RAF, who went on to compete in three Olympic marathons and win a record eight Polys, all on training which rarely exceeded 40 miles in a week.

SAM FERRIS—CAREER RECORD

31 May	1924	Windsor–Stamford Bridge	Pol	2:54:03	(2)
13 Jul	1924	Paris	OG	2:52:26	(5)
16 Aug	1924	Manchester*		2:47:44	(3)
30 May	1925	Windsor–Stamford Bridge	Pol	2:35:58.2	(1)
29 May	1926	Windsor–Stamford Bridge	Pol	2:42:24.2	(1)
1 Aug	1926	Copenhagen (33.7 km/21 miles)		2:10:13	(1)
7 Nov	1926	Turin		2:46:18	(1)
28 May	1927	Windsor–Stamford Bridge	Pol	2:40:32.2	(1)
30 Jul	1927	Manchester		2:48:46.4	(1)
28 Sep	1927	Liverpool		2:35:27	(1)
26 May	1928	Windsor–Stamford Bridge	Pol	2:41:02.2	(1)
5 Aug	1928	Amsterdam	OG	2:37:41	(8)
26 Sep	1928	Liverpool		2:33:00	(1)
14 Oct	1928	Turin		2:48:24	(2)
18 May	1929	Windsor–Stamford Bridge	Pol	2:40:47.4	(1)
5 Jul	1929	Windsor–Stamford Bridge	AAA	2:39:12	(2)
4 Jul	1930	Windsor–Stamford Bridge	AAA	2:41:46.4	(3)
21 Aug	1930	Hamilton	EG	no time	(2)
30 May	1931	Windsor–Stamford Bridge	Pol	2:35:31.8	(1)
28 May	1932	Windsor–Stamford Bridge	Pol	2:36:32.4	(1)
7 Aug	1932	Los Angeles	OG	2:31:55	(2)
10 Jun	1933	Windsor–White City	Pol	2:42:24.2	(1)

* At Manchester in 1924 the first two runners inadvertently cut the course. Ferris was first to complete the full distance.

The Poly marathon in 1925–6–7 also incorporated the AAA title.

Whilst Ferris dominated the southern scene during this period Harold Wood, the Makerfield coalman, was equally consistent in the north of the country. Although he never finished ahead of Ferris in five attempts, he won 13 out of 28 marathons, his successes being at Manchester (six), Blackpool (four), Liverpool (two) and Sheffield. In 1934 he was the best placed Englishman in the Empire Games race, finishing fourth. In 1928 he was second best British finisher in the Olympic race taking eleventh place in 2:41:15.

Harry Payne was thirteenth at Amsterdam and it was he who won the 1929 AAA race held over the Poly course on a balmy evening on 6 July in 2:30:57.6, a British record which lasted over 21 years. Favourite for the first British Empire Games marathon he was knocked down by a motor car whilst training on the eve of the race and, although starting, did not complete the course. The winner was Duncan McLeod Wright, twice British champion and twice winner of the Poly, a tough performer who finished fourth in the 1932 Olympics, after being briefly in the lead, the best position ever achieved by a Scot. His marathon career stretched from 1924 to 1946.

Another Scotsman and, as Wright, a member of Maryhill Harriers, Donald McNab Robertson, won a record number of six AAA marathon titles between 1932 and 1939 as well as the first two Scottish championships in 1946 and 1947. After his ninth place debut in the 1930 AAA race, Robertson won nine races, his only defeats being in the Empire Games of 1934 and 1938, the Olympic Games of 1936 and the 1946 AAA race, prior to his sudden death in 1949.

The immediate post-war years were dominated by four times international cross-country champion Jack Holden. Holden won four consecutive AAA marathons from 1947 and both the Empire and European titles in 1950. He lost only two races during this period, dropping out of the 1948 Olympic marathon and finishing second at Kosice in 1947. He retired, following his defeat by Jim Peters in the 1951 Poly. These were his only losses in 17 marathons. Peters' career is documented in the chapter on Runners and after his retirement it was not until 1960 that another consistent British marathon runner appeared.

That year Brian Kilby won the first of five AAA

Scotland's greatest pre-war marathon runners Duncan McLeod Wright (252) and Donald McNab Robertson (251) in 1932. (Maryhill Harriers)

Jim Peters and Jack Holden (248) in the Finchley '20'. (H W Neale)

races and went on to equal Holden's feat of winning both the Empire and European marathons in the same year (1962). On 6 July 1963 at Port Talbot he bettered Peters' record with 2:14:43, his best ever time, and only narrowly missed the bronze medal in the Tokyo Olympics as Basil Heatley took the silver medal and Ron Hill finished 19th for Britain's best ever team performance at these Games. Heatley, who had set a new world record of 2:13:55 in the Poly on 13 June 1964, thus equalled the feats of Ferris (1932), Harper (1936), and Richards (1948) in taking second place at the Olympics.

Jim Alder overtook Bill Adcocks on the track at Kingston for a well-deserved Commonwealth gold medal in 1966 and in so doing scored Scotland's third win in that event since 1930. The Morpeth-based Alder was a consistent runner and had become the first Scot to better 2:20 in finishing fourth in the 1964 AAA race with 2:17:46. His best time of 2:12:04 was achieved in 1970 when finishing second to Hill in the Commonwealth Games.

Like Kilby and Heatley, Adcocks was a member of the powerful Coventry Godiva Harriers. In 1968 he scored two notable victories abroad, both in European record times. First he won the Karl Marx Stadt

race in 2:12:16.8 and at the year's end the famous Fukuoka run in the then second fastest ever time of 2:10:47.8. In between, Adcocks finished a creditable fifth in the Olympics, held at the high altitude of Mexico City. The following April he won the arduous Marathon to Athens race in 2:11:07.2, his fourth win in 12 marathons, which remains one of the finest ever results, having regard to the toughness of the course. In addition, Adcocks beat all four runners who finished in front of him in Mexico. Injury put him out of the running for the European title race held over the same course later that year, the gold medal going to Ron Hill (see Runners) who had become the doyen of British distance running. Hill took the Commonwealth race the following year to hold both titles simultaneously, as had Holden and Kilby before him, and became the first and so far only British runner to win at Boston.

In 1974 Ian Thompson (see Runners) joined this illustrious trio with wins at Christchurch and Rome, his time of 2:09:12 at the former venue remaining the British record for the distance until 1983, when only three British runners approached that time. After John Graham had won the first Rotterdam event in 2:09:28, Hugh Jones captured the second London marathon in a time four seconds faster, to record his fourth win in nine races. Injury prevented him from taking part in the European Championships later in 1982, but in 1983, after winning the Stockholm marathon he finished eighth in Helsinki in 2:11:15. The third London race in 1983 was won by Mike Gratton in 2:09:43, only his second win in 13 marathons; the previous October he had won the bronze medal in the Commonwealth Games and gained the first medal in a major marathon by a British runner since 1974. He did not finish in the World Championship race in Helsinki. At New York in 1983 Geoff Smith made a gallant attempt to win in his marathon debut, but had to be content with second place. His time of 2:09:08 constituted a new British record.

AAA CHAMPIONS *(GB UNLESS STATED)*

1925	Sam Ferris	2:35:58.2
1926	Sam Ferris	2:42:24.2
1927	Sam Ferris	2:40:32.2
1928	Harry Payne	2:34:34
1929	Harry Payne	2:30:57.6
1930	Duncan McLeod Wright	2:38:29.4
1931	Duncan McLeod Wright	2:49:54.2
1932	Donald McNab Robertson	2:34:32.6
1933	Donald McNab Robertson	2:43:13.6
1934	Donald McNab Robertson	2:41:55
1935	Bert Norris	3:02:57.8
1936	Donald NcNab Robertson	2:35:02.4
1937	Donald McNab Robertson	2:37:19.2
1938	Jack Beman	2:36:39.6
1939	Donald McNab Robertson	2:35:37
1946	Squire Yarrow	2:43:14.4
1947	Jack Holden	2:33:20.2
1948	Jack Holden	2:36:44.6
1949	Jack Holden	2:34:10.6
1950	Jack Holden	2:31:03.4
1951	Jim Peters	2:31:42
1952	Jim Peters	2:20:42.2
1953	Jim Peters	2:22:29
1954	Jim Peters	2:17:39.4
1955	Bob McMinnis	2:39:35
1956	Harry Hicks	2:26:15
1957	Eddie Kirkup	2:22:27.8
1958	Colin Kemball	2:22:27.4
1959	Chris Fleming-Smith	2:30:11
1960	Brian Kilby	2:22:44.8
1961	Brian Kilby	2:24:37
1962	Brian Kilby	2:26:15
1963	Brian Kilby	2:16:45
1964	Brian Kilby	2:23:01
1965	Bill Adcocks	2:16:50
1966	Graham Taylor	2:19:04
1967	Jim Alder	2:16:08
1968	Tim Johnston	2:15:26
1969	Ron Hill	2:13:42
1970	Don Faircloth	2:18:15
1971	Ron Hill	2:12:39
1972	Lutz Philipp (GFR)	2:12:50
1973	Ian Thompson	2:12:40
1974	Akio Usami (Jap)	2:15:16
1975	Jeff Norman	2:15:50
1976	Barry Watson	2:15:08
1977	Dave Cannon	2:15:02
1978	Tony Simmons	2:12:33

1979	Greg Hannon	2:13:06
1980	Ian Thompson	2:14:00
1981	Hugh Jones	2:14:07
1982	Steve Kenyon	2:11:40
1983	Mike Gratton	2:09:43

In Championships won by foreign runners, the first British nationals to finish were as follows:
1972 Ron Hill 2:12:51; 1974 Bernie Plain 2:18:32.

WCCA CHAMPIONS

1978	Margaret Lockley	2:55:08
1979	Joyce Smith	2:41:37
1980	Joyce Smith	2:41:22
1981	Leslie Watson	2:49:08
1982	Kath Binns	2:36:12
1983	Grete Waitz (Nor)	2:25:28.7

First British national to finish in 1983 was Glynis Penny 2:36:21.

Joyce Smith (see Runners) has dominated the women's marathon scene since 1979 and in 14 completed races has been beaten by a British runner only once, when recovering from illness. In 1979–80 Smith had good international support from two consistent performers, Gillian Horowitz (*née* Adams), who briefly held the national record in 1979, and club colleague Carol Gould. Kathryn Binns, 20 years Smith's junior, finished ahead of her at Osaka in 1983 and went on to finish 22nd in Helsinki, as the current champion Glynis Penny dropped out. At the World University Games the same year, 20-year-old Sandra Rowell won the inaugural marathon title in 2:47:36.2, after taking ninth place in London.

Other races

In 1946 just six marathons were staged in Great Britain. By 1950 the total had reached ten but progress was slow and it took another 29 years before the number was doubled. Since 1980 (54 marathons) the number has escalated to 80 in 1981, 110 in 1982 and 135 in 1983. Of pre-war races the AAA, Poly, Midland and Welsh events are still held annually, whilst four marathons inaugurated in the post-war period before 1960, the Northern Irish and Scottish national races (both started in 1946), Isle of Wight (1957) and RRC (1959) have also continued into the 1980s. With the advent of the running boom three major marathons, all catering for the masses, started in 1981 at London (see Races), Bolton and Manchester.

Manchester

The 13 pre-war races between 1923 and 1936 were dominated by Harold Wood who won six times in 1926, 1928, 1931–2, 1934 and 1936, his time of 2:36:12 in 1932 being the fastest recorded in the series as well as a personal best. The event was revived between 1969 and 1973 by the Maxol engineering firm and staged the AAA title race twice during the period. In the final race, Eckhard Lesse (GDR) set a course record of 2:12:24. After an eight-year break, Piccadilly Radio held its first charity marathon over a flat one-lap route, Steve Kenyon winning in 2:11:54. The event attracted 9500 starters in 1983, 7363 finishing within 6:30. Leslie Watson, winner in 1982 and 1983 with a best time of 2:45:07 in 1982, is the fastest woman.

Bolton

The Adidas British marathon is also a one-lap race but with a long hill in the closing stages. About 7000 started in 1983, some 400 fewer than in 1982, but event records were set by Ian Thompson (2:18:09) and Eileen Claugus (USA, 2:38:50) as 5133 finished.

Scottish Championships

First held in 1946, most titles have been won by Alastair Wood with five in 1964–5, 1967–8 and 1972. Wood set a European and British record of 2:13:45 over the favourable Inverness to Forres course on 9 July 1966, and finished fourth in the 1962 European Championship race. The fastest time achieved in the series is 2:16:05 by Jim Dingwall in 1977.

Glasgow marathon

The Glasgow Peoples marathon was first held in 1982 with Glen Forster (2:17:16) and Priscilla Welch (2:46:58) setting records over an undulating course. Despite windy conditions in 1983, there was a record 9606 starters, 9300 of whom finished.

Ireland

The first marathon over 26 miles 385 yd to be held in Ireland was staged at the Jones' Road football stadium, Dublin, on 16 May 1909. It was won by the Galway professional runner Tom Hynes in 2:51:51. A national championship race was first held in 1925 and won by Jim O'Reilly in 2:56:04. O'Reilly finished ninth in the first British Empire Games marathon, five years later. The Tailteann Games, originally held from 500 BC to AD 1180, were revived in Dublin in 1924 and the marathon was won by a Scotsman, D Quinn, in 2:54:16. The second Games, four years later, also included a marathon; Joie Ray (USA), fifth in the Olympics that year, winning in 2:31:25 with Marthinus Steytler (SA) second, five minutes behind. The current governing body, the Bord Luthcheas Eireann (BLE), was formed in 1967 and a marathon championship has been held annually since.

NATIONAL CHAMPIONS (1974 TO 1983)

1974	Danny McDaid	2:19:02.4
1975	Richard Hodgins	2:19:45
1976	Danny McDaid	2:13:06
1977	Des McGann	2:20:34
1978	Dick Hooper	2:23:19
1979	Pat Hooper	2:17:46
1980	Dick Hooper	2:16:27
1981	Dick Hooper	2:15:37
1982	Dick Hooper	2:12:56
1983	Danny McDaid	2:19:09

The best performance in the Olympics is the 12th place by Pat McMahon in 1968 with a time of 2:29:21. Earlier that year, he had become the first Irishman to better 2:20 when he was timed in 2:19:49.8 at Artesia, NM. A major international win was scored by Neil Cusack at Boston in 1974 (2:13:09), whilst Brendan O'Shea and Mick Molloy have both triumphed in the annual Berchem (Bel) event. The current national record is 2:12:20.2, set by Louis Kenny in winning at Huntsville, AL, on 13 December 1980.

Dublin

A successful annual marathon has been held in Dublin since 1980.

WINNERS *(IRISH UNLESS STATED)*

	men	
1980	Dick Hooper	2:16:14
1981	Neil Cusack	2:13:58
1982	Gerry Kiernan	2:13:45
1983	Ronny Agten (Bel)	2:14:19
	women	
1980	Carey May	2:42:11
1981	Emily Dowling	2:48:22
1982	Debbie Mueller (USA)	2:40:57
1983	Mary Purcell	2:46:09

	Starters	Finishers
1980	1816	1489
1981	6819	6490
1982	9075	8750
1983	9121	8688

Nordic Championships

A Nordic championship has been held biennially since 1949, following a successful trial two years earlier. It is not surprising, in view of Finland's post-war superiority, that this nation has won most medals, including all three in 1955–7–9, 1963–8–9 and in 1963 they took the first six places.

Medal winners: Finland 16 gold, 8 silver, 15 bronze; Sweden 1–7–2; Norway 1–2–1 and Denmark 0–1–0. Iceland have yet to win a medal.

WINNERS

1949	Stockholm	Martti Urpalainen (Fin)	2:32:18
1951	Tampere	Veikko Karvonen (Fin)	2:28:07.4
1953	Oslo	Veikko Karvonen (Fin)	2:30:16
1955	Copenhagen	Veikko Karvonen (Fin)	2:21:21.6
1957	Gothenburg	Paavo Kotila (Fin)	2:24:04
1959	Pori	Eino Oksanen (Fin)	2:25:35
1961	Oslo	Tenho Salakka (Fin)	2:26:14
1963	Gothenburg	Eino Oksanen (Fin)	2:22:01
1965	Helsinki	Tenho Salakka (Fin)	2:24:50.6
1967	Copenhagen	Kalevi Ihaksi (Fin)	2:26:03
1968	Reykjavik	Pentti Rummakko (Fin)	2:17:47.2
1969	Kongsvinger	Pentti Rummakko (Fin)	2:21:49
1970	Sollentuna	Ulf Hakansson (Swe)	2:29:42
1973	Kuortane	Vilho Paajanen (Fin)	2:20:12.6
1975	Moss	Reino Paukkonen (Fin)	2:21:52
1977	Aarhus	Jan Fjaerestad (Nor)	2:20:35.2
1979	Östhammar	Hakan Spik (Fin)	2:14:48
1981	Rauma	Pertti Tiainen (Fin)	2:16:33

Series discontinued in 1983.

Finland

Kaarlo Nieminen was successful in the first marathon to be held in Finland over 40.2 km at Oulunkylä on 16 September 1906. His time was 3:01:06 and he went on to triumph in the first five marathons to be staged in his country. Although he won his sixth race, the first to cross the line was a horse called Poika that was ridden to a 2½ min victory. Nieminen was Finland's first Olympic entrant, finishing tenth in 1908 in 3:09:50.8, and the following June he won the first 42.195 km race to be held in Finland when he toured a 400 m track in

Paavo Nurmi (Fin), winning his one and only marathon in 1932.

Helsinki in 2:50:48. He emigrated to the United States in August 1909 where he turned professional, after winning eight out of eleven marathons at home.

The eldest of the famous Kolehmainen brothers Taavetti 'Tatu' was one of the favourites for the 1912 Olympic marathon, on the basis of winning the 40.2 km trial in 2:29:07.6, a superb time in view of the very muddy conditions. He did not finish the Stockholm race, retiring at 30 km but in 1913 finished second in the Poly with a national record 2:41:48 for the full distance. In 1920 he finished tenth in the Olympics, over eleven minutes behind his brother Johannes 'Hannes', whose winning time of 2:32:35.8 was a new world record (see Runners).

The middle brother Viljami 'William' turned professional in 1910 and like Nieminen went to the United States. In 1912 he won the Edinburgh Powderhall track marathon in 2:32:56.5 and then recorded a professional world record of 2:29:39.2 at Vailsburg stadium, Newark, NJ, on 11 October.

Finland's second gold medal followed in the 1924 Olympics and was something of an upset. Albin Stenroos had set national 5000 m and 10000 m track records, when only 18 years old and the same year he ran two marathons, finishing neither. In 1909 he competed in two more, finishing both but did not compete again over the distance until 1924, by which time he had won a bronze medal in the 1912 Olympic 10000 m and set a world record over 30 km. Stenroos did not train or compete at all between 1918 and 1920 and took part in only minor races until 1923, when he set a world record at 20 km. During the winter of 1923 he walked as much as 120 km (75 miles) per week in training and made the Olympic team by finishing runner up in the trial. Thus his Olympic gold was his first win in six marathons and he never won another.

Martti Marttelin and Armas Toivonen both won bronze medals in the next two Olympic marathons. Marttelin, who lost his life in the Second World War, won the 1928 Turin international race and finished second in the 1930 AAA race. Toivonen only competed in six marathons, dropping out of the first two which were the 1928 Olympic trials. He won the 1932 trial in 2:35:50.2 but it was the appearance of Paavo Nurmi in that race which made it so unforgettable. The race was held in slight rain with the first and last 10 km on the track at Viipuri and the remaining 22 km on soft country roads. At 20 km Nurmi asked Toivonen if the pace was too fast, to which the latter replied that it was the usual pace. Seven kilometres later, Nurmi asked if the pace was too slow. On getting the same answer as before, Nurmi decided to continue alone, reaching the 40.2 km point in the stadium in 2:22:03.8, six minutes ahead of Toivonen. At this point, as it was the normal 'short' marathon distance popular at the time in the Nordic countries, Nurmi retired, his Achilles tendons sore from wearing spikes, and Toivonen completed the full distance. Toivonen went on to win the first European title in 1934, which feat both Väinö Muinonen and Mikko Hietanen repeated in 1938 and 1946. Muinonen, fifth at Berlin, was also runner-up at Oslo behind Hietanen and recorded his best ever time of 2:33:03 at the age of 47 years 203 days in 1946.

Finland has won more medals—five—than any other European nation in Olympic marathons and only the United States with nine medals outscores her. The last Finnish runner to win a medal was Veikko Karvonen, who was third in 1956. Two years earlier he had won the European Championship, although somewhat luckily as the leader Filin turned the wrong way on entering the stadium when in the lead. However Karvonen, a postal officer, compiled a remarkable record between October 1949 and April 1959, winning 14 out of 34 marathons and was the most consistent of that era. Three times Nordic champion Karvonen also won two national titles in 1951 and 1954 and was first at such classic events as Boston, Enschede, Athens and Fukuoka. An untimely injury prevented him from making a better showing at Helsinki in 1952, when he finished fifth. Remarkably, the first Finnish marathon championship was not held until 8 August 1937, victory going to Muinonen in 2:35:44.4.

Hietanen's four wins between 1945 and 1948 is the record number won and he began his athletic career as a skier in 1933 and turned to running four years later.

NATIONAL CHAMPIONS (1974 TO 1983)

1974	Paavo Leiviska	2:15:10.2
1975	Paavo Leiviska	2:15:58.6
1976	Hakan Spik	2:17:47.4
1977	Hakan Spik	2:17:11.6
1978	Hakan Spik	2:16:20.3
1979	Jukka Toivola	2:17:08
1980	Esa Tikkanen	2:19:04
1981	Pertti Tiainen	2:16:33
1982	Niilo Kemppe	2:14:14
1983	Hakan Spik	2:17:53

In the 1982 European Championship marathon, Pertti Tiainen finished fourth in 2:16:27, one place ahead of national record holder (2:10:52) Jukka Toivola, for the best Finnish result in a major marathon since Karvonen's bronze in 1956.

The first Helsinki City marathon in 1981 was run in very hot weather but there were 1500 runners at the start, which number doubled the following year. In 1983 the race was held on the rest-day during the World Championships.

Veikko Karvonen (Fin), winner, shakes hands with Jim Peters (GB), second, after 1954 Boston race. Erkki Puolakka (Fin) third, looks on. (AP)

HELSINKI WINNERS *(FINNISH UNLESS STATED)*

men

1981	Günter Mielke (GFR)	2:23:35
1982	Dominique Chauvelier (Fra) / Cor Vriend (Hol)	2:17:02
1983	Francisco Medina (Spa)	2:25:40

women

1981	Sinikka Kiippa	2:53:15
1982	Sinikka Kiippa	2:41:18
1983	Sinikka Keskitalo	2:39:39

WOMEN'S NATIONAL CHAMPIONS (1980 TO 1983)

1980	Tuija Toivonen	2:46:23
1981	Elli Hallikainen	2:49:54
1982	Tuija Toivonen	2:37:52
1983	Sinikka Keskitalo	2:36:44

Tuija Toivonen set a national record of 2:34:14 in finishing eighth in the 1983 World Championships.

Sweden

The first mention of a distance race of approximate Olympic length was in 1892, when two races of about 40 km were held between Stockholm and Södertälje, and Norrköping and Linköping. The Stockholm course became a regular feature, although the distance varied between 33 km and 37 km depending on the start and finishing points. The clubs using this road limited the entries to their own members. In 1892 the Hephata club was formed exclusively for deaf mutes and in 1894 one of their runners, Julius Olsson, won a race in 2:27:17.6, which at the time was the fastest recorded although the exact distance is not known.

On 13 August 1899 an Open race was held for the first time over 40.2 km between Stockholm and Södertälje. The winner in 2:54:14.2 was Johan Ferdinand Nyström, a groom, who competed unsuccessfully in the 1900 Olympic race. Stockholm staged the first full marathon on 31 August 1909 when Thure Johansson toured a 368 m (402 yd) track in 2:40:34.2, the fastest ever recorded, and soon after he turned professional to perform well in the United States.

On 5 June 1910 the first national championship took place over 40 km, the official distance until 1948. The first winner was Sigge Jacobsson who was

Gösta Leandersson (Swe) and Mikko Hietanen (Fin, 4) in the lead at Kosice in 1946. (Kosice)

born in Helsinki. Jacobsson's time was 2:46:59.4 and two years later he finished sixth in the Olympics in 2:43:24.9, despite making the mistake of wearing new running shoes, which resulted in his feet being badly blistered.

The Championship has continued without a break since, as has that of Denmark, and these are the longest such continuously held national marathon championships. Two athletes have each won the title ten times, Gustav Kinn and Henry Palmé. Kinn, a three time Olympian, won his titles between 1917 and 1929, whilst Palmé won from 1934 to 1942 and in 1944. He also won two Poly marathons and gained a bronze medal in the 1938 European race.

NATIONAL CHAMPIONS (1974 TO 1983)

1974	Owe Malmqvist	2:19:54
1975	Carl-Magnus Bergh	2:17:45
1976	Leif Andersén	2:21:27
1977	Lars Enqvist	2:19:06
1978	Hans Jonsson	2:18:33
1979	Kjell-Erik Stahl	2:16:49
1980	Bo Engwall	2:21:04
1981	Kjell-Erik Stahl	2:17:04
1982	Kjell-Erik Stahl	2:19:20
1983	Kjell-Erik Stahl	2:12:49

The best result in the Olympics are the bronze medals won by Ernst Fast in 1900, the youngest ever

Two of Sweden's top marathon runners Kjell-Erik Stahl (13) and Tommy Persson (12) at Tokyo, 1983. (Hideaki Miyagi)

marathon medal winner, and by Gustaf Jansson 52 years later in Helsinki, although Johan ('John') Svanberg had finished second in the 1906 intermediary Games marathon at Athens. Thore Enochsson's silver medal in the first European Championship remains the best achievement in that series. One of the non-finishers in the 1912 Olympics was Alexis Ahlgren, but he made amends the following 31 May 1913, when he set a world record of 2:36:06.6 over the Windsor to Stamford Bridge course. The time lasted as a world record until 1920 but as a national record it was not bettered for 35 years 97 days, a record for any major nation in the marathon. Baltic Games winner in 1914, his Swedish 40.2 km record of 2:24:15, set at Hälsingborg on 22 September 1912, lasted even longer as it was not bettered until 1955. In 17 marathons he won eight and dropped out of eight!

After the Second World War Gösta Leandersson won at Kosice in 1948, having missed Olympic selection, then at Boston in 1949, before succeeding again at Kosice in 1950, when his time of 2:31:20.2 beat the 19-year-old course record. In 1980 Tommy

Persson set a national record of 2:11:02 at Columbus, OH in his sixth marathon after only finishing 30th at Moscow. Kjell-Erik Stahl finished ahead of him in the Olympics and in the 1982 European, although he did not run his first marathon until 33 years old. Stahl, seven years older than Persson, won both the Frankfurt and Beijing races in 1981 and those at Bremen, Munich and Antwerp in 1983 during which year he overtook Ron Hill's world record of 29 sub 2:20 marathons. In Helsinki, Stahl set a fine new national record of 2:10:38, missing the bronze medal by a single second in the process for Sweden's best major Games marathon placing since 1952. The first Stockholm international marathon, organised by the newspaper *Aftonbladet*, attracted over 2000 entrants in 1979, the number greatly increasing in succeeding years. The two-lap course is basically flat with one sharp incline at the West Bridge.

STOCKHOLM WINNERS *(SWEDISH UNLESS STATED)*

	men	
1979	Jukka Toivola (Fin)	2:17:35
1980	Jeff Wells (USA)	2:15:49
1981	Bill Rodgers (USA)	2:13:26
1982	Kjell-Erik Stahl	2:19:20
1983	Hugh Jones (GB)	2:11:37

	women	
1979	Heide Brenner (GFR)	2:47:02
1980	Ingrid Kristiansen (Nor)	2:38:45
1981	Ingrid Kristiansen (Nor)	2:41:34
1982	Ingrid Kristiansen (Nor)	2:34:26
1983	Tuulikki Räisänen	2:36:58

	Starters	Finishers
1979	1946	1802
1980	4517	4135
1981	6558	5917
1982	8411	7252
1983	9899	8945

Denmark

Denmark became the fifth nation to stage a marathon, when a 40.2 km event was held at Copenhagen on 24 April 1898, victory going to Martinus Olsen in 2:56:20. The venue and course distance was the same for the first national championship on 22 May 1910. Johannes Christensen won in 2:49:03 and added another three victories in the next four years. The championship has continued to be held annually without a break since. From 1937 the distance has been the regular 42.195 km and Henning Larsen, tenth in the 1948 Olympic race, has won most titles with nine between 1941 and 1950.

NATIONAL CHAMPIONS (1974 TO 1983)

1974	Jorgen Jensen	2:20:38
1975	Jorgen Jensen	2:23:58
1976	Jorgen Jensen	2:24:45

1977	Arne Stigsen	2:21:29.4
1978	Jorgen Hein	2:20:10.2
1979	Bjarne Brondum	2:21:30.4
1980	Jorn Lauenborg	2:13:44.6
1981	Svend Erik Kristensen	2:25:38
1982	Jorn Lauenborg	2:19:00.4
1983	John Skovbjerg	2:22:57

Denmark made her Olympic marathon debut in London in 1908 but by far her most successful Olympic race was that at Antwerp in 1920. In that race Sofus Rose finished sixth in 2:41:18 and Rudolf Hansen eighth in 2:41:39. Forty years later, at Rome, Thyge Torgersen equalled Rose's position with a time of 2:21:03.4 and followed up with a seventh place in the 1962 European Championships.

A dramatic breakthrough occurred in 1982, when first Allan Zachariasen and then Svend Erik Kristensen took the national record to under 2:13. After winning the Minneapolis to St Paul race on 3 October 1982 in 2:11:49, Zachariasen ran even faster in his first race in 1983 at Barcelona with a time of 2:11:05. The following month, in London, 21-year-old Henrik Jorgensen finished third in 2:10:47, the fifth improvement on the record in fifteen months, but at Helsinki he slipped to 19th (2:14:10) two places behind Kristensen (2:13:34).

Norway

Norway was one of the four countries that followed Greece in staging a marathon in 1896. At Kristiania, later Oslo, on 4 October, a 40.2 km race attracted 28 runners who left the start at three minute intervals. Hallstein Bjerke won in 3:34:36 and later won the first national title on 16 August 1897 with an improved 3:31:34. The championship race continued until 1902 but then was not held again until 1950, a record break of 48 years. In the immediate post-war period, John Systad and Viktor Olsen each won five titles, with Systad finishing eighth (2:38:41) in the 1948 Olympics, Norway's best placing in those Games. In the European Championships, Systad (1950), Olsen (1954) and Oyvind Dahl (1982) all finished ninth. Dahl, holder of the national record with 2:11:40 set at Karl Marx Stadt in 1980, finished fifth in the 1982 IAAF marathon, one place in front of colleague Inge Simonsen, joint winner at London in 1981 with 2:11:48. In the 1983 World Championships, Dahl placed 26th as Stig Roar Husby finished a solid tenth with a new national record of 2:11:29.

NATIONAL CHAMPIONS (1974 TO 1983)

1974	Thorbjorn Larsen	2:27:04
1975	Henry Olsen	2:25:22
1976	Henry Olsen	2:20:33
1977	Thorbjorn Larsen	2:25:53.2
1978	Jan Fjaerestad	2:19:17
1979	Jan Fjaerestad	2:17:02
1980	Svein Arve Pedersen	2:14:33
1981	Svein Hjeldnes	2:21:08
1982	Jan Fjaerestad	2:16:26
1983	Kjell Age Gotvassli	2:18:30

Despite no national championship being held, an annual international 40.2 km track race was staged at Bislett stadium in Kristiania from 1910 until 1916.

Since 1981 an international marathon has been held at Oslo over a flat two-lap course starting and finishing at Bislett.

OSLO WINNERS *(NORWEGIAN UNLESS STATED)*

	men	
1981	Hugh Jones (GB)	2:13:06
1982	John Skovbjerg (Den)	2:19:40
1983	Ole Fölling-Hansen	2:19:24
	women	
1981	Sissel Grottenberg	2:51:02
1982	Bjorg Moen	2:51:38
1983	Bente Moe	2:41:59

Grete Waitz (see Runners), who chopped nine minutes from the existing world record in three races and who was the first woman to better 2:30, deservedly won the first World Championship marathon, her sixth win in eight marathons. A non-starter was the consistent Ingrid Kristiansen, third in the 1982 European, who has a best of 2:30:08 set at New York in 1981. She gave birth to a son on the last day of the Championships, only 210 days after winning the Houston race in 2:33:27.

France

Although the famous French ultra distance races began in 1892, a race of 38 km (22½ miles) had been held on 11 April 1885 from Paris to Versailles and back. The winner, Louis Saussus, 2:36:30, was called the 'electric man' for his fleetness of foot.

Organised by the *Petit Journal*, France staged the first international marathon, following the Olympics on 19 July 1896, from Paris to Conflans. There were 191 runners at the start at 6.10 am and the winner by six minutes was the London runner Len Hurst, as the first nine finishers all bettered the Olympic winning time. Except for 1897 the race continued until 1905. The most successful of the French runners was Albert Charbonnel, winner in 1899 and 1902, who had a best time of 2:31:41.8 in 1900 when third.

Whilst athletes, wearing the French tricolour, have won three Olympic gold medals (as have the United States and Ethiopia) two of the runners, Mimoun and El Ouafi, were Algerian born. The third winner, Michel Théato, champion in 1900 in his first marathon, followed up with a third place in the 1901 Tour de Paris, before turning professional the following year, but he met with little further success. In the European Championship, the best placing is fourth by Maurice Waltispurger in 1938.

A French Championship was first held on 14 June 1914, won by 18-year-old Michel Mouloud in 2:42:00, but it was 1920 before the event was officially recognised. Before the war, full distance races were held only between 1921 and 1926 and in 1932 and 1937. Alain Mimoun has won most titles with six (1958–60 and 1964–6).

NATIONAL CHAMPIONS (1974 TO 1983)

1974	Fernand Kolbeck	2:26:12
1975	Daniel Fosse	2:19:48
1976	Jean-Pierre Eudier	2:20:57.6
1977	Fernand Kolbeck	2:19:08
1978	Jean-Paul Gomez	2:16:33.6
1979	Bernard Bobes	2:19:48
1980	Bernard Bobes	2:15:42
1981	Dominique Chauvelier	2:14:09
1982	Bernard Faure	2:16:28.1
1983	Alain Lazare	2:12:51

Following the 1900 Olympics, a 'Tour de Paris' race was held until 1921. The distance varied between 37 km (23 miles) and 42.195 km, the latter first run in 1912. The professional Henri Siret, a Parisian barman, won the event seven times, his fastest time of 2:44:46 being set in 1913. Siret had won the first professional marathon to be staged in Britain, when he beat a field of 89 over the Olympic course on 10 October 1908, in 2:37:23. The newspaper *L'Auto* staged two successful international races in 1934 and 1935 but it was another 41 years before any attempt to revive a Paris marathon was made. Since 1976 a race has been held in the capital and after a circuit of the Bois de Boulogne, the course crosses Paris along the north bank of the Seine to the Bois de Vincennes, returning along the south bank to finish near L'Arc de Triomphe.

PARIS WINNERS (1979 TO 1983)

1979	Fernand Kolbeck	2:18:53
1980	Sylvain Cacciatore	2:25:50
1981	Dave Cannon (GB) Ron Tabb (USA)	2:11:44
1982	Ian Thompson (GB)	2:14:08
1983	Jacky Boxberger	2:12:38

In 1980 there were 4000 starters but by 1983 the total had more than trebled to 13 000, 11 500 finishing, 8970 within 5:30. In 1975 a race was held for the first time in Essonne, south of Paris. Held early in the year, it soon attracted overseas' competitors and by 1982 over 2000 runners were at the start. Until 1983, when it finished at Evry, the race began at Verrieres-le-Buisson and terminated at Massy.

ESSONNE WINNERS *(FRENCH UNLESS STATED)*

1975	Andre Pouliquen	2:22:05
1976	Fernand Kolbeck	2:15:38
1977	Barry Watson (GB)	2:15:27

Alain Mimoun wins his sixth and final French marathon title at the age of 46. (Popperfoto)

1978	Jan Fjaerestad (Nor)	2:19:04
1979	Chun Son Goe (NK)	2:13:34
1980	Chun Son Goe (NK)	2:10:52
1981	Gian-Paolo Messina (Ita)	2:17:06
1982	Li Zong Hyong (NK)	2:14:50
1983	Andras Jenkei (Hun)	2:16:24

The fastest performance by a woman at Essonne is 2:39:19 by Gillian Adams (GB) in 1980, whilst most wins have been recorded by Chantal Langlacé with three in 1975, 1979 and 1981. Langlacé had previously set two world records for the marathon. On 27 October 1974, at Neuf Brisach, she ran 2:46:24 which lasted only five weeks as the record, and then at Oyarzun (Spa) on 1 May 1977 her time was 2:35:15.4. She remains the only French athlete to hold a world marathon record. The women's national championship was first held in 1980.

WOMEN'S NATIONAL CHAMPIONS (1980 TO 1983)

1980	Joelle Audibert	2:37:29
1981	Chantal Navarro	2:42:11
1982	Chantal Langlacé	2:42:10
1983	Sylviane Levesque	2:38:58

Germany

The longest pre-marathon era race was one of 36 km (22 miles) held on 19 August 1895 at Frankfurt and won by Alfred Bense in 2:38:43.4. The first German marathon, held over 40 km at Leipzig on 3 July 1898, was won by Arthur Techtow from Berlin, in a time of 3:19:05. No more marathons were held until 1905. It was another five years before the first 42.195 km race was held, two years after the sole German runner at the London Olympics had failed to finish. Julius Riess set the inaugural German record of 2:49:13.8 at Frankfurt on 13 June 1910.

An annual German marathon was held from 1920 but it was not until 1925 that the first official national championship race took place on 6 September with Paul Hempel, twice a winner at Kosice, first in 2:48:25.5. Three runners have each won four titles: Heinrich Brauch (1932–5), Jürgen Wedeking (1958, 1960–1, 1963) and Ralf Salzmann (1980–3).

NATIONAL CHAMPIONS (1974 TO 1983)

1974	Anton Gorbunow	2:21:50.8
1975	Ulrich Hutmacher	2:19:30
1976	Paul Angenvoorth	2:15:56.6
1977	Günter Mielke	2:15:18.3
1978	Reinhard Leibold	2:17:29.2
1979	Michael Spöttel	2:20:15
1980	Ralf Salzmann	2:16:22
1981	Ralf Salzmann	2:15:42
1982	Ralf Salzmann	2:18:45
1983	Ralf Salzmann	2:15:17

Despite the considerable interest shown in the marathon in Germany, little success has been forthcoming in major competition, the best performance in the Olympics being 15th in 1932 by Paul de Bruyn. De Bruyn was resident in New York when he won the 1932 Boston race, ensuring him a trip to Los Angeles, a year after he had returned to his homeland to win his only national marathon title. The best results in the European Championships have been the fifth places by Heinrich Brauch (1934) and Erich Puch (1938), Brauch's performance being a disappointment as he was the fastest European in the world that year with 2:36:12. In line with current trend, successful marathons have been instigated at Frankfurt and Berlin, whilst in 1983 new races were held in Bremen and Munich. The course at Frankfurt, a single loop over a flat, even route, starts and finishes in front of the Höchst chemical works. Finishing numbers (under 5:00) at Frankfurt have been: 1981 2588, 1982 4677 and 1983 5117.

WINNERS (GFR UNLESS STATED)

FRANKFURT
men

1981	Kjell-Erik Stahl (Swe)	2:13:20
1982	Delfim Moreira (Por)	2:12:54
1983	Ahmet Altun (Tur)	2:12:41

women

1981	Doris Schlosser	2:47:13
1982	Heide Hutterer	2:36:38
1983	Charlotte Teske	2:28:32

BERLIN

men

1981	Ian Ray (GB)	2:15:41.8
1982	Domingo Tibaduiza (Col)	2:14:46.7
1983	Karel Lismont (Bel)	2:13:37

women

1981	Angelika Stephan	2:47:23.5
1982	Jean Lochhead (GB)	2:47:04.1
1983	Karen Goldhawk (GB)	2:40:32

Christa Vahlensieck (GFR, 5), Carla Beurskens (Hol, 6) and winner Rita Marchisio (Ita, 12), Osaka 1982. (Hideaki Miyagi)

Women

German women marathon runners have by comparison been more successful than the men. Encouraged by the drive and determination of Ernst van Aaken, a physician at Waldniel as well as a respected trainer who had a pole vault best of 3.60 m (11 ft 9¾ in) set before the Second World War, an international marathon was staged in his home town in 1974. He was also responsible for the first all-women's race held the year before.

The first German to feature internationally was Liane Winter who won at Waldniel in 1974 and then at Boston on 21 April 1975, when she set a world record of 2:42:24. She later won world veteran titles in 1977–8–9. Christa Vahlensieck (*née* Kofferschlager) twice set world records, first at Dulmen on 3 May 1975 (2:40:15.8) and then at West Berlin on 10 September 1977 (2:34:47.5), the latter lasting a year. She was unbeaten during this period, winning the first four national titles contested and the second international race at Waldniel. Charlotte Teske handed Vahlensieck two defeats in 1981, and in 1982 became the first German to better 2:30 when she won at Miami with 2:29:01.6, improving to 2:28:32 at Frankfurt in 1983. At Helsinki, Teske failed to finish as the 1982–3 national champion Monika Lövenich placed 15th, four positions ahead of Vahlensieck.

NATIONAL CHAMPIONS (1975 TO 1983)

1975	Christa Vahlensieck	2:45:43
1976	Christa Vahlensieck	2:40:28
1977	Christa Vahlensieck	2:34:47.5
1978	Christa Vahlensieck	2:38:32.8
1979	Liane Winter	2:56:29
1980	Christa Vahlensieck	2:36:47
1981	Charlotte Teske	2:33:13
1982	Monika Lövenich	2:42:24
1983	Monika Lövenich	2:43:03

WALDNIEL INTERNATIONAL RACE (*GFR UNLESS STATED*)

1974	1	Liane Winter	2:50:31.4
	2	Chantal Langlacé (Fra)	2:51:45.2
	3	Christa Vahlensieck	2:54:40
1976	1	Christa Vahlensieck	2:45:24.4
	2	Kim Merritt (USA)	2:47:11.2
	3	Gayle Barron (USA)	2:47:43.2

Austria

Austria's first marathon, held on 14 July 1901 over 40 km at Vienna, also incorporated the national championship and was won by Fritz Luft in 3:59:00.4. Luft ran under the name of 'Engländer', the use of such a pseudonym being a common practice in Austria at the time to avoid discrimination. He probably selected that particular name in admiration of the English runners. The championship

was held sporadically until 1912, four years after Austria's first appearance in the Olympic marathon. From 1924 the event was held annually over 42.195 km, with Franz Tuschek the most outstanding of the pre-war exponents, winning the title every year between 1926 and 1935, except 1928 when injured and unable to compete. Before retiring, he finished 14th in the 1936 Olympics, the best Austrian marathon placing to date. Between 1952 and 1963 Adolf Gruber won 12 consecutive championships, the most national marathon titles won by a runner in Europe. He was unable to bend his right arm from the elbow, due to a war injury, but he had an almost fanatical regard for physical education, founded his own club in Vienna and is still very active.

Belgium

The first 'marathon' was held between Mechelen and Brussels in 1903, a distance of 36 km (22 miles) and was won by Jules Lesage in 2:27:00. Lesage won again in 1904–5 and was Belgium's first distance runner of note. Their sole runner in the 1908 Olympic marathon did not complete the course, and it was another 30 years before a national marathon was held. Even then it was not held regularly until 1947 and only since 1950 has the event been held over the full marathon distance. The most dominant runner has been Aurele Vandendriessche who was champion for nine consecutive years from 1956. Twice winner at Boston (1963–4) he also triumphed in international races at Berne, Enschede and Kosice in 1965, was twice runner-up in the European championships and seventh in the 1964 Olympics. His best time of 2:17:44 was at Boston in 1965, when he finished fourth.

NATIONAL CHAMPIONS (1974 TO 1983)

1974	Karel Lismont	2:11:13.2
1975	Hendrik Schoofs	2:18:15
1976	Hendrik Schoofs	2:20:33
1977	Eric Gijselinck	2:23:22.2
1978	Marc Smet	2:13:23
1979	Marc Smet	2:10:00
1980*	Herman Parmentier	2:12:31
1981	Marc de Blander	2:17:58
1982	Frederik Vandervennet	2:16:44
1983*	Frederik Vandervennet	2:14:13

*In 1980 the course was 41.9 km (26 miles) and in 1983, 41.5 km (25.8 miles).

At an international level Karel Lismont has compiled the best ever record in Games' marathons, winning a total of five medals, more than any other runner. He was Belgian champion in 1970–1 and 1974, and he won six of his first nine marathons.

KAREL LISMONT—CHAMPIONSHIP RECORD

15 Aug 1971 Helsinki	EC	2:13:09	(1)

10 Sep	1972	Munich	OG	2:14:31.8	(2)
8 Sep	1974	Rome	EC	d n f	(–)
31 Jul	1976	Montreal	OG	2:11:12.6	(3)
3 Sep	1978	Prague	EC	2:12:07.7	(3)
1 Aug	1980	Moscow	OG	2:13:27	(9)
12 Sep	1982	Athens	EC	2:16:04	(3)
14 Aug	1983	Helsinki	WC	2:11:24	(9)

Karel Lismont (Bel), winning the 1977 Mainichi race. (Popperfoto)

In silver medal position, ahead of Lismont at Athens, was Armand Parmentier running his second marathon. He set a Belgian record of 2:09:57 in finishing fourth at Rotterdam on 9 April 1983 and was sixth at Helsinki in 2:10:57. A popular international race is that held annually at Berchem near Antwerp. First held in 1970, the race is staged over a three-lap course in the evening and the fastest time recorded there is 2:10:00 by Marc Smet in 1979, then a national record.

In 1983 a new international marathon was held in Antwerp and won by Kjell-Erik Stahl (Swe) in 2:13:48.

Netherlands

Of the team of four Dutch marathon runners who started the 1908 Olympic race, only Willem Wakker (20th) finished the course. It was another six years before a marathon was held in the Netherlands, Harry Wessel winning a full distance race in 3:11:23.8.

Pleun van Leenan won the first national championship race at Amsterdam on 3 July 1932 in 3:17:13.2, but was beaten by visiting British runner Bert Norris (2:42:54.6) in 1933 by a margin of 21 min 57 sec.

Aad Steylen, the first from his nation to better 2:20, won five titles between 1965 and 1969, more than any other Dutchman, and equalled by Cor Vriend in 1983.

NATIONAL CHAMPIONS (1974 TO 1983)

1974	Henk Kalf	2:23:34
1975	Cor Vriend	2:23:33.5
1976	Ko v.d. Weijden	2:31:30
1977	Cor Vriend	2:21:47
1978	Roelof Veld	2:14:01
1979	Gerard Nijboer	2:16:48
1980	Rudi Verriet	2:20:22.6
1981	Cor Vriend	2:17:06
1982	Cor Vriend	2:12:15
1983	Cor Vriend	2:16:43

The best performances in major Games' marathons are those by Gerard Nijboer who, although troubled by injuries, in six races had an Olympic silver medal, a European gold medal and a European record time of 2:09:01 (1980–3) to his credit (see Runners).

Besides the biennial Enschede marathon (see Races) an international favourite since 1947, two marathons are now staged annually at Amsterdam and Rotterdam.

WINNERS *(NETHERLANDS UNLESS STATED)*

AMSTERDAM

1975	Jorgen Jensen (Den)	2:16:51
1976	Karel Lismont (Bel)	2:18:48
1977	Bill Rodgers (USA)	2:12:46.6

1978	not held	
1979	Ferenc Szekeres (Hun)	2:14:45.6
1980	Gerard Nijboer	2:09:01
1981	Ferenc Szekeres (Hun)	2:18:11
1982	Cor Vriend	2:12:15
1983	Cor Vriend	2:13:41

The best women's time in the race is 2:37:28 by Anny van Stiphout in 1982.

ROTTERDAM

1981	John Graham (GB)	2:09:28
1982	Rodolfo Gomez (Mex)	2:11:57
1983	Rob de Castella (Aus)	2:08:37

In 1983 the race featured the much heralded clash between the unbeaten holder of the world record, Alberto Salazar (USA) and the Commonwealth champion and second fastest Rob de Castella. At the finish, the Australian held off Carlos Lopes (Por) by two seconds with Gomez third, and Salazar a well beaten fifth. Rosa Mota (Por) recorded the best women's time at Rotterdam with 2:32:27, to remain then unbeaten at the distance.

Westland

The Westland marathon, currently held at Maassluis, has been held since 1969. It was won most times by Cor Vriend in 1977 and 1981–2–3, including the fastest time of 2:13:28 in 1982. Recent overseas winners have been Veli Balli (Tur) 2:16:11 in 1978, Julien Grimon (Bel) 2:19:14 in 1979 and Jorn Lauenborg (Den) 2:17:24 in 1980.

WOMEN'S NATIONAL CHAMPIONS (1981 TO 1983)

1981	Carla Beurskens	2:42:56
1982	Anny van Stiphout	2:37:28
1983	Eefje van Wissen	2:41:37

Portugal

The winner of the first national championship at Lisbon, on 2 May 1910 in 2:57:35, was the ill-fated Francisco Lazaro. He won again in 1911 and 1912, before collapsing in the final stages of the 1912 Olympic race and succumbing in hospital the next day. Subsequently, a meeting was held in the Stockholm stadium as a result of which the sum of 14 000 Crowns was presented to his family. No championships were held between 1915 and 1935 or during the War years.

In the 1936 Olympic Games, Manuel Dias was in second place at 17 km but he had made the fatal mistake of wearing new shoes, which he had to discard by 20 km. After resting for ten minutes he borrowed a pair of heavy shoes from a boy of the Nazi youth movement and continued to finish 17th. Early in 1937, he recorded 2:30:38, fastest in the world that year, in winning the second of his six consecutive national titles. He then took part in the

Poly, which was held in extreme heat and led for 19 miles before being overtaken by Bert Norris, who beat him by almost eight minutes as only seven of the 97 starters finished.

Most national titles have been won by Armando Aldegalega, with nine between 1964 and 1974. The best placing by a Portuguese runner in the Olympics is 16th by Anacleto Pinto in 1980 and in the European, eighth by Jose Araujo in 1954. Portugal's first international success occurred in 1982, when Delfim Moreira won the Frankfurt marathon in a record 2:12:54 and later triumphed at Rio de Janeiro. Carlos Lopes set a superb European record of 2:08:39 in finishing second to de Castella at Rotterdam on 9 April 1983 in his second marathon. He had dropped out of his previous attempt at New York in 1982, and did not take part in the World Championships.

The same year at Athens, Rosa Mota won Portugal's first ever European Championship medal, when she won the marathon in her first try at the event. After winning at Rotterdam, she further reduced the national record to 2:31:50 at Helsinki but had to be content with fourth place after a late burst.

Switzerland

The first marathon in Switzerland was held at Geneva on 27 October 1901 over 40.2 km and incorporated the national championship. Albert Charbonnel (Fra) won in 2:47:25. The championship was next held in 1908–9 and then in 1927, since when it has been an annual event. Hans Frischknecht has won most titles with five between 1947 and 1953. Whilst Switzerland's results in the major Games have been limited (22nd in the 1948 Olympics and 10th in the 1946 European are the best) Bruno Lafranchi finished an impressive third in the 1982 Fukuoka classic, his second marathon, setting a new Swiss record of 2:11:12. However, in the inaugural World Championships at Helsinki he could only manage 23rd.

Since 1981 an international race has been held in Geneva.

GENEVA WINNERS

1981	Ian Thompson (GB)	2:17:17.2
1982	Mike Kearns (GB)	2:13:50.8
1983	Ryszard Kopijasz (Pol)	2:15:00

Soviet Union

Russia's lone entry in the 1908 Olympics finished a creditable 19th, a far cry from the Stockholm race four years later, when none of the ten strong squad finished. Fifteen athletes lined up at Kiev on 20 August 1913, for the first marathon to be held in

Three Soviet stars of the 1950s. From left: Viktor Baikov, Ivan Filin and Sergey Popov. (Kosice)

Russia on the occasion of the First Olympic Festival. The winner, Aleksandr Maksimov, was timed in 3:03:00 for the 38 verstas or 40.5 km (25.2 miles) course. The first Soviet race took place at Sergiyevo, near Moscow, on 10 September 1922, but only attracted seven runners and it was another 13 years before the first national championship was held. Moscow hosted the race over the full distance on 12 September 1935 and Nikolay Babarykhin won in 2:48:23. The championship has been held regularly since, with Viktor Baikov being the most successful title winner with four wins between 1961 and 1964.

NATIONAL CHAMPIONS (1974 TO 1983)

1974	Yuriy Velikorodnikh	2:15:27.8
1975	Grigoriy Vinjar	2:15:27.8
1976	Nikolay Penzin	2:30:32.8
1977	Viktor Zubov	2:19:28.3
1978	Yuriy Laptyev	2:16:48.5
1979	Leonid Moseyev	2:13:19.6
1980	Vladimir Kotov	2:10:58
1981	Anatoliy Aryukov	2:20:06.8
1982	Leonid Moseyev	2:16:03
1983	Yuriy Pleshkov	2:15:22

Post-war Soviet marathon achievements have been numerous and despite the absence of many nations at the 1980 Olympics, their runners finished third, fourth and fifth, the best result by a European country since France's team effort 80 years earlier. It was the Khirgizian-born Satymkul Dzhumanazarov who took the bronze medal in 2:11:35, ahead of the more favoured national record holder Vladimir Kotov (2:12:05) and 1978 European Champion Leonid Moseyev (2:12:14). In the European Championships Sergey Popov won the 1958 race at Stockholm, with a world record 2:15:17, which lasted 12 years as a Soviet record, and Moseyev repeated two decades later. Whilst Soviet runners had triumphed at many European venues, it was not until 1982 that they scored a major success outside the continent. Vadim Sidorov set a national record of 2:10:33 in winning the second Tokyo Yomiuri marathon, but like the remainder of the national team performed below par in the European Championships later in the year.

The dominant woman runner since their entry in 1980 has been Zoya Ivanova, winner of the 1981 European Cup race and the 1982 Tokyo International, in a Soviet record time of 2:34:26.

WOMEN'S NATIONAL CHAMPIONS (1981 TO 1983)

1981	Zoya Ivanova	2:42:11
1982	Zoya Ivanova	2:35:38
1983	Zoya Ivanova	2:36:31

Raisa Smekhnova set a new Soviet record of 2:31:13 in finishing third at Helsinki, leading her colleagues Lucia Byelayeva (tenth) and Ivanova (23rd) to an unofficial World Championship team win.

Ian Thompson *(Left)* former British record holder with a time of 2:09:12 set at Christchurch, NZ, when winning the 1974 Commonwealth Games title in his second marathon, and Joyce Smith *(Above)* finishing the 1982 London marathon in a British record 2:29:43.
(Mark Shearman and Jeff Fuller)
(Lower left) Dick Beardsley (USA), left, and Inge Simonsen (Nor) run towards the finish of the first London marathon in 1981 when they tied for first place in 2:11:48, then the fastest time ever run in England; and *(Below)* Grete Waitz (Nor) and Mike Gratton (GB), 1983 winners, after the race in which Waitz equalled the women's world record of 2:25:29 which was beaten the very next day by Benoit. (All Sport)

The 1983 Rotterdam race featured an elite group of runners. From left: Rodolfo Gomez (Mex) third; Carlos Lopez (Por) second in a European record of 2:08:39; Rob de Castella first in 2:08:37; Jose Gomez (Mex) sixth; Armand Parmentier (Bel) fourth; and the previously unbeaten Alberto Salazar (USA) fifth. (Mark Shearman)

(Inset) Rob de Castella (Aus) holds off a challenge by Kebede Balcha (Eth) to win the inaugural World Championship in 2:10:03. Balcha, runner-up in 2:10:24, matched de Castella's time in winning the Montreal race in September for a new Ethiopian record. (David E. Martin)

Julie Brown (USA, 485) 1983 Avon women's champion, and Grete Waitz (Nor, 318) lead the World Championship race at Helsinki which Waitz won and Brown did not finish. (All Sport)

1982 Commonwealth silver medallist and African record holder Juma Ikangaa (Tan) leads the field at Tokyo, 1983. From left: Ikangaa, fifth; Dereje Nedi (Eth) fourth; Kebede Balcha (Eth) sixth; Toshihiko Seko (Jap) first in an Asian record 2:08:38; Rodolfo Gomez (Mex) third with a Central American record of 2:09:12; and Takeshi Soh (Jap) second in 2:08:55. (Hideaki Miyagi)

(Right) **Runners leave the grounds of Windsor Castle, starting point of the oldest British marathon organised by the Polytechnic Harriers and first held in 1909. The first ever marathon of 26 miles 385 yd also started at Windsor when the Olympic Games were held in 1908. In contrast to the 56 runners who started the 1908 race, over 16 000 cross Tower Bridge in London, 1983 *(Above)* in the world's biggest ever marathon race yet staged. (Mark Shearman)**

(Above) Leaders in the 1980 Asahi international marathon at Fukuoka. From left: Hideki Kita (Jap) 15th, Kirk Pfeffer (USA) 7th, Shigeru Soh (Jap) 5th, Waldemar Cierpinski (GDR) 6th, Dave Cannon (GB) 10th, Rob de Castella (Aus) 8th, Kyle Heffner (USA) 11th and Takeshi Soh (Jap) 2nd. The race was won by Toshihiko Seko (Jap) in 2:09:45 from Takeshi Soh and Kunimitsu Itoh (Jap) (see rear cover photo). (Asahi Shimbun)

(Left) Toshihiko Seko wins in a sprint finish to the 1979 Asahi race from colleagues Shigeru and Takeshi Soh, with Bernie Ford (GB) a distant fourth. (Asahi Shimbun)

The start of the 1980 Olympic Games marathon in Moscow, the first time that an eastern European nation had staged the quadrennial event, and Waldemar Cierpinski (GDR) who successfully defended the title he had won four years earlier in Montreal, thus equalling Abebe Bikila's feat of the 1960s. (All Sport)

Early leaders at the Munich Olympic marathon in 1972 feature some of the finest runners of the time. From left in the front row: Derek Clayton (Aus), world record holder, Ron Hill (GB) and Jack Foster (NZ). Behind Clayton is Akio Usami (Jap) and to Usami's left are Donal Walsh (Ire), Gaston Roelants (Bel), Seppo Nikkari (Fin) and Demissie Wolde (Eth). Winner Frank Shorter (USA) is behind Roelants, and 1968 champion Mamo Wolde (Eth) behind Demissie. Eckhard Lesse (GDR) and Kenny Moore (USA) bring up the rear of the group. (All Sport)

Current American world record holders at the finish of their epic runs. Alberto Salazar *(Top left)* breaks the tape in 2:08:12.7 at New York (1981) in only his second marathon, and at Boston two years later Joan Benoit *(Left)* finishes in 2:22:43, over two minutes faster than any other woman had run. Between 1973 and 1983 Bill Rodgers *(Above)* four times winner at both Boston and New York, has won 22 of 43 marathons contested and been timed in under 2 h 13 min on a record 18 occasions.
(All Sport and Mark Shearman)

Yelena Tsukhlo
(Sov, 11), Zoya
Ivanova (Sov, 12) and
Annie van Stiphout
(Hol) in 1982 Tokyo
marathon. (Popperfoto)

Left:
**Vadim Sidorov (Sov) sets a national record in winning the
1982 Tokyo marathon. (Popperfoto)**

German Democratic Republic

Since its formation in 1951, the GDR has made a
considerable impact on the athletics world.
Although the first title race took place that year, it
was the decision to stage an annual marathon at Karl
Marx Stadt in 1967 (see Races) which resulted in a
sudden and dramatic improvement on the part of
the national marathon runners. Winner of the most
national titles with four is Hans-Joachim Truppel.

NATIONAL CHAMPIONS (1974 TO 1983)

1974	Bernd Arnhold	2:16:13.2
1975	Hans-Joachim Truppel	2:18:50
1976	Karl-Heinz Baumbach	2:18:14

| 1977 | Holger Runge | 2:28:33.7 |
| 1978 | Waldemar Cierpinski | 2:14:57.4 |

Eckhard Lesse (GDR) wins the sixth Karl Marx Stadt race in his debut over the distance with a new national record.

1979	Hans-Joachim Truppel	2:20:02
1980	Martin Schröder	2:16:17
1981	Mathias Böckler	2:17:40
1982	Waldemar Cierpinski	2:13:59
1983	Stephan Seidermann	2:21:43.8

Waldemar Cierpinski (see Runners) equalled Abebe Bikila's feat of two Olympic gold medals when he captured both the 1976 and 1980 races, by far his and his country's greatest accomplishment to date. In the European Championships Jürgen Busch, three times a winner at Karl Marx Stadt, finished third in 1969 and Eckhard Lesse was runner-up in 1974. Lesse was the first GDR marathoner to perform consistently well outside Europe, finishing in the first five three times at Fukuoka, with a best time of 2:12:02.4 in the 1974 race, behind the winner Frank Shorter. It was Lesse who won the last Maxol marathon at Manchester in 1973, with an event record 2:12:24.

Czechoslovakia

Czech runners had competed well in the 1902 and 1904 Austrian races but it was not until 25 October 1908 that a 40 km event was held at Dobris, near Prague. The winner, Arnost Nejedly (3:22:50), had taken part in the 1906 Athens marathon and then finished 18th at London, two years later, in a time of 3:26:26.2. Nejedly's London time lasted as a national record until the founding of the Kosice race (see Races) in 1924. The first championship race was held the following year at Prague on 27 September and won by Josef Maly in 2:51:08. Most wins have been the seven by Pavel Kantorek between 1956 and 1967, during which time he competed in three Olympics, two European Championships and became the first Czech to better 2:20 in 1959.

NATIONAL CHAMPIONS (1974 TO 1983)

1974	Pavel Lichnovsky	2:26:25.4
1975	Vaclav Mladek	2:18:02.2
1976	Ondrej Zelanansky	2:20:57.8
1977	Josef Jansky	2:18:53.4
1978	Josef Jansky	2:17:32.2
1979	Stanislav Tomanek	2:15:41
1980	Vlastimil Bien	2:23:46
1981	Pavol Madar	2:19:17
1982	Miroslav Becka	2:19:08
1983	Frantisek Visnicky	2:16:52

Czechoslovakia's finest success in the marathon came in 1952, when Emil Zatopek, making his competition debut in the event, followed his triumphs at 5000 m and 10000 m to take the gold medal. His time of 2:23:03.2 was the fastest time recorded over a regular out and back course. A pointer to the current state of top level marathoning in the country is that, prior to 1983, it was back in 1964 that a Czech last won an international Kosice marathon.

Hungary

Gyula Kellner was the only non-Greek European entry in the 1896 Olympics and was the only foreign runner to finish. His bronze medal achievement remains Hungary's best achievement in the Olympics. The first marathon in Hungary was held in Budapest on 4 October 1896, Bela Janko winning in 3:29:00, as Kellner did not complete the course. Kellner did win the second marathon to be held the following year in 3:52:00. No more marathons were held in Hungary until 1922, the distance remaining at 40 km until the first championship race three years later. Held at Budapest on 13 September 1925 Pal Kiraly was the inaugural champion in 2:56:15. Three runners have each won the title seven times, Jozsef Galambos (between 1928 and 1936), Gyula Toth (1966–72) and Ferenc Szekeres (between 1973 and 1982).

NATIONAL CHAMPIONS (1974 TO 1983)

1974	Ferenc Szekeres	2:29:57.6
1975	Ferenc Szekeres	2:26:41
1976	György Sinko	2:21:11.8
1977	György Sinko	2:16:30.8
1978	Ferenc Szekeres	2:16:38.8
1979	Ferenc Szekeres	2:20:24
1980	Janos Szekeres	2:24:41
1981	Ferenc Szekeres	2:19:56
1982	Ferenc Szekeres	2:17:58
1983	Zoltan Kiss	2:22:18

The pre-war period was outstanding for the performances of Jozsef Galambos, whose four wins at Kosice is still unequalled. His best international result was his fourth position in the first European Championships. In 1966 Gyula Toth became the first Hungarian to win a European medal, finishing third, and later in the year was sixth at Fukuoka. He won the annual Szeged race a record six times between 1965 and 1971. The most consistent competitor of the last decade has been Ferenc Szekeres, twice winner of the Amsterdam international race, and the only Hungarian to have bettered 2:14. His best times have been 2:12:35 in finishing second at Amsterdam in 1980, and 2:12:36 when seventh at Tokyo in 1982.

Poland

The first Polish marathon was the national championship held on 2 November 1924 at Rembertow and won by Stefan Szelestowski in 3:13:10.5. Zdzislaw Bogusz won a record number of four titles between 1966 and 1970, during which time he became the first Pole to better 2:20.

NATIONAL CHAMPIONS (1974 TO 1983)

1974	Edward Legowski	2:16:48
1975	Edward Legowski	2:13:26
1976	Kazimierz Orzel	2:13:18.6
1977	Kazimierz Orzel	2:13:43.8

Jozsef Galambos (Hun), winner of a record four Kosice marathons. (Kosice)

Soviet runners (Leonid Moseyev first, Aleksandr Gozki second, and Yuriy Velikorodnikh third) at Debno, 1978. (Debno)

1978	Ryszard Marczak	2:15:27
1979	Zbigniew Pierzynka	2:16:09.8
1980	Zbigniew Pierzynka	2:13:30
1981	Ryszard Marczak	2:14:17
1982	Ryszard Kopijasz	2:14:49
1983	Jerzy Kowol	2:14:48

The best performance in the Olympics is Kazimierz Orzel's 15th position in 1976, whilst in the European both Michael Wojcik (1969) and Ryszard Marczak (1982) finished seventh. Marczak is by far the fastest Pole with 2:11:35 and 2:12:44 at New York in 1981 and 1982. Three major marathons are held annually in Poland.

Debno

First held in 1966, the event was a half marathon until 1969, and has been the venue of the national championship since 1978. Event record of 2:12:19.8 was set by Leonid Moseyev (Sov) in 1978.

Otwock

Organised by the *Trybuna Ludu* newspaper since 1973, the best time recorded is 2:13:27 by Chris Garforth (GB) in 1980.

Warsaw

First held in 1979, it attracted over 2000 runners in 1982. Jerzy Finster won the 1981 event in 2:17:06, the best time so far recorded in the series, named the International Marathon of Peace.

Balkan Games

The Balkan Games were first held in 1930, following a successful trial held the previous year. Since 1930 a total of 42 Games have been held (none between 1940 and 1953). Medal winners by nation: Yugoslavia 11 gold, 9 silver, 8 bronze; Greece 10–10–10; Turkey 10–15–5; Romania 6–6–11; Bulgaria 5–2–8. Albania have not won a medal. Most individual medals have been won by Franjo Skrinjar (Yug) with 6 gold, 2 silver, 1 bronze; Huseyin Aktas (Tur) 4–4–0; Stylianos Kyriakidis (Gre) 4–2–1; Ismail Akcay (Tur) 3–3–1 and Ludovic Gall (Rom) 3–1–2. The biggest winning margin is 14 min 47 sec by Gall in 1935 and the narrowest two tenths of a second in 1958 by Skrinjar.

CHAMPIONS

1930	Athens	Nicolae Ilie (Rom)	3:14:14.6
1931	Athens	Christos Sarras (Gre)	3:11:20.6
1932	Athens	Ludovic Gall (Rom)	3:20:41
1933	Athens	Ludovic Gall (Rom)	3:02:41
1934	Zagreb	Stylianos Kyriakidis (Gre)	2:49:42
1935	Istanbul	Ludovic Gall (Rom)	3:07:40
1936	Athens	Stylianos Kyriakidis (Gre)	2:49:10
1937	Bucharest	Stylianos Kyriakidis (Gre)	2:57:22
1938	Belgrade*	Athanassios Ragazos (Gre)	2:30:38
1939	Athens	Stylianos Kyriakidis (Gre)	2:52:07
1940	Istanbul	Athanassios Ragazos (Gre)	2:41:37.6
1953	Athens	Franjo Skrinjar (Yug)	3:09:45.6
1954	Belgrade	Franjo Skrinjar (Yug)	2:48:48.4
1955	Istanbul	Haydar Erturan (Tur)	2:51:33.8
1956	Belgrade*	Franjo Mihalic (Yug)	2:16:25
1957	Athens	Franjo Skrinjar (Yug)	2:41:37
1958	Sofia	Franjo Skrinjar (Yug)	2:41:05.6
1959	Bucharest	Franjo Skrinjar (Yug)	2:33:16.6
1960	Athens	Dobrivoje Stojanovic (Yug)	2:29:11.2
1961	Belgrade	Franjo Skrinjar (Yug)	2:33:17.4
1962	Ankara	Ivan Mustapic (Yug)	2:36:42.2
1963	Sofia	Ivan Mustapic (Yug)	2:32:31
1964	Bucharest	Constantin Grecescu (Rom)	2:28:23.4
1965	Athens	Ivailo Charankov (Bul)	2:39:50
1966	Sarajevo	Ismail Akcay (Tur)	2:22:44.2
1967	Istanbul	Ivailo Charankov (Bul)	2:24:52
1968	Athens	Ismail Akcay (Tur)	2:21:55
1969	Sofia	Nedo Farcic (Yug)	2:26:18.2
1970	Bucharest	Huseyin Aktas (Tur)	2:27:51.2
1971	Zagreb	Ismail Akcay (Tur)	2:25:35.2
1972	Izmir	Huseyin Aktas (Tur)	2:20:08.4
1973	Athens	Huseyin Aktas (Tur)	2:20:34.6
1974	Sofia	Atanas Galabov (Bul)	2:30:37
1975	Bucharest	Atanas Galabov (Bul)	2:28:20.4
1976	Celje	Huseyin Aktas (Tur)	2:33:52.2
1977	Ankara	Veli Balli (Tur)	2:22:56
1978	Salonika	Vassil Leschev (Bul)	2:24:20
1979	Athens	Michail Koussis (Gre)	2:21:20
1980	Sofia	Anastassios Psathas (Gre)	2:25:43
1981	Sarajevo	Michail Koussis (Gre)	2:19:05
1982	Bucharest	Gheorghe Buruiana (Rom)	2:31:46.8
1983	Izmir	Mehmet Terzi (Tur)	2:19:51

* The distance in 1938 was 40km, and in 1956 was short.

Greece

Greece is where it all started in 1896 and not one marathon but three were held that year between Marathon and Athens. There is a possibility that other races took place but the official Greek records do not show them and they may have been no more than time trials. Georgios Grigoriou is reported as having run the reverse course in 3:45:00 sometime in February and another source credits him with a time of 3:53:00. Dimitrios Deliyannis is similarly credited with 3:42:23. Both, however, did compete in the first official race on 10 March with nine other runners. Harilaos Vasilakos was first in 3:18:00, with Deliyiannis (3:33:00) third, and Grigoriou fifth. This race was for the Greek Championship and thus the first ever such race. A fortnight later, a marathon was part of the Pan-Hellenic sports celebrations. It was an Open event and 38 runners took part. The winner Lavrentis recorded 3:11:27 as one Spiridon Louis finished fifth in 3:18:27 as the first four bettered the winning time of the previous race.

Around this time, and again there is no date, two women are recorded as having run between Marathon and Athens. It is claimed that one Melpomene completed the course in 4:30:00, as did a 35-year-old mother of seven children, Stamatia

Ismail Akcay and Huseyin Aktas (Tur), who between them have won seven Balkan marathons.

Rovithi whose time was 5:30:00. Yet there is nothing so vague about the eventual outcome of the first Olympic marathon on 10 April and won by Louis in 2:58:50 (see Games).

The national championship continued to be held but only irregularly until 1955, when it became an annual event. The same year saw the holding of the first Classical Marathon (see Races). Theofanis Tsimigatos has won most titles with five (1974, 1977–8, 1980–1). Stylianos Kyriakidis, four time winner in the Balkan Games, set a European record of 2:29:27 in winning at Boston in 1946 and held the national record for 33 years 216 days, one of the longest ever such reigns. Michail Koussis became the first Greek to better 2:20 in 1978 and holds the current best of 2:14:36 set at Amsterdam in 1982. Twice Balkan champion, he finished 10th in the 1978 European and 20th in the 1980 Olympics.

Turkey

The first marathon, including the national championship, was held at Istanbul on 21 June 1938 and won by Selim Sunal in 3:21:50. Most wins have been by Ismail Akcay (eight) and Huseyin Aktas (six) between 1963 and 1976. The best performance in the Olympics is fourth by Akcay in 1968. Two months later he became the first Turkish runner to better 2:20, with 2:13:43.6 in fourth place at Fukuoka. A better time of 2:11:30 set by Veli Balli at Lahore in 1976, although accepted as legitimate, has been viewed with some scepticism, but no such doubt exists with the time of 2:12:41, set by Ahmet Altun at Frankfurt in 1983. On 30 October 1983 the first ever marathon linking two continents finished in Istanbul. The race, which included crossing the Bosporus Bridge, attracted some 6000 runners and was won by Ian Thompson (GB) in 2:23:34.

Yugoslavia

The first Yugoslav marathon championship was held at Zagreb on 24 August 1930 and won by Stane Sporn with a time of 3:08:47. Sporn won four of the first five titles contested and was the first Yugoslav runner to win a medal in the Balkan Games. Franjo Skrinjar has won most titles with five between 1953 and 1962, during which time he was dominant in the Balkan Games and won the first three international races held at Szeged (Hun) from 1957. The best performance in the Olympics is the silver medal won in 1956 by Franjo Mihalic, who went on to win the Athens (1957) and Boston (1958) classics.

Mediterranean Games

First held in 1951, there has only been one double

Franjo Skrinjar (Yug) in training.

winner, Bakir Benaissa (Mor), eighth in the Rome Olympics, in 1959 and 1963. Medal winners by nation have been: Turkey 2 gold, 3 silver, 4 bronze; Italy 2–3–0; Morocco 2–0–0; Egypt and Spain 1–1–2 each; Greece 1–1–1.

Biggest winning margin is 14 min 7 sec by Ahmet Aytar in 1951 and the closest finish was in 1967, when Antonio Ambu won by 13 sec.

CHAMPIONS

1951	Alexandria	Ahmet Aytar (Tur)	3:07:25
1955	Barcelona	Abdul Kerim (Egy)	2:50:35
1959	Beirut	Bakir Benaissa (Mor)	2:24:14.8
1963	Naples	Bakir Benaissa (Mor)	2:26:50
1967	Tunis	Antonio Ambu (Ita)	2:21:31
1971	Izmir	Gian-Battista Bassi (Ita)	2:23:33
1975	Algiers	Antonino Banos (Spa)	2:24:12.8

1979	Split*	Michail Koussis (Gre)	2:06:52.3
1983	Casablanca	Mehmet Terzi (Tur)	2:22:32.9

* Through error the course distance in 1979 was only 41.3 km (25.7 miles).

Spain

The first 'marathon' in Spain was over 33 km (20.5 miles) at Solosa on 25 April 1924 and incorporated the Olympic trial. The winner in 2:08:14 was Dionisio Carreras, who finished ninth at Paris in a time of 2:57:18.4 which remained a national record for nine years. No Spanish Olympian has improved on Carreras' position. The second race to be held was over 38.5 km (24 miles) at Barcelona on 12 February 1928, Carreras winning in 2:25:28.2. The first championship race took place on 29 June 1928 at Barcelona, Emilio Ferrer winning in 3:06:50. Most titles won have been five by Miguel Navarro, silver medallist in the 1959 Mediterranean Games and 17th at Rome, and Carlos Perez. Perez finished fourth in the 1966 European Championships, the best by a Spanish runner, and then became the first Spaniard to better 2:20 with 2:17:32 at Fukuoka three months later. Ricardo Ortega finished sixth at London in 1983, setting a fine new national record of 2:11:51, but it was the 1983 champion Juan Traspaderne who succeeded at Helsinki, when in finishing 12th he lowered the national record to 2:11:34, leaving Ortega in 21st position nearly three minutes behind.

NATIONAL CHAMPIONS (1974 TO 1983)

1974	Juan Hidalgo	2:16:00
1975	Agustin Fernandez	2:18:03
1976	Jose Gomez	2:18:33
1977	Santiago Manguan	2:21:33.6
1978	Antonio Romero	2:15:31
1979	Eleuterio Anton	2:17:01.7
1980	Eleuterio Anton	2:14:32
1981	Eleuterio Anton	2:20:49
1982	Santiago de la Parte	2:15:47
1983	Juan Traspaderne	2:15:10

Since 1978 an international marathon has been held at Barcelona.

BARCELONA WINNERS

1978	David Patterson (USA)	2:23:15
1979	David Patterson (USA)	2:19:37
1980	Don Faircloth (GB)	2:19:42
1981	Martin Knapp (GB)	2:18:56
1982	Mike Pinocci (USA)	2:14:30
1983	Allan Zachariasen (Den)	2:11:05

Italy

In 1894 distance running got under way in Italy, as 50 km (31 miles) races were held from Milan to Cernobbio and from Milan to Lecco. The winner of the latter, Carlo Airoldi, won similar races the following year. In 1896 Airoldi decided to compete in the Olympics on an individual basis. There followed one of the most amazing sagas in the annals of the marathon, as Airoldi set off on foot for Greece from his home in Milan. Leaving Milan on 28 February, he reached Ragusa (Yug) on 19 March, covering the 1119 km (695 miles) at an average of 53 km (33 miles) per day. On the night of 23 March he took a boat via Corfu to Patrasso, where he arrived on 27 March. In another five days and 219 km (136 miles) he reached Athens, arriving in good time for the Games, only for his entry to be refused on the allegations that he was a professional!

The first marathon to be held in Italy took place on 30 October 1898 over 40 km, on the occasion of the Lombardy Championship at Milan. The winner, Ettore Zilia (2:44:40), was forced to miss the 1900 Olympics through injury. The first Italian championship was held on 3 June 1908 at Rome, Umberto Blasi winning in 3:01:04 as the favoured Dorando Pietri (see Runners) dropped out. Between 1962 and 1969 Antonio Ambu won a record seven titles, and in 1967 became the first Italian to better 2:20, when he finished fourth at Boston in 2:18:04.

NATIONAL CHAMPIONS (1974 TO 1983)

1974	Giuseppe Cindolo	2:15:41.8
1975	Giuseppe Cindolo	2:18:11.8
1976	Giuseppe Cindolo	2:11:50.6
1977	Paolo Accaputo	2:19:16.4
1978	Massimo Magnani	2:16:46
1979	Michelangelo Arena	2:14:43.5
1980	Michelangelo Arena	2:16:17
1981	Gian Paolo Messina	2:15:40.7
1982	Giuseppe Gerbi	2:11:25
1983	Giuseppe Gerbi	2:15:11

Following Pietri's disqualification at London in 1908, Italy won two Olympic medals in the 1920s. Valerio Arri, nicknamed 'Titi', had won the national championship and the first Turin event in 1919, prior to finishing second in the 1920 Poly, just before the Olympics. So delighted was he on winning the bronze medal, he performed a series of cartwheels on breaking the tape. Four years later at Paris Romeo Bertini, who had run his first marathon in 1913, finished runner-up to Albin Stenroos. He gained selection by finishing second in the Olympic trial over 37 km (23 miles), in which Arri failed to finish. It was only after his silver medal success that Bertini won his sole national title and he lasted only 20 km in the 1928 Olympics. It would appear that Italy can possibly count another bronze medal as in 1912 Gaston Strobino, a native of Biela, finished third, wearing the colours of the United States.

In the European Championships the best Italian result has been the bronze medal won by Aurelio Genghini in the first race at Turin, at which venue he had won the Italian title the year before. Italy, however, scored a fine dual success at the first European Cup held at Agen in 1981. Massimo Magnani, who had made his marathon debut in 1973, was a clear winner, leading Italy to the team title. He had finished sixth in the 1978 European Championships and eighth in the Olympics two years later and has a best time of 2:11:28 when finishing second in the national title race of 1982. Ninth in the European Cup in only his second marathon was 23-year-old Gianni Poli, who went on to set an Italian record of 2:11:19 at Fukuoka later in the year. After finishing third in a sprint finish at the second European Cup race in 1983, Poli improved to 2:11:05 in seventh place at Helsinki.

In 1982 two new international races were staged in Rome and Turin, the race at Rome being marred by the fact that the course was some 110 m (120 yd) short. In 1983 Giuseppe Gerbi won by one second from Domingo Tibaduiza (Col). For its part Turin had held a particularly successful race over a 42.750 km (26.5 miles) course from 1919 to 1933, the series terminating with the first European Championships in 1934.

Another new marathon was held in 1983, at Milan. Most of the leading Italian male runners took part, Michelangelo Arena winning in 2:14:46.

WINNERS *(ITALIAN UNLESS STATED)*

ROME

	men	
1982	Emiel Puttemans (Bel)	2:09:53
1983	Giuseppe Gerbi	2:15:11
	women	
1982	Laura Fogli	2:31:08
1983	Alba Milana	2:32:57

TURIN

1982	Marc de Blander (Bel)	2:14:57

WOMEN'S NATIONAL CHAMPIONS (1980 TO 1983)

1980	Maria Pia D'Orlando	2:49:22.4
1981	Silvana Cruciata	2:45:23
1982	Alba Milana	2:41:45
1983	Alba Milana	2:32:57

In 1982 Rita Marchisio scored a major success at Osaka, winning in a national rècord 2:32:55 but was only 10th in the European Championship as consistent Laura Fogli took the silver medal. Fogli then finished fourth at New York (2:33:01), fourth in the 1983 Avon (2:34:19) and sixth at Helsinki (2:33:31).

Dropping out of the Chicago marathon, Fogli secured a late entry to New York one week later and finished third in a new Italian record time of 2:31:49.

America

United States

The first marathon to be held outside Europe was that organised by the Knickerbocker AC between Stamford, CT and Columbus Oval, NY. Held on 20 September 1896, the event attracted 30 runners and was won by John McDermott in 3:25:55.6 over a hilly, muddy 25 mile course. The next April McDermott won the inaugural Boston marathon, the only race that continued into the 20th century without a break.

Buffalo staged a PanAmerican Exhibition marathon in 1901 but only Boston continued to 1905, when two new races appeared on the American scene. Chicago and St Louis hosted 25 mile races which were to be held annually, and they were joined two years later by the Yonkers, NY event.

Following the success of John Hayes at London in 1908, there was a veritable explosion of marathons throughout the country which lasted for some two years, catering for both amateur and professional, indoors and out. During 1909 at least 32 such races

John A Kelley (USA), winning a 20 mile race in 1938, has been running marathons since 1928. (AP)

Clarence DeMar (left) with one of his closest American rivals Albert 'Whitey' Michelsen, 1927.

were held, a number not approached until the 1960s, and it was hardly surprising in view of the interest shown that Hayes' London time of 2:55:18.4 was soon bettered.

On 1 January 1909 Robert Fowler won the Empire City race in Yonkers with a time of 2:52:45.4 for the first official improvement. The race was terminated after the seventh runner had finished, due to the ensuing chaos caused by the crowd. The following month the Brooklyn marathon was run to Seagate and back on 12 February and for the first time 2:50 was bettered, James Clark winning with a fine 2:46:52.6. Little-known Albert Raines won the Bronx marathon at Westchester on 8 May by eleven minutes with a time of 2:46:04.6, but that was the last world record to be held by an American for nearly 16 years.

Whilst the 1908 Olympic race had been so successful from an American viewpoint, the race at St Louis four years earlier had also been a good one. Despite limited overseas entries, the United States only missed taking two places (fourth and fifth) in the

first eight, although recent investigation suggests that third-placed Albert Corey may still have been a French citizen. From 1896 through 1976, the nation did not miss a single Olympic marathon and has won more medals (nine) than any other country, with Clarence DeMar (see Runners) competing on three occasions.

Although Boston, by far the most important race, was unofficially considered to be the annual national championship, it was not until 1925 that the inaugural AAU title was awarded. Fittingly it was Boston that staged the race but only twice since (1928–9) have they had that honour. From 1932 to 1937 the race was held at Washington, DC and from 1938 to 1966, other than 1948, Yonkers was the venue. Since then the race has been staged at different locations and a steady decline in the attraction of the event has been apparent. From 1980 the organising body has been The Athletics Congress (TAC). To date, John J Kelley has won most titles with eight successive wins from 1956 to 1963, whilst the oldest champion is the non related John A Kelley, who was 43 when he took his second title in 1950.

Whilst there were no pre-war runners who could match the consistency of DeMar or the longevity of John A Kelley, still competing at Boston in 1983 at the age of 75, there were still some excellent performers in their own right apart from those already covered in the Boston review.

One of those was Albert 'Whitey' Michelsen who often clashed with DeMar, yet never won at Boston or in the AAU. He was still a tough competitor and finished well in both his Olympic appearances. In 1928 he was ninth and four years later was the top American finisher (seventh) at Los Angeles. He became the first to better 2:30, when he was timed in 2:29:01.8 at the first Port Chester race on 12 October 1925. The course, from Columbus Circle, NY to Liberty Square, Port Chester, was his favourite and he won the race three times, beating DeMar in the process.

The most consistent of the period was undoubtedly Frank 'Pat' Dengis, who was born at Swansea in Wales. Never a Boston winner, Dengis won 15 of 36 marathons between 1932 and 1939, when he was killed in an air crash. He won all but four of his last 16 marathons when at his peak and had victories in the AAU (three) and at Yonkers (three), Port Chester (four) and Salisbury (two).

As John J Kelley's career in the late 1950s was drawing to a close, a young teacher from South Dakota, Leonard Edelen (popularly known as 'Buddy') came to fame whilst resident in England, becoming the first American to better 2:20 in 1962 when he recorded 2:18:56.8 for fourth place at Fukuoka. The following year he won three major international marathons in Europe, breaking the

'Buddy' Edelen setting an American record at Fukuoka, 1962 in taking fourth place ahead of Pavel Kantorek (Cze). (Hideaki Miyagi)

course record each time. After winning at Athens, he lowered the world record to 2:14:28 on 15 June 1963 over the Windsor to Chiswick course, before taking the Kosice classic in October. Often troubled by sciatica, Edelen's sixth place in the Tokyo Olympic marathon was the best by an American since 1928, when Joie Ray was fifth, and of 13 races he won seven.

The runner who eclipsed Edelen's national record was one of the most popular and respected of runners, Kenny Moore, later to become a distinguished writer with *Sports Illustrated*. His fastest time was 2:11:35.8 at Fukuoka in 1970 when second to Akio Usami, whilst he narrowly missed the bronze medal in Munich, finishing fourth. Between 1968 and 1972 he took part in ten marathons, winning three.

The careers of Frank Shorter, Bill Rodgers and the current world record holder Alberto Salazar are covered separately.

AAU/TAC CHAMPIONS *(USA UNLESS STATED)*

1925	Charles Mellor	2:33:00.6
1926	Clarence DeMar	2:45:05.2
1927	Clarence DeMar	2:40:22.2
1928	Clarence DeMar	2:37:07.8
1929	Johnny Miles (Can)	2:33:08.8
1930*	Karl Koski	2:25:21.2
1931	William Agee	2:32:08.8
1932	Clyde Martak	2:58:18
1933	Dave Komonen (Can)	2:53:43
1934	Dave Komonen (Can)	2:43:26.6
1935	Pat Dengis	2:53:53
1936	William McMahon	2:38:14.2
1937	Mel Porter	2:44:22
1938	Pat Dengis	2:39:38.2
1939	Pat Dengis	2:33:45.2
1940	Gérard Côté (Can)	2:34:06.2
1941	Joe Smith	2:36:06.3
1942	Fred McGlone	2:37:54
1943	Gérard Côté (Can)	2:38:35.3
1944	Charles Robbins	2:40:48.6

1945	Charles Robbins	2:37:14
1946	Gérard Côté (Can)	2:47:53.6
1947	Ted Vogel	2:40:11
1948	John A Kelley	2:48:32.3
1949	Vic Dyrgall	2:38:49.9
1950	John A Kelley	2:45:55.3
1951	Jesse van Zant	2:37:12
1952	Vic Dyrgall	2:38:28.4
1953	Gösta Leandersson (Swe)	2:48:12.5
1954	Ted Corbitt	2:46:13.9
1955	Nick Costes	2:31:24.4
1956	John J Kelley	2:24:52.2
1957	John J Kelley	2:24:55.2
1958	John J Kelley	2:21:00.4
1959	John J Kelley	2:21:54.4
1960	John J Kelley	2:20:13.6
1961	John J Kelley	2:26:53.4
1962	John J Kelley	2:27:39.8
1963	John J Kelley	2:25:17.6
1964	Buddy Edelen	2:24:25.6
1965	Garfield Williams	2:33:50.6
1966	Norman Higgins	2:22:50.8
1967	Ron Daws	2:40:07
1968	George Young	2:30:48
1969	Tom Heinonen	2:24:43
1970	Bob Fitts	2:24:10.6
1971	Kenny Moore	2:16:48.6
1972	Ed Norris	2:24:42.8
1973	Doug Schmenk	2:15:48
1974	Ron Wayne	2:18:52.3
1975	Gary Tuttle	2:17:27
1976	Gary Tuttle	2:15:15
1977	Hakan Spik (Fin)	2:17:49
1978	Carl Hatfield	2:17:20
1979*	Tom Antczak	2:15:28
1980*	Frank Richardson	2:13:54
1981	Robert Johnson	2:29:14
1982	Joel Menges	2:32:28.7
1983	Pete Pfitzinger	2:14:45

* The courses in 1930, 1979 and 1980 were under distance.

In Championships won by foreign runners the first United States nationals to finish were as follows: 1929 DeMar 2:43:47; 1933 Porter 2:53:46; 1934 Porter 2:48:04; 1940 Lou Gregory 2:35:10; 1943 McGlone 2:35:10; 1946 John A Kelley 2:50:28.2; 1953 John Lafferty 2:50:31; 1977 Ed Schelegle 2:18:11. The 1930 winner Koski, born in Finland, was an American citizen. Jack O'Reilly (2:33:08) was second.

Women

Whilst American women's marathon involvement had begun in the early 1960s, it was not until 1972 that they were officially recognised at Boston. Since then Japanese born Miki Gorman won the event twice, the only woman to do so. In between wins she became a mother for the first time. Jackie Hansen became the first woman to better 2:40 when she ran 2:38:19 at Eugene on 12 October 1975. This was the second world record set by the Californian based runner who had earlier recorded 2:43:54.5 at Culver City on 1 December 1974.

Remarkably despite the successive exploits by Kim Merritt, Julie Brown, Patti Catalano and Joan Benoit, all of whom set fine national records, Hansen was the last American to hold the world record until Benoit's shattering performance at Boston.

AAU/TAC CHAMPIONS (USA UNLESS STATED)

1974	Judy Ikenberry	2:55:18
1975	Kim Merritt	2:46:15
1976	Julie Brown	2:45:33
1977	Leal Ann Reinhardt	2:46:34
1978	Martha Cooksey	2:41:49
1979*	Sue Petersen	2:46:17
1980*	Sue Munday	2:43:17
1981	Nancy Conz	2:36:45.9
1982	Lorraine Moller (NZ)	2:36:12.5
1983	Julie Brown	2:26:24

* The courses in 1979 and 1980 were short. In 1982 the first United States national to finish was Laurie Binder (2:39:45.5).

Other races

With well over 250 marathon races scheduled for 1983 many long established events no longer attract the fields of other newer, sponsored races, often held on easier courses. Longest running besides Boston include Yonkers, NY (47th in 1983); Western Hemisphere at Culver City, CA (36th); Heart of America at Columbia, MO (24th) and The Race of Champions at Holyoke, MA (23rd).

Eugene

Arguably the top race after Boston and New York is the Nike event staged at Eugene, first held in 1971. Starting and finishing at Hayward Field, the course consists of two small and two large loops and is basically flat. In 1976 the Olympic trial race was held at this venue. The nearest any male runners have come to winning twice outright are Jon Anderson (1972 [tie] and 1975) and Jeff Wells (1977 and 1979 [tie]). There have been several achievements in the women's division. In 1973 12-year-old Lilli Ledbetter won in 3:03:32 and is the youngest known winner of any women's race. Two years later Jackie Hansen set a world record and in 1978 and 1982 American records were set by Julie Brown (2:36:23.1) and Joan Benoit (2:26:11).

WINNERS SINCE 1979

	men	
1979	{ Jeff Wells / Tony Sandoval	2:10:20
1980	Dick Quax (NZ)	2:10:47
1981	Benji Durden	2:12:12
1982	Rodolfo Gomez (Mex)	2:11:35
1983	Gary Siriano	2:12:32
	women	
1979	Joan Benoit	2:35:41
1980	Lorraine Moller (NZ)	2:31:42
1981	Lorraine Moller (NZ)	2:31:15
1982	Joan Benoit	2:26:11
1983	Akemi Masuda (Jap)	2:30:30

Honolulu

First held in 1973 this race is held on Oahu Island in early December and starts at 6 am. Duncan Macdonald has won the race three times (1973–6–80) and Patti Catalano four times in succession from 1978. Fastest times recorded are by David Gordon, 2:15:29.8 in 1982, and Catalano, 2:33:24 in 1981. In 1982 a record 10 258 runners started.

Miami

The Orange Bowl marathon, first held in 1977, currently attracts an international field, the fastest times to date being recorded in the 1982 race by Dave Long (GB), 2:12:16.8, and Charlotte Teske (GFR), 2:29:01.6. In 1983 the course was 150 m short.

Chicago

First held in 1977 as the Mayor Daley marathon, the event is now known as America's marathon. Over 8000 started in 1983, the event attracting world class fields in both divisions. Joseph Nzau beat Hugh Jones (GB) by half a second in 2:09:44.3 in a thrilling men's race, setting a new Kenyan record. In the women's event Anne Audain (NZ), making her marathon debut, fell in the last mile when leading. Rosa Mota (Por) beat Jacqueline Gareau (Can) by 24 sec in 2:31:12, with Dorthe Rasmussen (Den) third in 2:31:45 and Audain fourth (2:32:14).

Houston

The Houston–Tenneco marathon which dates from 1973 is held over a level out and back course and was twice won by Ron Tabb in 1978 and 1980. Current course record holders are Benji Durden, 2:11:11 in 1982, and Ingrid Kristiansen (Nor), 2:33:27 in 1983.

Columbus

One of the newest marathons the Columbus Bank One race was first held in 1980 over a single loop course. The winner, Tommy Persson (Swe), set an event record of 2:11:02 which still stands. Charlotte Teske (GFR) ran 2:35:15 in 1981 and is the fastest woman at the venue.

San Francisco

Held against the backdrop of the Golden Gate Bridge, the race is held over a rolling course and in 1983 attracted over 7500 runners. Miguel Tibaduiza (Col) set an event record of 2:14:31.7 in 1982, and in 1983 Janis Klecker (USA) became the fastest woman with 2:35:44.

Canada

Canada's success at the early Boston races owed much to the *Hamilton Herald* who organised a 'go as you please' race around the Bay adjacent to the east end of Lake Ontario in 1894. The race distance was just over 19 miles (30.6 km) and has been held ever since except for the periods 1917–19 and 1925–35. The first Canadian marathon was held on 6 June 1908 over 25 miles at Hamilton and served as the Olympic trial. In first place was Harry Lawson (2:38:11) who finished seventh in London. The first championship race was staged on 24 May 1910 at the same venue and was won by Mike Ryan (USA) in 2:49:19, but despite this early interest it was another 20 years before the start of a regularly held annual championship. Gordon Dickson, fifth in the 1958 Commonwealth marathon, won a record six titles between 1957 and 1964.

NATIONAL CHAMPIONS (1974 TO 1983)

1974	Tom Howard	2:17:57
1975	Brian Maxwell	2:18:40
1976	Doug Scorrar	2:30:55
1977	Mike Dyon	2:18:05
1978	Rich Hughson	2:21:54
1979	Ken Inglis	2:20:45
1980	Brian Maxwell	2:16:52
1981	John Hill	2:19:15.8
1982	Mike Dyon	2:16:12.6
1983	Art Boileau	2:16:21

In 1908 Canada's team effort was surpassed only by that of the United States as they took fifth, sixth and seventh places. William Wood's fifth place was equalled four years later by James Duffy and remains the best by a Canadian in the Olympics. Both Harold Webster (1934) and Andy Boychuk (1967) won gold medals in the Empire and Pan American Games, but Canada's first international success came in 1906 when William Sherring won the Athens marathon over a 41.86 km (26 miles) course in 2:51:23.6 by nearly seven minutes (see Games). Sherring travelled to Europe on his own and worked on the railway in Greece to maintain his upkeep.

Before the advent of the Gérard Côté era (see Runners) there were other fine runners in Canada. Johnny Miles, bronze medallist in the inaugural Empire Games, won twice at Boston in 1926 and 1929, the latter incorporating the AAU title, and also the first Hamilton marathon in 1927. Finnish-born Dave Komonen, a shoemaker who made his own running shoes, was one of the unlucky band of athletes who hit form in a non-Olympic year. Besides capturing the national championship in 1931–3–4, Komonen also won the AAU title in 1933–4 in addition to Boston (1934). At Hamilton in 1933, on a very hot day, he led for eleven miles in a bid to make the 1934 Empire team before retiring, yet this important race came only one week after he had won the AAU event.

The 1934 Hamilton winner was Derbyshire-born Harold Webster who went on to an upset win in the Empire Games. He was a consistent performer who,

William Sherring (Can) wins the 1906 Athens marathon and is applauded by Prince George of Greece.

although only winning one national title (1936), took the prestigious Hamilton event four times and fourth place at Boston in 1930 and 1933. He did not finish either the 1928 or the 1936 Olympic marathons.

Jerome Drayton, by far the fastest Canadian, has been something of an erratic runner since his dramatic breakthrough in 1969. Previously named Peter Buniak, he won the classic Fukuoka event three times between 1969 and 1976 (only Shorter and Seko have won more) and was second in the 1978 Commonwealth race. He did not complete either of the 1970 or 1974 marathons at Edinburgh and Christchurch, and was a disappointing sixth at Montreal in 1976. Drayton has held the Canadian record since 1969 with a best of 2:10:08.4 when winning at Fukuoka in 1975. Besides the Montreal international race (see Races), other annually held marathons include the following:

Ottawa

The Ottawa National Capital race was first held in 1975 and Mike Dyon has won the event three times (1977, 1981–3). In 1978 the race served as the Commonwealth trial which Brian Maxwell won in 2:16:02.6, fastest time recorded at that venue. Chris Lavalle, winner in 1978 and 1980, is the fastest woman with 2:42:50 in the latter. There were a record 4223 starters in 1983.

Toronto

Visiting athletes captured the top honours in each of the first four Toronto marathons through Tom Fleming (USA) 1978; Dave Cannon (GB) 1979; Bill Rodgers (USA) 1980, and Kevin Ryan (NZ) with an event record 2:13:26 in 1981. Benji Durden (USA) won the 1983 race in 2:15:16 as Carey May (Ire) set a women's event record of 2:36:07.

Vancouver

Tom Howard won the first three Vancouver marathons from 1972. Event records are held by Garry Henry (Aus), 2:13:13 in 1980, and Gail Mackean, 2:44:53 in 1979, after having also won the previous year. The course was over distance in 1983, when 2400 runners started.

Winnipeg

The fifth edition of this event in 1983, which included the national title race, attracted over three thousand athletes and the women's winner Cindy Hamilton set a record at the venue of 2:40:47. Dennis Rinde (USA), winner in 1981–2, is the fastest man with a time of 2:13:51 set in 1981.

The women's national championship was first officially accepted in 1978.

WOMEN'S NATIONAL CHAMPIONS (1978 TO 1983)

1978	Gail Mackean	2:49:56
1979	Wendy Robertson	3:00:17
1980	Janet Weishaupt	2:53:01
1981	Linda Staudt	2:44:26
1982	Cindy Hamilton	2:39:01.7
1983	Cindy Hamilton	2:40:47

Visiting runners won in 1980 (Marilyn Belwood [USA], 2:45:27) and 1982 (Annick Lebreton [Fra], 2:36:05.5). Although not yet a winner of the national title, the outstanding Canadian woman runner has been Jacqueline Gareau. In 1980 Gareau was a delayed winner at Boston, following the disqualification of Rose Ruiz who had fraudulently claimed victory. Gareau subsequently finished fifth in 1981 and second in 1982–3, her time of 2:29:28 in the latter being a new Canadian record. In Helsinki she finished fifth in 2:32:35.

Jerome Drayton (Can) leads Olympic champion Waldemar Cierpinski (GDR) at Fukuoka 1976. (Asahi Shimbun)

Central America and Caribbean

The Central American and Caribbean region includes 28 nations eligible for competition in the area. Cuba (1904) and Mexico (1928) are the only countries which were represented in the Olympic marathon before the war.

Central American and Caribbean Games

Held quadrennially since 1926 they are the oldest such regional championships outside the Olympics. A marathon was not held until the fourth Games in Panama City in 1938 when runners from Mexico, Venezuela, Puerto Rico and Panama took part. After the war half-marathons were held until 1970. Doroteo Flores (Gua) is the only runner to have won twice (1946 and 1954) and was runner-up in 1950. Flores, a mill worker, won at Boston in 1952 and was Pan American champion in 1955. In the 1952 Olympics he finished 22nd, Guatemala's best placing. Medal winners by nation: Mexico 3 gold, 4 silver, 4 bronze; Guatemala 3–2–2; Colombia 2–2–2; Puerto Rico 2–1–1; Panama 1–0–0; Cuba 0–2–1 and El Salvador 0–0–1.

WINNERS (MARATHON)

1938	Panama City	Jose Thompson (Pan)	3:01:03.4
1970	Panama City	Alfredo Penaloza (Mex)	2:47:23.4
1974	Santo Domingo	Gilberto Serna (Col)	2:28:07.8
1978	Medellin	Radames Vega (PR)	2:22:33.8
1982	Havana	Jorge Gonzalez (PR)	2:26:40

Central American and Caribbean Championships

Commencing in 1967 at Jalapa, the Championships are held biennially and have been dominated by Mexico. The distance has been half-marathon until 1979 (30 km) and full since. Medal winners by nation: Mexico 6 gold, 3 silver, 3 bronze; Cuba 1–2–5; Colombia 1–2–1; Costa Rica 1–0–0; Jamaica and Puerto Rico each 0–1–0. Most successful individual runner has been Mario Cuevas (Mex) with two gold medals (1973 and 1979) and one silver (1977).

WINNERS (MARATHON)

1981	Santo Domingo	Radames Gonzalez (Cub)	2:23:15
1983	Havana	Victor Mora (Col)	2:48:51.1

Central American Championships

First held in 1958, the eleventh championships were held at Guatemala City in 1980 when Carlos Cuque (Gua) became the first Guatemalan to better 2:20. This was the first occasion that such a time had been run in any of the regional Games or Championships of the Central American and Caribbean area.

WINNERS (MARATHON)

1972	Panama City	Clovis Morales (Hon)	2:36:08
1975	San Jose	Rafael Sandi (CRC)	2:36:30.7
1980	Guatemala City	Carlos Cuque (Gua)	2:19:20

Bermuda

Since 1975 Bermuda have staged an international marathon, and the following year made their one appearance in the Olympics. Debbie Butterfield is the region's fastest woman with 2:49:58.3, set at Los Angeles in 1979.

WINNERS

	men	
1975	Andy Boychuk (Can)	2:25:14
1976	not held	
1977	Doug Scorrar (Can)	2:27:44
1978	Ron Hill (GB)	2:26:13
1979	Andy Holden (GB)	2:18:50
1980	Andy Holden (GB)	2:15:20
1981	Andy Holden (GB)	2:16:57
1982	Colin Kirkham (GB)	2:17:28
1983	Andy Robertson (GB)	2:19:09

	women	
1975	not held	
1976	not held	
1977	not held	
1978	Debbie Butterfield	3:00:16
1979	Julie Shea (USA)	2:46:42
1980	Patti Lyons (USA)	2:46:52
1981	Kiki Sweigart (USA)	2:43:09
1982	Judy Vivian (USA)	2:45:09
1983	Kathy Ricica (Can)	2:50:42

Cuba

Had not Cuba's first Olympic entry in 1904 Felix Carvajal, a postal carrier, stopped to talk to spectators and eat unripe fruit, he may well have gained a medal. As it was, he had to be content with fourth place in a time close to four hours. It was 72 years before Cuba had another marathon entry, when the

1975 Pan American Games champion Rigoberto Mendoza finished 28th at Montreal. The first Cuban to better 2:20 was Radames Gonzalez, who recorded 2:16:15 at Karl Marx Stadt in 1980 but failed to finish at Moscow. Twice national champion (1978–9), Gonzalez has a consistent record in Central American races with fourth (1978) and second (1982) in the Games marathon, and second (1979) and first (1981) in the Championship race.

Mexico

The first marathon in Mexico was held on 28 November 1910 at Mexico City and was won by Juan Ruiz in 3:30:05. Juan Torres won the inaugural championship (4:11:00) in 1924 and four years later was one of the two-man squad in Mexico's first Olympic marathon. Mexico have been by far the most successful nation in the region, winning 23 of a possible 60 medals in the Games and Championships. In addition to medals won in regional competition, Mexico also won the 1963 Pan American Games title through Fidel Negrete. Pablo Garrido, better known as a film actor, was the first Mexican to better 2:20 when he ran 2:17:30 at Boston in 1969, before improving greatly to 2:12:52.8 at Fukuoka the same year when he finished fourth. Rodolfo Gomez has become Mexico's top marathon runner since turning to the event, after winning the 1979 Pan American 10000 m title. He became the first non-European to finish in the Moscow Olympics with sixth place, by far Mexico's best such performance.

RODOLFO GOMEZ—CAREER RECORD

31 Jul 1976 Montreal	OG	2:18:21.2	(19)
2 Dec 1979 Fukuoka		2:16:18	(15)
2 Mar 1980 Coyoacan		2:19:20	(1)
1 Aug 1980 Moscow	OG	2:12:39	(6)
26 Oct 1980 New York		2:10:13	(2)
1 Mar 1981 Tokyo		2:11:00	(1)
25 Oct 1981 New York		2:12:47	(7)
7 Mar 1982 Athens	IAAF	2:11:49	(1)
22 May 1982 Rotterdam		2:11:57	(1)
12 Sep 1982 Eugene		2:11:35	(1)
24 Oct 1982 New York		2:09:33	(2)
13 Feb 1983 Tokyo		2:09:12	(3)
9 Apr 1983 Rotterdam		2:09:25	(3)

South America

Chile was the first South American nation to be represented in an Olympic marathon when Juan Bascunan finished 33rd in 1920. Subsequently, Chile did well in 1924 and 1928 as Manuel Plaza finished sixth and second, the latter Chile's only athletics medal in the Olympics. Argentina followed Chile's example with excellent gold medal achievements in 1932 and 1948.

Manuel Plaza, Chile's only Olympic medallist.

South American Championships

The Championships were first officially held in 1919 at Montevideo but it was not until the eighth celebrations at the same venue in 1933 that a 'marathon' race was introduced. The distance was 33 km (20½ miles) and the winner, Plaza, took his 14th and last individual gold medal in the championships. In 1949 and 1952 the race was held over 20 km and in 1954–6–8, 1963 and 1981 over the half-marathon, the most popular distance in Central and South America until quite recently. In 1979 the distance was 36 km (22 miles) through error. Four runners have won the event twice: Corsino Fernandez (1943–5), Delfo Cabrera (1949, 1952), Osvaldo Suarez (all Arg, 1956–8) and Hector Rodriguez (Col, 1975–7). Rodriguez became the first to better 2:20 over a full course in the series in 1977. To date Argentina have been the most successful nation with 9 gold, 8 silver and 6 bronze medals, followed by Colombia 6–7–3; Chile 6–4–8; Brazil 2–4–5; Peru and Uruguay each 1–1–0; and Bolivia, Ecuador and Venezuela each 0–0–1. Chile (1939) and Argentina (1941, 1952) have each won all three medals in a single race.

CHAMPIONS (MARATHON)

1961	Lima	Juan Silva (Chl)	2:39:35.8
1965	Rio de Janeiro	Ricardo Vidal (Chl)	2:38:14.2
1967	Buenos Aires	Armando Gonzalez (Uru)	2:35:43
1969	Quito	Pedro Cardenas (Col)	2:36:35.6
1971	Lima	Martin Pabon (Col)	2:26:10.4
1974	Montevideo	Jose Ramirez (Chl)	2:30:42
1975*	Rio de Janeiro	Hector Rodriguez (Col)	2:12:08
1977	Montevideo	Hector Rodriguez (Col)	2:19:56
1983	Santa Fe	Juan Plagman (Chl)	2:15:50

*Course distance 41.5 km (25.8 miles).

Bolivar Games

First held in 1938, the Games are now held quadrennially. Medal winners by nation: Colombia 5 gold, 5 silver, 3 bronze; Venezuela 1–1–1; Bolivia 1–1–2; Panama 1–0–0; Ecuador 1–2–2 and Peru 0–0–1. In 1973 Colombia won all the medals.

WINNERS (MARATHON)

1970	Maracaibo	Jose Moreno (Pan)	2:51:48.8
1973	Panama City	Gilberto Serna (Col)	2:35:11.6
1981	Barquisimeto	Eduardo Castellanos (Ven)	2:23:07

Argentina

Buenos Aires staged the first international marathon to be held in South America on 24 May 1910. The runners toured 40 laps of a racecourse, totalling 42.4 km (26.3 miles) with Dorando Pietri (Ita) winning in 2:38:48.2. Antonio Creuz (Chl) and Anibal Carraro (Arg) took second and third in 2:45:04 and 2:54:09 respectively. There were also runners from Spain and Uruguay. Argentina's Olympic debut was an auspicious occasion as Juan Carlos Zabala, a Buenos Aires orphan, won in a close finish (see Games). The previous year he had won the Kosice race in his first attempt at the distance but dropped out from the Los Angeles pre-Olympic race suffering from the heat. He was unsuccessful in his attempt to retain the title in Berlin. The 1948

Olympic race was won by Delfo Cabrera, a fireman, in his debut over the full distance and in 1952 he became the first defending champion to finish in the first six. Twice South American champion, he was also the inaugural Pan American Games champion in 1951. Second in that race was Reinaldo Gorno and he was again second in the 1952 Olympics to Emil Zatopek. A tough performer, Gorno won the 1954 Asahi and 1955 Enschede classics and also unofficial South American titles in 1946 and 1953. In 1981 Alfredo Maravilla became the first Argentinian to be timed in under 2:20 when he recorded 2:17:43 at Boston. He has twice been national champion (1980–2) since the series was revived in 1978.

Brazil

Of Brazil's two Olympic runners in the 1932 race one was last, whilst the non-finisher Matheus Marcondes had won the first marathon to be held in Brazil at São Paulo on 16 August 1925 in 2:52:44.8. He improved to 2:48:24 at the same venue in 1930 and this time lasted until 1959 as the national record. Although a national title race had been held biennially since 1971, it was in 1980 with the launching of the Rio de Janeiro international race that the marathon upsurge in the continent began. The course, which is mainly flat, starts and finishes at Leme on the Copacabana beach, going inland to the city centre before returning to the beach, then through Ipanema to the turn at Leblon. In 1982 the race started at 4 pm when the temperature was in the region of 30°C (86°F).

RIO WINNERS

	men	
1980	Greg Meyer (USA)	2:16:40
1981	Bill Rodgers (USA)	2:14:13
1982	Delfim Moreira (Por)	2:15:57
1983	Lawrie Whitty (Aus)	2:18:43

	women	
1980	Lorraine Moller (NZ)	2:39:10
1981	Lorraine Moller (NZ)	2:35:56
1982	Charlotte Teske (GFR)	2:38:42
1983	Charlotte Teske (GFR)	2:40:13

	Starters	Finishers
1980	1099	556
1981	2917	1801
1982	5389	3496
1983	6000	4383

One athlete responsible for much of the current interest is Eleanora Mendonca. In 1978 she ran with distinction at Boston and New York and in the latter finished fifth in 2:48:45, then the fastest ever by a South American woman. Eloi Rodrigues Schleder is the current fastest male with 2:13:08.

Asia

Marathon activity in the world's largest continent has been spearheaded by Japanese runners who made their first Olympic appearance in 1912. Although it was not until 1951 that the first Asian Games were held (see Games), the forerunner to these celebrations, the Far Eastern Games, were first staged in 1913. The marathon was not part of the programme but was sometimes held as part of an Open meeting which invariably followed the Games. At Tokyo, in 1917 and 1921, marathons were held over 25 miles and won by Genichi Hashimoto (2:31:23.2) and Teruji Hasegawa (2:57:16.4). There were also Japanese winners in 1923 (Seiichi Mori 2:58:00) and 1930 (Fukutaro Shibui 2:36:33) when the distance was 42.195 km. The series closed in 1934. The first Asian Championships were held in Manila in 1973, with South Koreans Je Hyung Cho (2:27:30.2) and Chang Yul Park finishing first and second. Two years later, in Seoul, the defending champion could only place fifth as Japanese Sueki Tanaka (2:32:05.8) and Susumu Sato took their revenge. Third in both races was the Nepalese runner Jit Bahadur Chhetri.

Japan

The first Open marathon was the 1912 Olympic trial at Tokyo on 19 November 1911 over 25 miles and won by Shinzo Kanaguri, three times an Olympian.

Kenny Moore (USA), left, runner-up, watches winner Akio Usami receive the winner's trophy at Fukuoka, 1970. (Asahi Shimbun)

Kanaguri did not finish in 1912 or in 1924 but in between was 16th at Antwerp in an Asian record of 2:48:45.4. In 1912 he dropped out of the race, held on a hot day, and joined a family relaxing in their roadside garden. Suitably refreshed, Kanaguri left and made his way back to Japan without telling any of the Olympic officials.

In 1932, at Los Angeles, Japan had her best ever Olympic marathon and led by Seiichiro Tsuda, sixth in 1928, took the unofficial team prize with fifth, sixth and ninth places, even though the last two runners were Korean-born. Similarly, in 1936 both the gold and silver medallists, Kitei Son and Shoryu Nan, were from Korea and thus the best by a Japanese-born athlete is the silver medal won by the consistent Kenji Kimihara in 1968. Kimihara, who also raced at Tokyo (eighth) and Munich (fifth), was twice Asian Games champion and winner at Boston and in the Poly. Between his breakthrough in December 1962 at Fukuoka and his last major win at Beppu in 1973, he won 13 out of 34 marathons and even now competes successfully in veteran events.

The first national championship race was held at Tokyo on 2 November 1913 over 25 miles and was won by Shizo Kanaguri in 2:31:28, the first of three consecutive wins. The event was not held in 1924, nor in the war years, and most victories have been won by another redoubtable performer, Akio Usami, with five. In addition to a string of successes in Japan, Usami won abroad at Seoul, Manchester, Athens and in the Poly. Since his retirement in 1977, by which time he had won eleven of 37 races over the distance, he has become a TV sports personality. Since 1965 the venue of the championships has alternated between Otsu (even years) and Fukuoka.

OPEN CHAMPIONS (1974 TO 1983)

1974	Akio Usami	2:13:24
1975	Jerome Drayton (Can)	2:10:08.4
1976	Akio Usami	2:15:22
1977	Bill Rodgers (USA)	2:10:55.3
1978	Takeshi Soh	2:15:15.4
1979	Toshihiko Seko	2:10:35
1980	Hiroshi Yuge	2:14:33
1981	Rob de Castella (Aus)	2:08:18
1982	Michio Mizukubo	2:15:23
1983	Toshihiko Seko	2:08:52

In years won by visiting athletes, the best placed Japanese have been: 1975 Takeshi Soh 2:12:52; 1977 Toshihiko Seko 2:15:00.1; 1981 Kunimitsu Itoh 2:09:37.

Usami's other wins were in 1968 (2:13:49), 1971 (2:13:22.8) and 1972 (2:20:24).

Five world records have been set by Japanese marathon runners, including the Korean-born Son. At Tokyo in 1935 records were set by Fusashige

Suzuki (2:27:49 on 31 March), Yasuo Ikenaka (2:26:44 on 3 April) and Kitei Son (2:26:42 on 3 November). Suzuki's reign of three days is the shortest on record whilst Son's time lasted 20 years 39 days as a Japanese best time. Toru Terasawa (2:15:15.8 at Beppu on 17 February 1963) and Morio Shigematsu (2:12:00 in the Poly between Windsor and Chiswick on 12 June 1965) also set world records, the latter only winning one other major race in his career at Boston the same year as his record.

Besides Fukuoka (see Races) other important annually held marathons are those at Beppu, Otsu (the Mainichi) and more recently, Tokyo.

Beppu

Held over a flat course from Beppu to Oita City and back, the first race in 1952 was over 35 km. Two runners have each won the event four times, Toru Terasawa (1963 to 1966) and Kenji Kimihara (1967, 1970-1-3). Terasawa's time in 1963 was a world record and two years later he set an Asian record of 2:14:38. One of the favourites for an Olympic medal in 1964, he was a disappointing 15th in 2:23:09. His best time was 2:13:41 when second to Shigematsu in the 1965 Poly. In 1978 Shigeru Soh, eldest of twins (see Miscellany) set an Asian record of 2:09:05.6 and was well inside Clayton's 1969 world record schedule until the final two kilometres when a strong, cold head wind slowed the already tired runner.

WINNERS (1974 TO 1983)

1974	Yasunori Hamada	2:13:04.2
1975	Kenichi Ozawa	2:13:10.4
1976	Yukio Shigetake	2:14:22.2
1977	Yasunori Hamada	2:13:57
1978	Shigeru Soh	2:09:05.6
1979	Hideki Kita	2:13:29.1
1980	Yutaka Taketomi	2:13:29
1981	Shigeru Soh	2:11:30
1982	Robert Hodge (USA)	2:15:43
1983	Yoshihiro Nishimura	2:13:55

Mainichi

The venue of the Mainichi race first held in 1946 was Osaka until 1962. Tokyo staged the event in 1963-4 and since then the venue has been Otsu. Akio Usami has won the race five times (1968, 1972-4-5-6) whilst overseas winners have been Abebe Bikila (1961-5), Bill Adcocks (1970), Frank Shorter (1973) and Karel Lismont (1977).

WINNERS (1974 TO 1983)

1974	Akio Usami	2:13:24
1975	Akio Usami	2:12:40
1976	Akio Usami	2:15:22
1977	Karel Lismont (Bel)	2:14:08
1978	Takeshi Soh	2:15:15.4
1979	Shigeru Soh	2:13:26

1980	Hiroshi Yuge	2:14:33
1981	Masao Matsuo	2:14:38
1982	Michio Mizukubo	2:15:23
1983	Koshiro Kawaguchi	2:13:22

Tokyo

Two international races held early in 1981 were the first men's marathons to be held in the capital since the 1964 Olympics. The first race was organised by the Yomiuri Shimbun and the second by Sankei to commemorate the Tokyo–New York sister city affiliation. To avoid clashing, it was decided to hold the race in different years. In 1983 Toshihiko Seko set an Asian record of 2:08:38, beating Takeshi Soh by 17 seconds as nine runners bettered 2:13 in a race run in ideal conditions.

First Tokyo women's marathon, 1979. From left: Gillian Adams (GB), Elizabeth Hassall (Aus), Sissel Grottenberg (Nor) and winner Joyce Smith (GB). (Asahi Shimbun)

RESULTS *(JAPANESE UNLESS STATED)*

1981	Yomiuri	1	Hideki Kita	2:12:04
		2	Amelio Bocci (Ita)	2:12:11
		3	Dereje Nedi (Eth)	2:12:14
1981	Sankei	1	Rodolfo Gomez (Mex)	2:11:00
		2	Tommy Persson (Swe)	2:12:07
		3	Randy Thomas (USA)	2:12:31
1982	Yomiuri	1	Vadim Sidorov (Sov)	2:10:33
		2	Hugh Jones (GB)	2:10:41
		3	Stefano Brunetti (Ita)	2:11:22
1983	Sankei	1	Toshihiko Seko	2:08:38
		2	Takeshi Soh	2:08:55
		3	Rodolfo Gomez (Mex)	2:09:12

Women

Tokyo staged its first marathon since the 1964 Olympics, when an all-women marathon was held in the autumn of 1979. The Tokyo race met with a rival promotion in Osaka in January 1982. As with the close proximity of the men's races at Fukuoka and Tokyo the women's races suffer likewise.

RESULTS

TOKYO

1979	1	Joyce Smith (GB)	2:37:48
	2	Gillian Adams (GB)	2:39:28
	3	Sissel Grottenberg (Nor)	2:43:05
1980	1	Joyce Smith (GB)	2:30:27
	2	Jacqueline Gareau (Can)	2:30:58
	3	Gillian Adams (GB)	2:40:53
1981	1	Linda Staudt (Can)	2:34:28
	2	Jane Wipf (USA)	2:38:20
	3	Kiki Sweigart (USA)	2:44:42
1982	1	Zoya Ivanova (Sov)	2:34:26
	2	Yelena Tsukhlo (Sov)	2:38:17
	3	Chantal Langlacé (Fra)	2:42:18
1983	1	Nanae Sasaki	2:37:09
	2	Regina Joyce (Ire)	2:37:44
	3	Mitsue Tanaka	2:38:46

OSAKA

1982	1	Rita Marchisio (Ita)	2:32:55
	2	Carla Beurskens (Hol)	2:34:14
	3	Christa Vahlenseick (GFR)	2:34:42
1983	1	Carey May (Ire)	2:29:23
	2	Charlotte Teske (GFR)	2:35:44
	3	Kath Binns (GB)	2:37:01

India

India made their Olympic entry in 1920 at Antwerp, when Phadeppa Changule finished 19th in 2:50:45.4, only slightly slower than his time of 2:48:49 at Poona the previous November, which was an Asian record. Phadeppa took part in the 1920 Poly but retired after 19 miles. The first national marathon championship took place at Calcutta on 6 February 1938 and was won by Amar Singh in 2:59:17.6. The race was held biennially until 1948, when it became an annual event and was won by Chhota Singh a record eight times. Singh did not finish the 1948 Olympics marathon but won the first Asian Games title in 1951 and this remains India's sole success in an international marathon. Since 1961 the All-India Open and All-India Inter-State marathons are considered to be championship events.

ALL-INDIA WINNERS (1980 TO 1983)

	Open	
1980	Shivnath Singh	2:30:39
1981	Swaroop Singh	2:21:32
1982	Swaroop Singh	2:30:19
1983	Swaroop Singh	2:27:08
	Inter-State	
1980	Swaroop Singh	2:19:27
1981	Vinod Kumar	2:33:09
1982	Seetharam Kukkappa	2:35:34
1983	Vijay Kumar	2:34:14

Although the majority of top runners are employed in either the Armed Forces, Police or Railway, the current Indian record holder Shivnath Singh (2:11:59.4 in the 1978 Open) is a steel plant worker. In the 1982 Asian Games, Kukkappa in third place won India's first medal since 1951 and had earlier won the Inter-State, Inter-Railway and Rath invitational events. The best Olympic performance is the eleventh place by Shivnath Singh in 1976 with a time of 2:16:22.

Korea

Long before Korea's independence their runners had starred in the Olympic marathon. Besides the gold and silver medal exploits of Kee Chung Sohn (see Runners) and Sung Yong Nam in 1936, Eun Bae Kim had placed sixth and Tae Ha Kwon ninth in Los Angeles four years earlier. Following Sohn's triumph, the Dong-A national newspaper, which had sponsored an annual marathon since 1931, published a photograph of the victor on the front page. However, much to the chagrin of the Japanese government the editors had deleted the Rising Sun on Sohn's vest and the incident led to the suspension of the paper for one year. The first marathon in Korea took place in September 1927 at the third Korean sports festival and was won by Bong Ock Ma in 3:29:37. Three years later the first championship was won by Sung Keun Lee in 2:36:50.

From 1945 Korea became a member of the IAAF and within two years Yun Bok Suh had bettered Sohn's world (and Korean) record of 2:26:42 set in 1935, when he won the Boston marathon in 2:25:39. Standing 5ft 1in (1.55m) Suh is the smallest of the marathon world record holders. Suh finished only 27th in the 1948 Olympics but at Helsinki Yoon Chil Choi narrowly missed the bronze medal, finishing fourth in 2:26:36. Four years later in Melbourne Chang Hoon Lee equalled this performance which no subsequent Korean has remotely approached, and in 1958 he won the Asian Games title upsetting the Japanese favourites. In the 1982 Games Yang Kon Kim was an equally surprising winner and in 1983 he finished fifth in the Seoul international marathon with a time of 2:18:20. The national record is 2:16:15, set by Moon Heung Ju in 1974 in the 45th Dong-A marathon.

NATIONAL CHAMPIONS (1980 TO 1983)

1980	Park Yuen Kuan	2:19:58
1981	Lim Sang Kyu	2:19:53
1982	Kyong Yul Choi	2:21:03
1983	Hak Su Kim	2:22:37

In 1982 an international marathon, attracting 7426 starters from 26 nations, was staged at Seoul for the first time since an irregular series of four races terminated in 1969. In 1983, 7118 runners participated in the event, 1059 of whom finished. Organ-

Kee Chung Sohn (Kitei Son) on victory rostrum (left) and as subsequently pictured in Korean newspaper (right). (Korean AAF)

ised by the Korean Broadcasting System the race starts and finishes at the Yoido Plaza.

SEOUL WINNERS

	men	
1982	Lawrie Whitty (Aus)	2:14:33
1983	Tommy Persson (Swe)	2:16:01

	women	
1982	Allison Roe (NZ)	2:43:12
1983	Magda Ilands (Bel)	2:40:55

People's Republic of China

Readmitted to the IAAF in 1978, China's only marathon appearance in the Olympics was in 1936, when their sole runner finished 40th. China made a fresh international start in 1980 at Essonne. Xu Liang, running in tennis shoes only a week after taking part in the world cross-country championships, finished fifth in a national record 2:13:32, having won the national title in 1979 with 2:21:17.

NATIONAL CHAMPIONS (1980 TO 1983)

1980	Yang Jian	2:17:56
1981	Pen Jiazhen	2:20:39
1982	Shan Chanmin	2:19:07
1983	Shan Chanmin	2:17:53

In 1981 China staged an international marathon in Beijing, starting and finishing in Tiananmen Square, which attracted 84 runners from 12 countries, 61 of whom finished. Nineteen nations were represented the following year, when 137 of the 195 starters completed the course. In 1983 a new course was used with the start and finish at the Workers' Stadium.

BEIJING WINNERS

1981	Kjell-Erik Stahl (Swe)	2:15:20
1982	Li Zong Hyong (PRK)	2:14:44
1983	Ron Tabb (USA)	2:18:51

Democratic People's Republic of Korea

Following the division of Korea in 1955, considerable progress has been made by the marathon runners from the north. They made a startling international debut at Kosice in 1975 when Chang Sop Choe (first) and Chun Son Goe were both timed in 2:15:47.8. Goe subsequently finished ahead of his colleague at the same venue in both 1977 and 1978 and also won at Essonne in 1979–80, the latter in a national record 2:10:52. Choe finished 12th in the 1976 Olympics with a time of 2:16:33.2 and then took the silver medal in the 1978 Asian Games, with Goe third. A third member of the marathon squad, Li Zong Hyong, won major overseas victories at Essonne and Beijing in 1982, in addition to the national championship, but was only 34th in the World Championship race at Helsinki in 1983.

Israel

Since 1977 the Sea of Galilee international marathon has been held annually and incorporates the national championship. From 1978 the course, which follows the Sea road, started at Ein Gev and finished at Ginnosar, but since 1981 the runners now turn at Tiberias to finish at Ein Gev. The race is unique in that it is run totally below sea level.

Chang Sop Choe and Chun Son Goe (PRK) finish together at Kosice in 1975. (Kosice)

WINNERS

men

1977	Werner Dörrenbächer (GFR)	2:19:33
1978	Kevin Shaw (Rho)	2:14:02
1979	Werner Dörrenbächer (GFR)	2:18:31
1981	Jim Dingwall (GB)	2:16:19
1981	Colin Kirkham (GB)	2:17:11
1982	Ralf Salzmann (GFR)	2:16:39

women

1977	Zehava Shmueli	3:02:58
1978	Claire Taylor (Rho)	3:08:18
1979	Mazal Shalom	3:16:06
1981	Zehava Shmueli	2:52:45
1981	Gillian Drake (NZ)	2:46:37
1982	Sally Strauss (USA)	2:46:15

The 1980 race was held in January 1981 instead of December 1980. In 1979 the course was 860 m (940 yd) long.

Yair Karni has won the Israeli title four times (1977–9–1981–2) and in the second race of 1981 ran 2:17:34, the current national record.

South East Asia

The first South East Asia Peninsular Games in 1959 did not include a marathon and it was not until the third Games in 1965 that one was included in the programme. In 1977 the event became the South East Asian Games. Burma dominated the first eight marathons, winning all the gold medals and losing only one silver (to Malaysia in 1965). In 1981 Jimmy Dela Torre (Phi) broke the run by winning from Michael (Bur) by 38 seconds. Medal winners by nation: Burma 9 gold, 8 silver, 0 bronze; Philippines 1–1–0; Malaysia 0–1–2; Indonesia and Thailand 0–0–3 each; and Singapore 0–0–2. Most medals won are four by Khin Soe, the region's only sub 2:20 runner (2:19:56.7 in the 1978 Asian Games), and Sumbwegam (Bur) who won two silver medals as well as two gold. Sumbwegam finished 18th at Mexico City in 1968, the best Olympic placing by a marathon runner from the region. A women's race was held for the first time in 1983, Kandasany Jayamani (Singapore) winning in 3:03:46.

CHAMPIONS

1965	Kuala Lumpur	Sumbwegam (Bur)	3:06:20
1967	Bangkok	Myitung Naw (Bur)	2:53:32
1969	Rangoon	Sumbwegam (Bur)	2:31:00.8
1971	Kuala Lumpur	Hla Thein (Bur)	2:40:02
1973	Singapore	Ko Ko (Bur)	2:28:04.2
1975	Bangkok	Khin Soe (Bur)	2:28:18.2
1977	Kuala Lumpur	Khin Soe (Bur)	2:26:18
1979	Jakarta	Khin Soe (Bur)	2:29:11
1981	Manila	Jimmy Dela Torre (Phi)	2:25:50
1983	Singapore	Khin Soe (Bur)	2:32:51

In 1982 international marathons were held for the first time in Manila, Penang, Singapore and Taipeh. Manila winners: 1982 Waldemar Cierpinski (GDR) 2:14:27; 1983 Domingo Tibaduiza (Col) 2:25:01.

Hong Kong

First held in 1977, the annually-held marathon has been international since 1981.

WINNERS

men

1981	Yoshinobu Kitayama (Jap)	2:19:43
1982	Andy Holden (GB)	2:17:43
1983	Jim Dingwall (GB)	2:15:48

women

1981	Kath Binns (GB)	2:45:38
1982	Winnie Ng (HK)	2:50:09
1983	Yuko Gordon (HK)	2:48:08

Arab Nations

International competition for runners from the Arab nations commenced in 1953 with the first Pan Arabian Games. The host nation, Egypt, swept the board in the marathon, taking all three medals. The Games were held every four years up to 1965 but eleven years passed before the fifth and latest celebrations were staged. Medal winners by nation: Morocco 2 gold, 0 silver, 2 bronze; Egypt 1–3–1; Sudan 1–0–1; Tunisia 1–0–0; Syria 0–1–0 and Lebanon 0–1–0.

In 1977 Damascus hosted the first Arab Championships. Medal winners: Iraq 1–1–0; Saudi Arabia and Qatar 1–0–1 each; Libya 1–0–0; Tunisia 0–1–1; Syria and Djibouti 0–1–0 each; and Bahrain 0–0–1.

A successful Pan Arab marathon championship was held in Baghdad in 1978 and was won by Abdel Madjid Mada (Alg) in 2:20:05.4 from John Narat (Sud).

Pan Arabian Games

WINNERS

1953	Alexandria	H Abdel Fattah (Egy)	2:31:49.8
1957	Beirut	A Ben Omar (Tun)	2:54:23.8
1961	Casablanca	Hassan (Mor)	2:44:44
1965	Cairo	Allal Ben Saoudi (Mor)	2:53:24
1976	Damascus	Moussa Madani (Sud)	2:28:18

Arab Championships

WINNERS

1977	Damascus	Shtewi Albishi (SAU)	2:36:44
1979	Baghdad	A El-Sonqy (Lib)	2:34:44
1981	Tunis	Abderrahmane Ayedh (Qat)	2:49:13
1983	Amman	Saadoun Nasser (Irq)	2:38:15

Africa

South Africa was the first nation from the Continent to be represented in an Olympic marathon, when three runners took part in 1904. Not until 1952 did another country, Egypt, send a marathon runner to the Olympics, followed by Kenya and Ethiopia four years later. Two Algerians, Boughera El Ouafi and Alain Mimoun, won gold medals in 1928 and 1956 wearing French colours. Abebe Bikila (Eth) became the first to win two Olympics, both in world record time, in 1960 and 1964. Apart from these celebrations the African Games (see Games) are the main attraction, although erratic in their appearance, as are the African Championships which are scheduled to take place biennially.

African Championships

In 1979 Yetneberk Belete (Eth) defeated the Commonwealth Champion Gidamis Shahanga (Tan), yet three years later neither of the Ethiopian entrants, Kebede Balcha and Dereje Nedi, completed the course. In that second poorly attended race, held in extreme heat, Djibouti athletes took the silver and bronze medals ten minutes behind the winner.

CHAMPIONS

1979	Dakar	Yetneberk Belete (Eth)	2:29:53
1982	Cairo	Juma Ikangaa (Tan)	2:21:05

The best established marathon in Africa is at the East and Central African Championships held for the most part on an annual basis, although not always featuring the marathon. The event started as a pre-war dual nation meet between Kenya and Uganda in 1934.

Ethiopia took all three medals in 1971 and 1976. Since 1970 they have won five gold medals, four silver and four bronze. The Championships were not held in 1973–4 nor was the marathon held in 1975 or 1980. In 1982 the event was held in conjunction with the African Championships, but the marathon was not held in 1983.

EAST AND CENTRAL AFRICAN CHAMPIONS

1968	Dar es Salaam	James Wahome (Ken)	2:23:39
1969	Kampala	John Stephen (Tan)	2:33:06
1970	Nairobi	Yetneberk Belete (Eth)	2:18:48.4
1971	Lusaka	Merawi Gebru (Eth)	2:21:21.2
1972	Dar es Salaam	Joseph Kombole (Zam)	2:39:22.2
1976	Zanzibar	Gebru Gurmu (Eth)	2:13:25

Boughera El Ouafi, Algerian-born Frenchman, entering the stadium to win the 1928 Olympic title and become the first coloured athlete to win a marathon medal.

1977	Mogadisco	Emmanuel Ndiemandoi (Tan)	2:18:54.8
1979	Mombasa	Dereje Nedi (Eth)	2:22:12.6
1981	Mombasa	Getachev Kebede (Eth)	2:17:35.5
1982	Cairo	Juma Ikangaa (Tan)	2:21:05

Another irregularly held event is the Central African Games first staged in 1976 in Gabon. No marathon was held but five years later Jose Ernesto of the host nation Angola won the second Games' race in 2:50:28.

Algeria

The first Algerian to gain an international success was Ahmed Djebellia who won the Polytechnic Harriers' race in 1914, two years after failing to start the Olympic marathon. Algerian-born runners Boughera El Ouafi and Alain Mimoun have won two of France's three gold medals in the Olympics, when they were successful in 1928 and 1956. El

Ouafi went to Paris to find work with the Renault motor industry and rarely competed outside Olympic years. He won the French Championship in 1924, before finishing seventh in Paris and repeated the title win four years later. He turned professional after winning at Amsterdam and beat Joie Ray (USA) by a quarter of a mile in his first race at Madison Square Gardens, NY, winning 4000 dollars in the process.

Mimoun had won five silver medals in Olympic and European track finals before his marathon debut at Melbourne in 1956. He won four IAAF cross-country titles in addition to a record six French marathon championships and continued to compete when well into his fifties. Since attaining independence in 1962, the most outstanding Algerian runner has been Abdel Madjid Mada. Mada won the first Pan Arab marathon championship in 1978 with a time of 2:20:05.2, then finished fourth in the African Games and in 1980 became the sole Algerian to have bettered 2:20 when he ran 2:15:01 at Debno. He was Algeria's first Olympic marathon representative in 1980 but retired after 25 km.

Ethiopia

Ethiopia made their Olympic marathon debut in 1956 four years before Abebe Bikila's outstanding triumph at Rome. Bikila (see Runners) firmly established Ethiopia on the marathon scene with his two Olympic victories in world record times. He had won 12 out of 13 races over the distance before injury forced him to retire from his last two races. Mamo Wolde, who so often ran in the shadow of his illustrious colleague, secured a third successive gold medal for Ethiopia at Mexico City, a feat unprecedented in Olympic history. Wolde was not so consistent as Bikila, yet always managed to find form when it mattered most. In 1972 he won the Olympic bronze medal in his best ever time of 2:15:08.4 and the following year he won the African Games marathon.

The current top Ethiopians are Kebede Balcha and the younger Dereje Nedi, who both made their overseas debut at the Essonne marathon in 1977. Later in the year, Balcha won the Athens popular race before twice winning at Montreal (1979 and 1981) and finishing fourth at London in 1983. Nedi finished seventh in the Moscow Olympics with his then best time of 2:12:44 as Balcha did not finish. Running for the third successive year at Tokyo in 1983, Nedi finished fourth in a new Ethiopian record of 2:10:39, over a minute ahead of Balcha, his fourth win in six international encounters with his colleague. He was a non-finisher at Helsinki, as Balcha took the silver medal behind de Castella with an even faster 2:10:27. In September Balcha won

for the third time at Montreal, lowering the record by 24 seconds to 2:10:03.

Tanzania

Tanzania's first major exponent of the marathon, John Stephen will be remembered as the last finisher in the 1968 Olympics over one hour four minutes behind the winner. The next year he won the East and Central African title and in 1970 finished fifth in the Commonwealth race in 2:15:05, a national record. The best that the nation could manage in the 1978 African Games was seventh by a newcomer, Gidamis Shahanga, who caused a complete upset in winning the Commonwealth gold medal the same year. He improved his best time to 2:14:25 in finishing sixth at Brisbane four years later, after winning the 10000 m track title. At Brisbane, the newly crowned African champion Juma Ikangaa came very close to emulating Shahanga's surprising win at Edmonton, losing to de Castella in the final stages of an epic race. With a time of 2:09:30, Ikangaa became the first African to better 2:10 and at the finish was only 12 seconds behind the winner. At Tokyo in 1983 he finished fifth in 2:10:54, splitting the two Ethiopians Nedi and Balcha, but slipped to a lowly 15th at Helsinki in 2:13:11. Fifth in the World Championships was Agapius Masong in a fast 2:10:42, his third successive improvement in 1983, after finishing fourth at Houston (2:13:07) and second at Stockholm (2:11:54).

South Africa

South Africa's Amateur Athletic Union, one of the oldest, was founded in 1894 and she was first represented at the Olympics in 1904. The first 'marathon' over a distance of 22 miles (35 km) was held at Johannesburg on 11 April 1908 and was followed eleven days later by the first Union Championship over 25 miles at Cape Town. The winner of both these races was Kenneth Kane McArthur, born in County Antrim, Ireland, who had emigrated to the country in 1901 and began running five years later. He did not compete in the London Olympics but Charles Hefferon, who did not finish the Cape Town event, was a fine second to Johnny Hayes. Returning home, Hefferon won his 13th national title in the inaugural ten-mile track championship early in 1909 and then turned professional. McArthur, after winning his one and only ten-mile title, competed in the 1912 Olympics, securing the gold medal after a tough battle with colleague Christian Gitsham (see Games) who was a non-finisher eight years later. In 1910 McArthur had travelled to Europe to compete in the Poly and at Athens but both races were cancelled. There is no

Ken McArthur (SA) nears the finish of the 1912 Olympic race in which he maintained his unbeaten record over the distance.

record of McArthur having lost a marathon up to the time of his Olympic victory.

KEN McARTHUR—CAREER RECORD

11 Apr	1908	Johannesburg		2:20:30	(1)
22 Apr	1908	Cape Town	NC	3:18:27.4	(1)
4 Sep	1909	Johannesburg		3:03:54.2	(1)
25 Oct	1909	Durban (25¼ miles)		2:44:36	(1)
5 Nov	1910	Cape Town		2:42:58.2	(1)
14 Jul	1912	Stockholm	OG	2:36:54.8	(1)

In the 1936 Olympics, Johannes Lodwyck Coleman and Henry Alfred 'Jackie' Gibson ran well against stiff European and Japanese opposition. Coleman, four years the senior, finished sixth, a year after making his debut in the Natal Championship which he won for the first of five consecutive years, and Gibson eighth. There was intense rivalry between the two, with Coleman almost unbeatable at sea-level but Gibson the better at altitude, and each won three national titles in the marathon. Gibson set an African record of 2:30:45 in 1937, the world's second fastest that year, but it was Coleman who won the 1938 Empire race (with Gibson third) and

Johannes Coleman and Sid Luyt (SA) lead world record holder Yun Bok Suh (Kor) at London Olympics, 1948. (AP)

he finished fourth at London ten years later. In six head to head encounters, Coleman won four. In the three Empire Games of the 1950s, South Africa captured four medals, although none of them gold, with Johannes Barnard, three times marathon champion, taking one silver and one bronze. In 1971 Ferdi le Grange was the first South African to better 2:20 and he improved the record to 2:12:47 in taking his second national title in 1974 before retiring. In the Manchester Maxol marathons of 1972–3 he placed eighth and fourth respectively and was winner of the Belgian Open Championship in 1972. In 1983 Johann Dreyer won the Bellville race in his marathon debut with a time of 2:11:42, four seconds faster than the previous national record set by Johnny Halberstadt in Chicago, 1982. This is the fastest marathon yet run on the African continent.

The annual title race has been held regularly since 1928, except for the war years. From 1974 to 1977 there were two races, one an Open (to all nationalities) and the other a Closed event. From 1962 to 1971 a 'non-white' championship was held annually. Other regular major events include the Western Province (first held in 1933) and Natal (1934) state races, and the Interprovincial Championship (1968).

OPEN CHAMPIONS (1974 TO 1983) *(SA UNLESS STATED)*

1974	**Ferdi le Grange**	**2:12:47**
1975	**Mike Tagg (GB)**	**2:19:47**
1976	**Gabashane Rakabaele (Les)**	**2:23:49**
1977	**Brian Chamberlain**	**2:19:20**
1978	**Johnny Halberstadt**	**2:19:36**
1979	**Gabashane Rakabaele (Les)**	**2:12:27**
1980	**Thompson Magawane**	**2:12:50**
1981	**Mark Plaatjies**	**2:16:17**
1982	**Gabashane Rakabaele (Les)**	**2:17:36**
1983	**Kevin Flanegan**	**2:16:21**

The first South Africans to finish, in years won by visiting athletes, were: 1975 Willie Farrell 2:20:23; 1976 Andrew Greyling 2:23:53; 1979 Halberstadt 2:13:10; 1982 Vivian van der Sandt 2:18:10.

Oceania

Australia

Australia was one of the five countries to be represented in the inaugural 1896 Olympic marathon. The first marathon in Australia was organised by the Sydney YMCA and held on 12 April 1909 over 26 miles 385 yd; it was won by Andrew Sime in 3:05:30.2. Four months later, on 21 August, the first championship race was held at Brisbane and drew a field of twenty-six. Andrew Wood won the title in 2:59:15.4 with Sime third, but the latter came back to form, winning the first Victorian Championship (9 October 1909) in 3:04:26 and the second New South Wales title (6 June 1910) with an improved 2:54:30. National title races were held intermittently until 1949, when it then became a biennial event excepting Olympic years. Two runners, Derek Clayton (1967–8, 1971–3) and John Farrington (1969–70, 1974–5) have each won four titles since the championship became an annual event in 1966.

NATIONAL CHAMPIONS (1974 TO 1983)

1974	John Farrington	2:17:23
1975	John Farrington	2:17:20
1976	Vic Anderson	2:23:28.6
1977	Bob Wallace	2:20:11.2
1978	Jim Langford	2:19:29
1979	Rob de Castella	2:13:23
1980	Lawrie Whitty	2:19:00
1981	Garry Bentley	2:16:58
1982	Bob Wallace	2:16:02
1983	John Stanley	2:17:03.7

Overseas athletes won in 1982: Fumiaki Abe (Jap) 2:15:56.2 and 1983: Ron Tabb (USA) 2:10:53.5.

Derek Clayton (see Runners) finished seventh in the Mexico City Olympics for Australia's best placing in that event. In 1967 he became the first runner to better 2:10 in winning the Fukuoka marathon on 3 December in 2:09:36.4 and improved on that time with 2:08:33.6 at Antwerp on 30 May 1969. Despite recurring injury problems, Clayton won 14 of 22 marathons between 1965 and 1974. Australia's first appearance in the Empire Games was in 1938, when two of their three runners took the last two places, but after the war there was a steady improvement culminating in Dave Power's fine win in 1958. Four years later he finished second, which was at the time the nearest a defending champion had come to retaining a major marathon title. In 1982 Rob de Castella (see Runners) won the Commonwealth gold medal in 2:09:18, the fastest time ever achieved in a race of that calibre. The previous year at Fukuoka on 6 December, he recorded a world record of 2:08:18 for an out and back course, only five seconds outside Alberto Salazar's time on a point to point route. De Castella convincingly beat Salazar at Rotterdam in early 1983, prior to becoming World Champion at Helsinki.

Of the annually held State Championships, that of New South Wales first held in 1909 and regularly from 1937 is the oldest established. The Victorian title (1909) became an annual event from 1946. All-comers and international races are also held at Canberra, Melbourne and Sydney.

The Canberra event is staged over a three-lap course and was first run in 1976, the fastest time being set by Graeme Kennedy (2:15:16) in 1981.

Melbourne's Big M race currently attracts in the region of 5000 runners and has been won three times by Andy Lloyd (1979–80–1). Bill Rodgers (USA) won the fifth race of the series in 1982, in a time of 2:11:08 over a flat point to point course, and Juma Ikangaa (Tan) won in 1983 with 2:13:50.

The newest race at Sydney drew 2500 starters in 1983 and was won by Ron Tabb (USA) in 2:10:53.5. Starting in north Sydney, the route crosses the harbour bridge and runs due south to Botany Bay and the 30 km point. The course then returns along the same road to the finish near the Sydney Athletic Field. The international field included runners from New Zealand, United States, Canada, France and Great Britain, 2137 of whom finished.

New Zealand

The first marathon to be held in New Zealand took place on 14 July 1909 between Riverton and Invercargill and was won by D Stewart in 3:22:30; yet it was another 30 years before the first championship was staged. The race was held on 11 March 1939 at Napier and Clarrie Gibbons was the winner in 2:44:57. Ray Puckett, an Olympian in 1960 and 1964, has won most marathon championships with five, whilst the oldest winner is John 'Jack' Foster who was 43 years 287 days of age when he won in 1976.

NATIONAL CHAMPIONS (1974 TO 1983)

1974	John Robinson	2:15:03.8
1975	Tony Reaveley	2:19:54.6
1976	Jack Foster	2:16:27
1977	Terry Manners	2:20:40
1978	Paul Ballinger	2:17:33
1979	Tony Good	2:18:47.3
1980	Don Greig	2:17:08
1981	Paul Ballinger	2:17:28

| 1982 | Trevor Wright | 2:19:34 |
| 1983 | Graham Macky | 2:21:22 |

Paul Ballinger (NZ) wins 1982 Fukuoka race in national record time. (Popperfoto)

New Zealand's entry into the Olympic marathon did not come about until 1956, six years after their debut in the Empire Games. Since then their impact, for a nation of just over 3 000 000 people, has been an exciting one. Barry Magee (1960) and Mike Ryan (1968) both won bronze medals, and Foster a silver in the 1974 Commonwealth race at Christchurch.

Both Magee and Ryan have also won the famed Asahi classic in Japan, Magee being the first to better 2:20 in the event in 1960 and Ryan featuring in the closest ever finish six years later. These two accomplished athletes were joined in 1982 by Paul Ballinger, whose winning time of 2:10:15 was a national record. In finishing second to Ian Thompson in 1974, Foster's time of 2:11:18.6 is still the fastest by a veteran runner (over 40 years of age). Foster took up running at the age of 33 after a cycling career and was 37 when he made his international debut in 1969 at Toronto. There he won the following year. Since then he has scored major wins at Kyoto, Westwood CA, and Honolulu and has bettered 2:20 in 12 races since reaching 40.

Track stars Theodorus 'Dick' Quax and Rodney Dixon both made startling headway in their first serious attempts at the marathon. Quax won at Auckland and Eugene (2:10:47) in 1980, a year after finishing third at the latter venue, and Dixon set an event record of 2:11:21 at Auckland in 1982. Rod Dixon's second full marathon was a memorable one. At New York in 1983 he became the first non-USA winner with a new national record of 2:08:59, taking the lead in the last quarter of a mile.

Among the women, Allison Roe (see Runners) became the first overseas runner to win at both Boston and New York the same year (1981), setting a world record in the process, and Lorraine Moller (see Miscellany) was the first to win the annual Avon international race on two occasions.

Besides the national championship event, five annual marathons have gained in popularity over the years. The most established is the Fletcher marathon around Lake Rotorua, first held in 1965 and won by Jack Foster four times. The Peoples marathon at Wiri, Auckland, has been staged since 1979 and in 1981 Kevin Ryan won with a record 2:12:11. In 1981 two races were held at Hamilton and at Christchurch. Currently the most popular of the marathons is the City of Auckland international event.

AUCKLAND WINNERS *(NZ UNLESS STATED)*

men

1977*	Dave Chettle (Aus)	2:02:24
1978	Ian Thompson (GB)	2:13:49
1980	Dick Quax	2:13:12
1981	Dave Cannon (GB)	2:12:53
1982	Rod Dixon	2:11:21
1983	Alain Lazare (NC)	2:14:50

Seppo Nikkari (Fin) leads Jack Foster (NZ), Akio Usami (Jap), Frank Shorter (USA, winner) and John Farrington (Aus) at the turn in Fukuoka, 1971. (Asahi Shimbun)

	women	
1977*	Gillian File	2:42:01
1978	Gillian File	2:44:11
1980	Joan Benoit (USA)	2:31:23
1981	Allison Roe	2:36:16
1982	Robin Hames	2:44:37
1983	Robin Hames	2:48:10

* In 1977 the course was 39.726 km (24.7 miles).

Pacific Islands

The marathon was first included in the South Pacific Games at the third Games at Port Moresby in 1969.

Alain Lazare (NC), the Pacific's outstanding distance runner. (Tony Isaacs)

The first marathon in the area was held at Apia, Western Samoa, on 22 March 1969 and won by Amani Tapusoa in 2:41:50 which lasted as a regional record for six years. The first championship race, on 5 April 1969 at Port Moresby, Papua New Guinea, was won by Gari Vagi in 2:46:23.6. The outstanding marathon runner of the area has been Alain Lazare from Noumea, New Caledonia, who has won 18 gold medals in South Pacific Games and championships on track and road. His best time of 2:12:51 was achieved in winning the 1983 French Championship race. Games medal winners by nation: New Caledonia 5–0–1; Papua New Guinea 0–4–2; French Polynesia 0–1–0; Nauru and Fiji 0–0–1 each.

WINNERS

1969	Port Moresby	Julien Gohe (NC)	2:49:18.8
1971	Pirae, Tahiti	Andre Petersen (NC)	2:50:50
1975	Tumon, Guam	Alain Lazare (NC)	2:36:35
1979	Suva, Fiji	Alain Lazare (NC)	2:30:57
1983	Apia	Alain Lazare (NC)	2:28:29.6

In 1976 (Noumea, NC) and 1978 (Pirae) South Pacific Championships were held, Lazare winning both marathons in 2:34:00 and 2:31:10 respectively. In 1981 a mini-Games was introduced in lieu of the championships, thus providing the smaller nations with an opportunity to stage an event within their financial and administrative capabilities. Held at Honiara, Solomon Islands, the winner was Shri Chand (Fij) in 2:36:15.

The 1980 Port Moresby marathon pre-race favourite Tau John Tokwepota (PNG) woke on the morning of the race to find that his car had been stolen during the night. He had no option other than to run the 5 km to the start, where the race had commenced 5 min 18 sec earlier. Tokwepota set off in pursuit, caught the leaders and finished in a national record 2:39:43. He was rewarded with a trip to the Honolulu marathon where he improved to 2:28:13.

Successful international marathons have been held annually at Suva (since 1979) and Tahiti (since 1981).

Miscellany

Age

The oldest runner to have won a gold medal in the Olympic Games is the Ethiopian Mamo Wolde who was 36 years 130 days old when he was first in 1968. In the European Championships in 1950, Jack Holden (GB) was 43 years 158 days and is the oldest known winner of a major regional championship marathon. Earlier in 1950 he won the Empire Games race when 42 years 335 days old, and later that year became the oldest runner to win a British marathon title at 43 years 126 days.

The oldest winner of a major national title is the Algerian-born Alain Mimoun (Fra) who was 45 years 176 days old when he won his sixth national title at Paris in 1966.

The oldest runner to run a sub 2:20 marathon is Jack Foster (NZ) who recorded 2:17:28.9 in finishing sixth in the 1978 New York race at the age of 46 years 167 days. He holds the fastest time by a veteran (over 40 years of age) of 2:11:18.6 in finishing second in the 1974 Commonwealth Games marathon at the age of 41 years 268 days.

The oldest world record setter is Jim Peters (GB), who was 35 years 262 days when he set his fourth such record from Windsor to Chiswick on 26 June 1954, his last completed marathon, in a time of 2:17:39.4.

The oldest female runner to complete a marathon is Ruth Rothfarb who made her debut over the distance in 1981 at the age of 80. She did not start running until aged 72 and recorded her best time of 5:29:06 at Miami in January 1982.

The fastest ever veteran female marathon runner (over 35 years) is Joyce Smith (GB) who ran 2:29:43 at London in 1982 at the age of 44 years 216 days, the oldest British woman to set any record in athletics. She had made her marathon debut in 1978 at the age of 41 years 255 days, setting a national record and winning the national title in the process.

Tom Richards (GB), silver medallist in 1948, oldest British Olympic medallist at 38 years 140 days. (H W Neale)

The oldest runner to win a medal in major races is Väinö Muinonen (Fin) who was 47 years 235 days old when he won the silver medal in the 1946 European Championships. In the Olympics, the oldest medal winner is Mamo Wolde (Eth) who was 40 years 90 days when third in 1972.

The youngest Olympic gold medallist is Juan Zabala (Arg) who was 20 years 300 days in 1932, whilst the youngest Olympic medal winner is Ernst Fast (Swe) who was 19 years 179 days when finishing third in 1900.

The youngest medal winner in the European Championships is Karel Lismont (Bel) who was 22 years 160 days old at Helsinki in 1971 when he won the title in his third race over the distance. The youngest medal winner in the Commonwealth Games marathon is Gidamis Shahanga (Tan) who was 24 days short of his 21st birthday when he won the gold medal in 1978.

It is reported that the gold medal winner of the 1981 South East Asian Games marathon, Jimmy Dela Torre (PHI), was under 18 years old at the time of his victory, but to date this has not been confirmed.

Kirk Pfeffer (USA) was 18 years 165 days old when he ran 2:17:44 in 1975, the fastest by a junior runner (under 19 years) at the time. A faster time of 2:16:56 was set by So Chang Sik (NK) at Beijing in 1982. His age was given as 18 years, but his birthday was later shown at Helsinki as 14 June 1959.

Of the world record breakers, the three Japanese who set such times in 1935 were all in their 22nd year, and only 21 days separated them at the time of their records. Yasuo Ikenaka was the youngest at 21 years 31 days, followed by Fusashige Suzuki (21 years 45 days) and finally Olympic champion elect Kitei Son (21 years 66 days).

The youngest national champion is Monika Frisch who was 12 years 309 days old when she won the 1983 Austrian women's championship in 3:10:03. It should be pointed out that running marathons under the age of 18 is medically not recommended.

Precocious American youngsters are recorded as having run marathons from at least the age of five

The oldest male runner to complete a marathon is the Greek runner Dimitris Iordanidis, who was 98 years old when he ran from Marathon to Athens in the Popular marathon in 1976, recording a time of 7:33:00. He holds the fastest time for anyone over the age of 90 as two years previously he covered the same course in 6:42:00.

Dimitris Iordanidis (Gre), oldest known marathon runner. (Greece AAF)

years (boys) and six years (girls). Bucky Cox, from Texas, is reported as having run 5:29:09 at the age of five in 1978, improving to 3:40:04 two years later, when seven years old. Among the girls, no less impressive is the achievement of Californian Mary Etta Boitano who, in 1970 when six years old, was timed in 4:27:32.

Twins

The fastest male twins are Shigeru and Takeshi Soh (Jap) who have best times of 2:09:05.6 (1978) and 2:08:55 (1983) respectively. The Sohs were born prematurely on 9 January 1953 with Takeshi (2200 gr/4 lb 14 oz) arriving five minutes before Shigeru (1800 gr/3 lb 15 oz). According to Japanese custom the first-born is the youngest. The twins made their debut at Nobeoka on 4 March 1973, since when Shigeru has taken part in 20 marathons, winning four, and Takeshi 22, winning three. Shigeru has finished ahead of Takeshi in eleven of the 19 marathons in which they have both competed.

The fastest female twins are Sylviane and Patricia Puntous (Can) with best times of 2:42:53.1 in finishing together at Orlando, FL on 20 February 1983. Sylviane, born two minutes before her sister, is right handed and Patricia, left handed, but the only distinguishing physical difference is that Sylviane has a tooth on the right side which is smaller, whilst Patricia has a tooth on the left side which is smaller. They were born on 28 December 1960.

Altitude

The highest altitude at which the Olympic Games have been held is 2240 m (7349 ft), at Mexico City in 1968. The same venue was used for the Pan American Games in 1955, the first time a major Games had been held at altitude and marathons were held both times. The highest venue for a regional championship which has catered for a marathon was at Quito at an altitude of 2850 m (9350 ft) on the

occasion of the 1969 South American Championships.

The highest venue for a regularly held marathon is at 4150 m (13 615 ft) above La Paz, where the Inca's marathon is staged. The fastest time recorded there is 2:36:56 by Ricardo Condori (Bol) on 27 April 1980.

The highest altitude that a sub 2:20 marathon has been run is at Addis Ababa at 2365 m (7728 ft) and in the 1972 Olympic trial Yetneberk Belete won in 2:14:52, fastest time recorded at that venue.

Ethiopian marathon in progress at Addis Ababa. (Don Morley)

The fastest time recorded at an altitude of over 1000 m (3281 ft) is 2:12:33 by Gabashane Rakabaele (Les) at Nigel (1754 m/5725 ft) on 4 July 1976.

The lowest altitude at which a race has been staged is 200 m (660 ft) below sea-level, at the Sea of Galilee, where an international marathon has been held annually since 1977.

Latitude

The most northerly venue for a national championship marathon is Oulu, 65 degrees north, where the 1964 Finnish event took place. The 1971 New Zealand title race was held at Invercargill which, at 47 degrees south, is the most southerly venue.

The most northerly annually held marathon is the Mayor's Midnight Run at Anchorage, Alaska, at 61 degrees north. From 1963 to 1979 the University of Alaska at Fairbanks (65 degrees north) staged the Equinox marathon until it was discontinued.

The Arctic Circle marathon at Rovaniemi (Fin) has been held annually since 1977. Although the start and finish at Rovaniemi is 10 km south of the Arctic Circle, the race crosses the zone on the out and back course.

Since 1979 a small localised marathon has been held each July at Nanisivik on Baffin Island, North West Territories, Canada. Named the Midnight Sun race, it is 450 m north of the Arctic Circle at 73 degrees north.

Two regional championships have been held within one degree of the Equator in which a marathon has been run, and both took place in 1969. Kampala to the north hosted the East and Central African Championships, whilst Quito to the south held the South American. **The nearest to the Equator that the Olympics have been held** has been at Mexico City in 1968 at 19 degrees north.

Winning Margins

Spiridon Louis' winning margin of 7 min 13 sec in 1896 remains **the biggest winning margin in the Olympics**, whilst in a major regional Games marathon Delfo Cabrera (Arg) won the first Pan American Games title in 1951 with a margin of 9 min 59.8 sec. In the fifth Pan Arabian Games marathon at Damascus in 1976 Moussa Madani (Sud) won by a massive 30 min 32.3 sec from Khalife Oteich (Syr) and this is the greatest margin on record in an international Games marathon. The record margin in the USA Championship marathon is 19 min 45.8 sec, which 'Buddy' Edelen held over Adolf Gruber (Aut) at the finish of the 1964 race

held in extreme heat. In the AAA event of 1934 Donald McNab Robertson had finished and accepted his prize before the arrival of Bert Norris 13 min 10 sec later.

At Antwerp in 1920, Hannes Kolehmainen (Fin) and Jüri Lossmann (Est) were involved in **the closest ever finish of an Olympic marathon** with 12.8 sec dividing them at the tape. Lossmann always maintained that he would have had a better chance of winning, had any of the officials bothered to accompany him instead of taking a holiday as he alleged. In other major Games marathons, 1.5 sec separated Leonid Moseyev (Sov) and his colleague Nikolay Penzin at the finish of the 1978 European Championship race for the narrowest winning margin recorded. Moseyev was also involved in a close finish the next year at the pre-Olympic Games marathon at Moscow, when the first three were all given the same time of 2:13:20. The actual times recorded were Moseyev 2:13:19.6, Shigeru Soh (Jap) 2:13:19.8, Viktor Zubov (Sov) 2:13:20 and fourth placed Satymkul Dzhumunazarov (Sov), destined to be the 1980 bronze medallist, one second behind in 2:13:21. In all, the six seconds between first and sixth finisher accounted for **the closest overall result in such a marathon**.

The stadium crowd at Panama City for the 1973 Bolivar Games witnessed a near tie between the three Colombian medal winners, but there the judges timed them to within a tenth of a second of each other. Gilberto Serna (2:35:11.6), Hector Rodriguez (2:35:11.7) and Martin Pabon (2:35:11.8), the reigning South American champion, were placed in that order. The closest finale to an AAA marathon took place in 1946, when Squire Yarrow edged out Donald McNab Robertson by two tenths of a second in 2:43:14.4, thus depriving the latter of a seventh title. On entering the White City stadium, the two runners found that the steeplechase final was still in progress and they were forced to manoeuvre between officials, runners and hurdles in order to reach the tape.

Since 1908, when the times of all Olympic marathon finishers were first recorded, **the greatest margin between first and last** was 1 hr 28 min 01.8 sec between gold medallist Abebe Bikila (Eth) and Albert Massaquoi (Lib), 62nd and last at Rome in 1960. The slowest recorded time by a finisher in the Olympics was 4:22:45 by George Lister (Can), 27th and last in 1908, but there is no doubt that this time was exceeded by finishers in earlier celebrations.

The eighth and last recorded finisher in 1900 at Paris, Ron McDonald (USA), had won the Boston marathon in 1898; Kurao Hiroshima (Jap), 33rd and last at Melbourne in 1956 had won at Beppu that year and would win again there in 1958, as well as record two wins in the Asahi. John Stephen

(Tan), 57th and last at Mexico City in 1968, had finished sixth in the 1962 Commonwealth marathon and improved to fifth in 1970.

In the 1951 Asian Games marathon at New Delhi, the sixth and last finisher Oichi Noda (Jap) found

Hannes Kolehmainen (Fin) and Jüri Lossmann (Est, 680) after closest ever Olympic marathon finish.

that everyone in the stadium had gone home except the two officials left to time him in 3:45:00, over one hour behind the winner.

At the 1979 Pan American Games, held at San Juan, the last finisher Wallace Williams (US Virgin Islands) found the stadium door locked on his arrival. His time of 3:22:12 in 15th place left him 38 min

56 sec behind the 14th man. He made great inroads at Boston in 1982 with a national record 2:43:17 but later that year he was again last, this time in the Central American and Caribbean Games marathon.

In complete contrast to Williams at San Juan, Johannes Coleman (SA), running in the 1938 Natal provincial marathon, arrived at the finish at Alexander Park, Pietermaritzburg to find the chief time-keeper in a nearby tea-room. No one had expected his arrival so soon and his own watch showed a time of 2:23:00 on entering the Park which meant that he may well have been deprived of a new world record.

The smallest margin between an Olympic winner and the last finisher is 34 min 24.4 sec between Delfo Cabrera (Arg) and 30th placed Stan Jones (GB) in 1948. In the 1982 European Championship race 20 min 15 sec separated first and last (25th) finisher, the smallest margin since the inaugural race of that series in 1934, when the margin between the eight finishers was 18 min 40.4 sec.

Tragedies

To date there have been just two tragedies in major Games marathons. In the 1912 Olympic race at Stockholm the young Portuguese champion Francisco Lazaro, fresh from his third successive national title win, collapsed in the final stages. Only 20 years 235 days old, Lazaro was rushed to the Seraphim Hospital where he died from heat exhaustion early the next day.

In the East and Central African Championship marathon at Nairobi in 1970 John Mwanika (Uga), bronze medallist the year before, was knocked down by a motor vehicle and killed. The race continued and Ethiopian runners captured the first four places ahead of three Kenyan runners.

Left and right:
Francisco Lazaro's entry form and doctor's fitness certificate to run the 1912 Olympic marathon. (Rooney Magnusson)

EMOTTAGEN DEN 4 - JUN. 1912

FORMULAIRE D'INSCRIPTION
POUR
LES SPORTS ATHLÉTIQUES

(DANS LE STADE, DU SAMEDI 6 AU LUNDI 15 JUILLET 1912)

LES ENGAGEMENTS SONT REÇUS JUSQU'AU 6 JUIN 1912.

Par conséquent l'inscription devra parvenir au Comité Suédois d'Organisation au plus tard le 6 Juin 1912, avant minuit. *Les engagements arrivés après cette date (voir l'exception au revers, art. 11) ne sont pas reçus.*

L'engagement doit être *dactylographié* ou *très lisiblement écrit en caractères latins.* Chaque formulaire n'est valable que pour UN concurrent et UN concours.

Pour l'inscription aux concours d'équipes, on devra remplir des FORMULAIRES SPÉCIAUX pour chacun des participants et des réserves de l'équipe; un AUTRE FORMULAIRE comprenant *toute l'équipe* (participants et réserves) sera rempli par l'organisation régissant les sports athlétiques dans le pays.

1. CONCOURS	*Marathone*
2. NATION, que le concur. rent représente	*Portugal*
3. NOMS et PRÉNOMS du concurrent (Prière d'écrire lisiblement.)	*Lazaro Francisco*
4. DATE DE NAISSANCE	*Le 8 janvier 1891*
5. LIEU DE NAISSANCE	*Lisbonne*
6. Date de la NATURALISATION (A remplir dans le cas où le concurrent n'appartient pas par sa naissance à la nation qu'il représente mais s'est qualifié de naturalisé — voir l'art. 6 des Dispositions Générales des Jeux Olympiques.)	

Déclaration à signer par le concurrent:

Je soussigné déclare que les renseignements ci-dessus sont exacts et que je suis amateur selon la définition suivante:

Amateur est celui qui n'a jamais:
a) concouru pour des prix en espèces ou en vue de bénéfices pécuniers, ou retiré un profit économique quelconque de l'exercice de son sport;
b) concouru avec des professionnels;
c) contre rémunéré ou enseigné dans aucune branche de sport athlétique;
c) vendu, mis en gage, loué ou pour de l'argent montré un prix gagné.

et je m'engage à me conformer aux Dispositions et Règlements prescrits pour les Jeux Olympiques à Stockholm en 1912.

Je m'engage également, pour le cas où je remporterais une Coupe Challenge, à fournir la garantie stipulée à l'art. 16 des Dispositions Générales des Jeux Olympiques.

Signature du concurrent:

Francisco Lazaro

Déclaration à signer par l'organisation qui régit les Sports Athlétiques dans le pays:

La déclaration ci-dessous doit être signée par l'organisation régissant les Sports Athlétiques qui inscrit le concurrent ou, à défaut d'une telle organisation, par le Comité Olympique compétent.

Nous certifions que les renseignements ci-dessus sont exacts, autant que nous le sachions, et nous inscrivons le concurrent au concours indiqué plus haut

Signé Par le Comité Olympique Le Portugais Le Président

T. S. V. P.

Starting Times

The earliest time that a major Games marathon has started was at 5.30 am for the 1966 Commonwealth Games marathon at Kingston (Jam). A similar starting time was used in Kuala Lumpur for the 1977 South East Asian Games race. Of current annually held marathons the one at Guam starts at 4 am.

The latest start for an international marathon was 8.20 pm for the first Canadian National Exhibition marathon at Toronto in 1969. It was held at that time so that the finish would not interfere with stadium entertainment starring Bob Hope, and each of the runners had an individual police motor cycle escort.

Games' officials have not always been sympathetic towards the needs of the marathon runners when arranging a starting time. A temperature of 39°C (102°F) was reported at the 1900 Olympic race in Paris. However, later inconsiderations were recorded as recently as 1982, when the Asian Games race at New Delhi started at 1.30 pm in very hot weather with the temperature showing 29°C

Toronto marathon 1969. From left: Jeff Julian and Jack Foster (NZ), Alastair Wood (GB).

(84°F) and at the African Championship race a high of 34°C (93°F) was reached. Despite a 6 am start, the temperature reached 43°C (110°F) at Jullunder (Ind) in 1979 but even this extreme heat did not stop Shivnath Singh from setting a new Indian record of 2:11:59.4.

Debuts

Currently the fastest time recorded in a marathon debut is 2:09:08 by Geoff Smith (GB) in finishing second in the 1983 New York marathon, a British record.

In the Olympic Games, there is no record of the following gold medal winners ever having run a competitive marathon before: Michel Théato (1900), Delfo Cabrera (1948), Emil Zatopek (1952) and Alain Mimoun (1956).

At Kosice in 1931, Juan Zabala (Arg) made his debut in pouring rain and won by a record 14 min

Jubilant Rod Dixon (NZ) at the finish of the 1983 New York marathon and a fallen Geoff Smith in second place. Dixon became the first non-United States runner to win the race, whilst Smith's time of 2:09:08 was a new British record and the fastest ever first marathon recorded (Keith Meyers/ NYT Pictures)

Bobby Mills (GB) set a British record in his marathon debut in 1920, after winning the DCM in the First World War.

Rosa Mota (Por) winning the 1982 European Championship in her marathon debut. So far she has won three of her four races improving her time in each of them. (Mark Shearman)

37 sec margin from Jozsef Galambos (Hun) in a new South American record time of 2:33:19. At the same venue in 1947, Charles Heirendt (Lux) won in his first and only attempt at the marathon, his time of 2:36:06 lasting as a national record until 1966.

Notable marathon debuts by British runners include Bobby Mills' British record of 2:37:40.4 in winning the 1920 Poly, after he had been awarded the Distinguished Conduct Medal for services in the First World War; Jim Peters' achievement in the same race which incorporated the AAA title in 1951 with a national record 2:29:24; and Ian Thompson who in 1973 at Harlow won the national championship in 2:12:40 which remained the fastest debut time until 1980.

No male runner has set a world record on their marathon debut, although Alexis Ahlgren (Swe) had only run 40 km or 40.2 km events common to the Nordic areas prior to winning the 1913 Poly in 2:36:06.6, a world record for the full marathon. Harry Barrett (GB) and Alberto Salazar (USA) both managed the feat in their second marathon. Grete Waitz (Nor) not only set a world record in her first marathon but followed up with similar records in her second and third races over the distance, and all at the same venue New York between 1978 and 1980.

Rosa Mota (Por) won the first European Championship marathon for women over the tough Marathon to Athens course in 1982 in her first ever marathon.

In 1979 Joyce Smith (GB) captured the national title in a record 2:41:37 on her marathon debut.

Participants

The greatest number of official runners to start a marathon is 16 500 at London in 1983. Of these a staggering 15 776 (95.6%) completed the race.

In each of the four New York marathons held since

Former world heavyweight boxing champion Ingemar Johansson (Swe), running at Stockholm 1981. (Stockholm marathon)

1980, there have been over 14 000 official starters on each occasion, the most being in 1983 when there were 15 193.

The biggest field in an Olympic marathon is 74, which occurred at both the 1968 and 1980 events. The smallest number to start since 1904, when the first such accurate assessment could be made, was in 1932 at Los Angeles when 29 started the race. Of these, twenty finished and it was only in 1904, when 14 finished, that there have been less.

The smallest field in a major regional Games marathon occurred at Jakarta in 1962 at the Asian Games. In most oppressive heat just eight athletes started, only four of whom finished.

Whilst it is virtually impossible to calculate the number of spectators on the marathon course for any one race, it has been estimated that between 2.5 and 3 million watched the 1982 New York race. Similarly, an estimated 1.5 million viewed the all women's race at Osaka in 1981.

The largest number of stadium spectators to be present at the finish of the marathon was 100 000 at Berlin in 1936 when it was reported that the stadium was full.

Roger Bourbon (USA), running in the London race. (All Sport)

Since 1980, when the number of entrants to the popular marathons began to escalate towards and then overtake the ten thousand mark, sports personalities and celebrities as well as general fun runners have participated. Many of them run in order to raise money for charitable organisations.

Among other sportsmen, Ingemar Johansson (Swe) and Floyd Patterson (USA), who fought each other three times for the world heavyweight boxing championship, ran in the 1982 Stockholm marathon. Patterson, making his debut, was timed in 4:22:55, exactly 24 min ahead of Johansson, who had run his best time of 4:30:13 in New York the previous year. Patterson improved his time to 3:35:27 at New York in 1983. Former world light-heavyweight champion John Conteh (GB) ran 3:26:21 at London in 1983, whilst Alan Minter (GB), who held the title at middleweight, ran at the same venue in 1981 and 1982, recording 4:09:32 in the latter.

Two other ex-world champions competed in the 1982 Stockholm marathon. The 1971 table-tennis champion Stellan Bengtsson (Swe) and middleweight wrestling champion Frank Andersson (Swe) both completed the distance in 3:38:16 and 4:08:34 respectively.

As long ago as 1947, computer pioneer Alan Turing (GB) ran 2:46:03 in the 1947 Windsor to Chiswick race. In 1980 Björn Ulveaus (Swe) of the ABBA popular music group made his debut in Stockholm, finishing in 3:23:54. Matthew Parris (GB), Conservative member of Parliament for Derby West, clipped more than four minutes from his best time in the 1983 London marathon, recording 2:38:43, whilst in the 1981 Boston race the United States agriculture secretary John Block finished in 3:06. At Boston the following year a nun, Sister Madonna Buder, was timed in 3:38 and in 1983 former pole vaulter Jim Knaub set a world record of 1:47:10 in propelling a wheelchair over the full course at the same venue. In 1982, at Honolulu, Donald Davis ran the distance backwards in a best ever 4:20:36 and another record was set at Ottawa in 1983, when Canadian Jacques Pilon became the first totally blind runner to better three hours with a time of 2:58:33.

Roger Bourbon, a Swiss national resident in the United States, carried a tray and bottle successfully throughout the 1982 London marathon in a record 2:47:18, as opposed to his normal marathon best of 2:30:30.

In the first London marathon, radio and TV personality, Jimmy Savile, OBE, resplendent in a gold lamé track suit, raised over £50 000 for the Stoke Mandeville hospital appeal. In 1982 he improved his time to 3:46:23 and the amount raised to £200 000, to become by far the most prolific money

Jimmy Savile in action in the London marathon. (Jeff Fuller)

raiser for charity. He ran his 21st marathon at Glasgow in 1983, when he recorded his best time so far of 3:27:00. Mike Kasser, a New York producer, ran in the 1983 London marathon, finishing with a time of 2:56:30. He then flew to New York by Concorde and competed in Boston the next day, where he recorded a time of 3:08.

Times

The fastest ever non-winning time is the European record of 2:08:39, set by Carlos Lopes (Por) at Rotterdam in 1983, when finishing two seconds behind Rob de Castella (Aus).

Fastest non-winning times for places 3 to 10 are as follows:

3	2:09:11	Shigeru Soh (Jap)	Fukuoka	1983
4	2:09:17	Takeshi Soh (Jap)	Fukuoka	1983
5	2:09:21	Alberto Salazar (USA)	Fukuoka	1983
6	2:09:35	Kunimitsu Itoh (Jap)	Fukuoka	1983
7	2:10:29	Kirk Pfeffer (USA)	Fukuoka	1980
8	2:10:44	Rob de Castella (Aus)	Fukuoka	1980
9	2:11:24	Karel Lismont (Bel)	Helsinki	1983
10	2:11:29	Stig Roar Husby (Nor)	Helsinki	1983

Since 1953, when Jim Peters (GB) became the first runner to break through the 2:20 barrier, this time has been regarded as of world class. Thirty years have elapsed since and a more realistic equivalent for current day performers would be a time of 2:15.

The most sub 2:20 times achieved in a single race over a certified course is 93 at London in 1983, a record 29 being timed under 2:15 in the same race. A further 84 (23) were so timed at Boston the very next day.

The most sub 2:20 times run on a single day occurred on 24 May 1980, when the United States Olympic trial and the Soviet national championship race were held. At Niagara Falls 56 competitors bettered the standard whilst at Moscow the total was 52. In Copenhagen, the same day, a single runner achieved the standard making a grand total of 109. Between the two major venues 2:15 was broken by 28 runners, 16 of them Soviet athletes.

The most sub 2:20 times at a single venue is the 393 recorded at Fukuoka between 1960 and 1983 at an average of 16 per race. Since 1966 at the same venue there have been 150 times under 2:15, an average of 7 per race.

The most sub 2:20 times by a single runner is by Kjell-Erik Stahl (Swe) between 1979 and 1983. On

Kjell-Erik Stahl (Swe), winning the 1982 Stockholm race in 30°C heat. (Popperfoto)

4 June 1983 Stahl ran his 30th such time, thus overtaking the previous record of 29 held by Ron Hill (GB), in his 38th marathon. He had also run under 2:20 on three other occasions but the course was short each time.

The most sub 2:15 times by a single runner is 25 by Bill Rodgers (USA) between 1975 and 1983.

The longest world record tenure is 13 years 326 days by Derek Clayton (Aus), who set his first record of 2:09:36.4 on 3 December 1967, improved to 2:08:33.6 on 30 May 1969 and this time was not bettered until 25 October 1981.

The longest standing continental record tenure is 20 years 274 days by Juan Zabala (Arg) who ran 2:33:19 on 28 October 1931, improved to 2:31:36 on 7 August 1932 and this lasted as a Central and South American record until the Olympic Games marathon of 1952.

The longest standing verified record of a major nation is one of 35 years 97 days by Alexis Ahlgren (Swe). His 2:36:06.6, which was also a world record, on 31 May 1913 in the Poly, was not beaten until 5 September 1948. Jüri Lossmann, silver medallist in 1920 at Antwerp, held the Estonian record of 2:32:48.6 set in that race until 1956, a total of 35 years 356 days, by which time Estonia had been a member of the Soviet Union for 16 years.

The British record of 21 years 321 days is held by Harry Payne whose 2:30:57.6 set on 6 July 1929 lasted until beaten by Jim Peters in his debut in 1951.

Titles and Races

The most national titles won by an individual among the major nations are the 12 consecutive Austrian Championships by Adolf Gruber from 1952 to 1963. Gruber was 43 years old at the time of his last victory and competed in three Olympic and two European Championship marathons.

Donald McNab Robertson, the Glaswegian coach painter, won most British titles with six in 1932–3–4, 1936–7, and 1939. He was denied a seventh title in 1946 when beaten by two tenths of a second.

Most medals won in major Games marathons are five by Karel Lismont. Running in a total of eight such races Lismont took one gold (1971 European), one silver (1972 Olympics) and three bronze (1976 Olympic, 1978 and 1982 European). In the remaining three marathons he finished ninth in the 1980 Olympics, dropped out of the 1974 European, and was ninth at Helsinki. Ron Hill (GB) has competed in a record number of eight major Games marathons. His record reads: 1962 European—did

Harry Payne, winning the 1929 AAA marathon. (Woodford Green AC)

Tatu Kolehmainen (Fin) leads Alexis Ahlgren (Swe) in 1912 Olympics.

not finish; 1964 Olympic—19th; 1966 European—12th; 1969 European—1st; 1970 Commonwealth—1st; 1971 European—3rd; 1972 Olympic—6th; 1974 Commonwealth—18th.

The best record in three Olympic races is that by Lismont (above). The best by a British runner is by Sam Ferris who finished fifth in 1924, eighth in 1928 and second in 1932. His record is matched by Kenji Kimihara (Jap) who had identical placings to Ferris between 1964 and 1972.

Veterans

A world championship for veteran road runners has been held since 1968 under the auspices of IGAL, the International Association of Veteran Long Distance Runners, alternating each year between the marathon and 25 km events.

OVERALL MARATHON CHAMPIONS

	men	
1968 Baarn	Walter Weba (GFR)	2:29:06
1970 Skovde	Nobuyoshi Sadanaga (Jap)	2:23:52
1972 Cologne	Arthur Walsham (GB)	2:24:59
1974 Paris	Alastair Wood (GB)	2:28:40
1976 Coventry	Eric Austin (GB)	2:20:50.8
1978 Berlin	Fritz Muller (USA)	2:25:20
1980 Glasgow	Don Macgregor (GB)	2:19:23
1982 Kawaguchi	Tim Johnston (GB)	2:22:18
	women	
1974	Dale Grieg (GB)	3:45:21
1976	Corry Konings-Rijper (Hol)	3:04:44
1978	Liane Winter (GFR)	2:51:32
1980	Lyn Billington (GB)	2:55:34
1982	Wendy Robertson (Can)	2:46:28

In the races from 1968 to 1972 inclusive, the four age groups were over 40, 50, 60 and 70 years old. From 1974 the groups were divided into five-year sections, ie 40–44, 45–9, etc. Women were first catered for in 1974 with two categories, 35–9 and 40 and over. Since 1978 their groups have also been divided into five-year sections, starting from 35–9.

Most gold medals won by nations in all categories are 17 by Great Britain, followed by GFR 16, Sweden 10, United States 5, Holland 3, Denmark, Japan, Switzerland 2 each, Austria and Canada 1 each.

Most individual gold medals are five, by the Swedish runner Robert Theodore ('Thedde') Jensen who won the over 60 group in 1968, 1970–2, and 65–9 group in 1974–6.

The World Masters Track and Field Championships first staged in 1975 have held a marathon in their programme of events. From 1977 it has been known as the World Veterans Marathon organised by WAVA (World Association of Veteran Athletes).

CHAMPIONS

	men	
1975 Toronto	Eric Austin (GB)	2:28:23
1977 Gothenburg	Eric Austin (GB)	2:25:57

1979 Hanover	John Robinson (NZ)	2:22:52
1981 Palmerston	Renato de Palmas (Ita)	2:19:34
1983 San Juan	Tim Johnston (GB)	2:27:04
	women	
1975	Donna Gookin (USA)	3:09:42
1977	Liane Winter (GFR)	3:00:31
1979	Liane Winter (GFR)	2:47:31
1981	Vicky Foltz (USA)	2:59:30
1983	Françoise du Pont (Fra)	3:06:16

Most Marathons

The most marathons run in an accurately documented career are 147 by Theodore ('Ted') Corbitt (USA) between 1951 and the end of 1981, during which period he also competed in 51 ultra-

Ted Corbitt (USA) in the 1952 Olympic race. (Gary Corbitt)

Johnny Kelley (USA), finishing his 48th Boston marathon, 1979. (AP)

Leslie Watson (GB), the most prolific female marathon runner.

distance events of 30 miles or more. In completing these 198 races, Corbitt has run 6115.7 miles (9842 km), of which 3877.6 miles (6240 km) were covered in marathons. His best time for the standard distance is 2:26:44 in winning the 1959 Philadelphia marathon and he finished 44th in the 1952 Olympics. One of the original organisers of the United States RRC, Corbitt was the first President of the New York section, established the first US and NY RRC Newsletters, was responsible for starting a road racing course measurement programme and has been Chairman of the TAC Standards Committee since 1965. Born in South Carolina, Corbitt, a physical therapist by occupation, has covered over 120 000 miles (193 116 km) in his racing and training career.

The longest running career by a top runner still competing is that of John Adelbert Kelley (USA) who in 1983 completed his 56th year of marathon running. Kelley ran his 111th marathon in 1983 at Boston, where he has raced on 52 occasions, winning in 1935 and 1945. His Boston tally is the greatest ever at a single major venue where he has finished in the top 10 on a record 18 times. In the period from 1928 he missed only the 1929–30–1 and 1968 races, failing to finish in 1928, 1932 and 1956 of the remainder.

The most marathons run in a year are 53 by Jay Helgerson (USA) who completed a marathon every week for 52 weeks between 28 January 1979 and 19 January 1980. In one week-end he ran two marathons, discounting the first as he was ill, and his total included two ultra-marathons. He ran at Boston, New York and the AAU event among others and his best time of 2:45:54 was only three and a half minutes outside his best time set in 1977 at Pasadena of 2:42:18.

The most marathons run by a woman of international calibre is 97 by Leslie Watson who ran her first marathon in 1975. Leslie, a Glasgow-born London-based physiotherapist, has won her event 42 times and has a best time of 2:44:18 set at New York in 1982. Since 1979 she has run at least 12 marathons each year, the most being 20 in 1981.

Paul Georges, a Trans World Airlines employee, suffered a heart attack in 1971 at the age of 43. Six years later he started training and made his marathon debut at New York that year. On 24 July 1982 he completed running a marathon in each of the 50 States by finishing the Utah Desert News marathon, his 86th event, during which time he covered more than 300 000 miles. Georges underwent heart surgery again in early 1983, recovering to run four more marathons. He has a best time of 3:57:30 at Detroit in 1978.

Dick Beardsley (USA) ran a record 13 consecutive personal improvements from his debut on 13 August 1977, when he ran 2:47:28 at Hurley, WI, to 20 June 1981 at Duluth, MN, where he recorded 2:09:37.

His sub 2:20 career record:

24 May 1980	Niagara Falls	OT	2:16:01	(16)
7 Sep 1980	Eugene		2:15:11	(10)
26 Oct 1980	New York		2:13:55	(9)
10 Jan 1981	Houston		2:12:50	(2)
1 Feb 1981	Beppu		2:12:41	(3)
29 Mar 1981	London		2:11:48	(1) eq
20 Jun 1981	Duluth		2:09:37	(1)
15 Aug 1981	Stockholm		2:16:17	(2)
24 Jan 1982	Houston		2:12:42	(2)
19 Apr 1982	Boston		2:08:53	(2)
19 Jun 1982	Duluth		2:14:50	(1)
24 Oct 1982	New York		2:18:12	(30)

Dick Beardsley takes refreshment during the first London marathon, 1981. (All Sport)

Paul Georges, in one of his 93 marathons.

Kenneth McArthur (SA) completed six marathons between his debut in 1908 and four years later, when he won the Olympic gold medal after which he retired, winning them all. He missed the 1908 Olympics, as no one came forward to pay his expenses for the journey to England. Sam Ferris (GB) won eight consecutive marathons between 1925 and 1928, including a short Danish race over 33.7 km (20.8 miles), for one of the longest recorded unbeaten runs by a world class athlete.

In recent years Abebe Bikila (Eth) twice won six consecutive marathons, interrupted only by his defeat at Boston in 1963, between 1960 and 1966, in one of the finest ever career records. Frank Shorter (USA) and Bill Rodgers (USA) also won six marathons in succession, Shorter between 1971 and 1973, and Rodgers between 1977 and 1978.

Lorraine Moller (NZ) won her first eight marathons between 1979 and 1981 before her first defeat at London in 1982. At the end of 1983 she had won nine of 12 marathons, with a best time of 2:29:35.5, set at Duluth in June 1981, including two Avon international titles.

World Record Progression

men

2:55:18.4	Johnny Hayes (USA)	*White City	24	Jul 08
2:52:45.4	Robert Fowler (USA)	Yonkers	1	Jan 09
2:46:52.6	James Clark (USA)	New York	12	Feb 09
2:46:04.6	Albert Raines (USA)	New York	8	May 09
2:42:31	Harry Barrett (GB)	*Stamford Bridge	26	May 09
2:40:34.2 (t)	Thure Johansson (Swe)	Stockholm	31	Aug 09
2:38:16.2 (t)	Harry Green (GB)	Stamford Bridge	12	May 13
2:36:06.6	Alexis Ahlgren (Swe)	*Stamford Bridge	31	May 13
2:32:35.8	Hannes Kolehmainen (Fin)	Antwerp	22	Aug 20
2:29:01.8	Al Michelsen (USA)	Port Chester	12	Oct 25
2:27:49	Fusashige Suzuki (Jap)	Tokyo	31	Mar 35
2:26:44	Yasuo Ikenaka (Jap)	Tokyo	3	Apr 35
2:26:42	Kitei Son (Jap)	Tokyo	3	Nov 35
2:25:39	Yun Bok Suh (Kor)	Boston	19	Apr 47
2:20:42.2	Jim Peters (GB)	*Chiswick	14	Jun 52
2:18:40.2	Jim Peters (GB)	*Chiswick	13	Jun 53
2:18:34.8	Jim Peters (GB)	Turku	4	Oct 53
2:17:39.4	Jim Peters (GB)	*Chiswick	26	Jun 54
2:15:17	Sergey Popov (Sov)	Stockholm	24	Aug 58
2:15:16.2	Abebe Bikila (Eth)	Rome	10	Sep 60
2:15:15.8	Toru Terasawa (Jap)	Beppu	17	Feb 63
2:14:28	Buddy Edelen (USA)	*Chiswick	15	Jun 63
2:13:55	Basil Heatley (GB)	*Chiswick	13	Jun 64
2:12:11.2	Abebe Bikila (Eth)	Tokyo	21	Oct 64
2:12:00	Morio Shigematsu (Jap)	*Chiswick	12	Jun 65
2:09:36.4	Derek Clayton (Aus)	Fukuoka	3	Dec 67
2:08:33.6	Derek Clayton (Aus)	Antwerp	30	May 69
2:08:12.7	Alberto Salazar (USA)	New York	25	Oct 81

*The courses finishing at the White City, Shepherds Bush; Stamford Bridge, Chelsea; and Chiswick, all in the London area, all started from Windsor. (t) denotes a marathon run entirely on a stadium track.

women

3:40:22	Violet Piercy (GB)	*Stamford Bridge	3	Oct 26
3:27:45	Dale Greig (GB)	Ryde	23	May 64
3:19:33	Mildred Sampson (NZ)	Auckland	21	Jul 64
3:15:22	Maureen Wilton (Can)	Toronto	6	May 67
3:07:26	Anni Pede-Erdkamp (GFR)	Waldniel	16	Sep 67
3:02:53	Caroline Walker (USA)	Seaside	28	Feb 70
3:01:42	Beth Bonner (USA)	Philadelphia	9	May 71
2:46:30	Adrienne Beames (Aus)	Werribee	31	Aug 71
2:46:24	Chantal Langlacé (Fra)	Neuf Brisach	27	Oct 74
2:43:54.5	Jackie Hansen (USA)	Culver City	1	Dec 74
2:42:24	Liane Winter (GFR)	Boston	21	Apr 75
2:40:15.8	Christa Vahlensieck (GFR)	Dulmen	3	May 75
2:38:19	Jackie Hansen (USA)	Eugene	12	Oct 75
2:35:15.4	Chantal Langlacé (Fra)	Oyarzun	1	May 77
2:34:47.5	Christa Vahlensieck (GFR)	West Berlin	10	Sep 77
2:32:29.8	Grete Waitz (Nor)	New York	22	Oct 78
2:27:32.6	Grete Waitz (Nor)	New York	21	Oct 79
2:25:41	Grete Waitz (Nor)	New York	26	Oct 80
2:25:28.8	Allison Roe (NZ)	New York	25	Oct 81
2:25:28.7	Grete Waitz (Nor)	London	17	Apr 83
2:22:43	Joan Benoit (USA)	Boston	18	Apr 83

In accordance with IAAF ruling both Roe and Waitz times were rounded up to 2:25:29. Benoit's time was first announced as being 2:22:42 but subsequently rounded up to 2:22:43 by Boston officials.

British Record Progression

men

3:16:08.6	William Clarke	*White City	24	Jul 08
2:42:31	Harry Barrett	*Stamford Bridge	26	May 09
2:38:16.2 (t)	Harry Green	Stamford Bridge	12	May 13
2:37:40.4	Bobby Mills	*Stamford Bridge	17	Jul 20
2:35:58.2	Sam Ferris	*Stamford Bridge	30	May 25
2:35:27	Sam Ferris	Liverpool	28	Sep 27
2:34:34	Harry Payne	*Stamford Bridge	6	Jul 28
2:33:00	Sam Ferris	Liverpool	26	Sep 28
2:30:57.6	Harry Payne	*Stamford Bridge	5	Jul 29
2:29:24	Jim Peters	*Chiswick	16	Jun 51
2:20:42.2	Jim Peters	*Chiswick	14	Jun 52
2:18:40.2	Jim Peters	*Chiswick	13	Jun 53
2:18:34.8	Jim Peters	Turku	4	Oct 53
2:17:39.4	Jim Peters	*Chiswick	26	Jun 54
2:14:43	Brian Kilby	Port Talbot	6	Jul 63
2:13:55	Basil Heatley	*Chiswick	13	Jun 64
2:13:45	Alastair Wood	Inverness to Forres	9	Jul 66
2:12:16.8	Bill Adcocks	Karl Marx Stadt	19	May 68
2:10:47.8	Bill Adcocks	Fukuoka	8	Dec 68
2:10:30	Ron Hill	Boston	20	Apr 70
2:09:28	Ron Hill	Edinburgh	23	Jul 70
2:09:12	Ian Thompson	Christchurch	31	Jan 74
2:09:08	Geoff Smith	New York	23	Oct 83

women

3:40:22	Violet Piercy	*Stamford Bridge	3	Oct 26
3:27:45	Dale Grieg	Ryde	23	May 64
3:11:54	Anne Clarke	Guildford	19	Oct 75
3:07:47	Margaret Thompson	Korso	26	Oct 75
2:50:55	Christine Readdy	Feltham	16	Apr 76
2:50:54	Rosemary Cox	Rugby	3	Sep 78
2:41:37	Joyce Smith	Sandbach	17	Jun 79
2:41:03	Gillian Adams	Eugene	9	Sep 79
2:36:27	Joyce Smith	Waldniel	22	Sep 79
2:33:32	Joyce Smith	Sandbach	22	Jun 80
2:30:27	Joyce Smith	Tokyo	16	Nov 80
2:29:57	Joyce Smith	London	29	Mar 81
2:29:43	Joyce Smith	London	9	May 82

ACKNOWLEDGEMENTS

Twenty years of collating marathon results and statistics has inevitably led to my corresponding with scores of enthusiasts around the world. Those whose names follow are only the latest in that long line who have directly contributed to this current work. Particular mention must be made of three long-time friends who have survived a barrage of queries over the years and have never failed to respond: Peter Matthews, Chairman of the National Union of Track Statisticians, and Editorial Director of Guinness Superlatives Ltd; Dr David Martin of Georgia State University, Atlanta, USA, and Rooney Magnusson from Stockholm, Sweden.

No less important have been the contributions from (in alphabetical order) José Corominas (Spa), Andy Etchells (GB), Turhan Göker (Tur), Fouad Habashi (Syr), Matti Hannus (Fin), Riel Hauman and Arrie Joubert (SA), P N Heidenstrom (NZ), Richard Hymans (GB), Tony Isaacs (GB), Paul Jenes (Aus), John Jewell (GB), Tore Johansen (Nor), Erich Kamper (Aut), Gurbaksh Singh Kler and Leong Teck Chew (Mal), Jacobus Koumans (Hol), R Murali Krishnan (Ind), Bienvenu Lams (Bel), Hans Larsen (Den), Christian Lindstedt (Swe), Bernard Linley (Tri), Peter Lovesey (GB), Bill Mallon (USA), Derrick Marcus and Jose Clemente Goncalves (Bra), Andy Milroy (GB), Hideaki Miyagi (Jap), John Murray (Ire), Jean-Claude Patinaud (Fra), Yves Pinaud (Fra), Fulvio Regli (Swz), Fernando Rodil (PR), Cecil Smith (Can), Dave Terry (GB), T Tomioka (Jap), Otto Verhoeven (GFR), Luis Vinker (Arg), and the secretaries of Maryhill Harriers, Polytechnic Harriers, Woodford Green AC.

My thanks also to the IAAF and the Federations of Bolivia, China, Greece and Korea and the Arabian States, for their co-operation in answering specific queries. In addition I have consulted the following periodicals: Athletics Weekly (GB), Leichtathletik (GFR), Runner (USA), Running (GB) and Track & Field News (USA), the publications of the ATFS, IAAF, NUTS and RRC, and the definitive history of the event 'The Marathon Footrace' (Martin & Gynn, 1979). Where errors in the latter have been detected they have been corrected in this book. I also acknowledge the great assistance given by the Asahi Shimbun Company (Tokyo) in supplying both data and photographs for use in this publication. Finally my sincere thanks to Beatrice Frei, Editor and David Roberts, Art Editor for their help in preparing and producing this book.

INDEX

References in bold type are to illustrations.
m. signifies marathon.

Women (Name followed by
    hyphen (-) denotes previous
    surname)

Subject Index